Some of the great correspondents in
Women of the World

Margaret Fuller A friend of Thoreau and Wordsworth, she had a man's ambition and a woman's heart.

Mary Roberts Rinehart The famous novelist who was among the first American correspondents to reach the front in World War I.

Martha Gellhorn Ernest Hemingway's third wife, who stowed away on a hospital ship in order to cover the Normandy invasion in June 1944.

Margaret Bourke-White One of the greatest news photographers. Torpedoed on a ship bound for Africa in World War II, she discarded all but one can of her food to make room for her camera.

WOMEN OF THE WORLD

Also by Julia Edwards:

THE OCCUPIERS

WOMEN OF THE WORLD

The Great Foreign Correspondents

Julia Edwards

IVY BOOKS • NEW YORK

Ivy Books
Published by Ballantine Books
Copyright © 1988 by Julia Edwards

Library of Congress Catalog Card Number: 87-37593

ISBN 0-8041-0491-3

First published by Houghton Mifflin Company. Reprinted by permission of Houghton Mifflin Company.

Manufactured in the United States of America

First Ballantine Books Edition: August 1989

To June Herman Shaplen

CONTENTS

ACKNOWLEDGMENTS

FIRST A SALUTE TO FELLOW MEMBERS OF THE OVERSEAS PRESS club who made this book possible, who provided more fascinating material than one book would hold, and informed, advised, and helped obtain photographs.

My special thanks go to Eleanor Bogart and Dr. Wilda Smith for sharing their knowledge of Peggy Hull while writing their own book about her and to David Len Jones for pointing me in the right direction. I am indebted as well to John Tebbel for his encouragement.

As with the women correspondents I write about, I owe much to the men who assisted me. George Weller of the *Chicago Daily News* married Charlotte Ebener, whose adventures I chronicle, and made himself an authority on the achievements of her sex. His help, and especially his enthusiasm for the project, illustrates the fact that the most respected editors and correspondents welcomed women to the profession.

My editor, Frances Tenenbaum, earned her halo the day she took on this project, doing all an editor can to spare me the critics' wrath.

Ann Sperber was there when I needed her. I toast all the Very Important People whose valuable time I consumed and the staffs of libraries, news agencies, newspapers, and press clubs for assistance beyond the call of duty.

This book was the idea of June Herman Shaplen, editor, foreign correspondent, beloved friend, and wife of Robert Shaplen. Had she lived to see it published, she would have shared my regret that I could not include many women who belong on the honor roll of professional foreign correspondents. In dedicating this book to her, I pay my respect to all the women who set their sights high long before it became fashionable for women to want to have it all and who possessed the spirit to realize their dreams.

1

The Red Umbrella

THE MAN IN THE TRENCH COAT, SO LONG A SYMBOL OF THE intrepid American foreign correspondent, was never the lone ranger that chroniclers of international intrigue have made him out to be. With as much stamina and more persistence than the challenge demanded of men, women have reported all the great and catastrophic events of the past 140 years. They have covered wars, riots and revolutions, poverty and plenty, humanity's struggle to survive, and the dream of peace before we die.

Hundreds of women have covered war and peace around the globe as staff correspondents for newspapers, magazines, radio, and television. Thousands more have reported from abroad as stringers, free-lancers, and reporters on special assignments. Some have played a part in the history they recorded. But in the history of their profession women have been relegated to the footnotes or at best resurrected for amusing sidebars— anecdotes about how one posed in the nude and another slept with a general to get her story.

So far, television has done more than newspapers to focus attention on the women who bring us the news. President Ronald Reagan found women at his press conferences eager to assist him in identifying the raised arm he wished to recognize. They wore red, a favorite color of First Lady Nancy Reagan. The jovial President responded by calling on at least one "woman in red" at every conference. The television cameras frequently focused before the words were out of his mouth. On the road, the red umbrella came into fashion as the trench coat went out.

The plethora of pretty women anchors on television news

programs cast a deceptively bright light on the status of women in the field. In 1987, although 50 percent of the reporters and editors in the United States were women, they accounted for only 20 percent of the foreign correspondents. The statistics, of course, gave no clue to the relative power and prestige of the women at home and abroad. The correspondents overseas belonged to a small but elite corps of professionals. The perception that employers applied more rigorous standards to women than to men gave the chosen few a sense of superiority frequently supported by their readership and their audiences.

As dramatic as many of the events women reported was the story of their struggle for the right to cover the world as the equals of male correspondents. For generations, the women had to contend with discrimination and prejudice when competing for jobs men fought to get. Many of the women pioneers in the field shared the motivation of George Meegan, a young Englishman who in 1983 walked 19,700 miles from the tip of South America to the Arctic. "I was seeking uniqueness," he explained, "and I went through an awful lot to get it."

For an exciting century, from 1850 to 1950, women were breaking out of the stereotype of Kinder, Kirche, Küche—children, church, kitchen. America's first woman foreign correspondent, Margaret Fuller, scandalized the nation; her successors simply infuriated the defenders of the status quo. The establishment's reluctance to entrust a man's job to a woman was matched by the public's enthusiasm when a woman finally made it. Yet the barriers to women in the profession did not come tumbling down because women demonstrated the courage to die or the ability to survive; society accepted each woman's feat as a celebration of the unique, not as evidence of women's capacities.

So long as there was something new to do, there was no end to the news stories about the first women to do it. The first woman correspondent accredited by the U.S. Army to cover a war zone, the first to board a battleship at sea, the first to go on a bombing mission, all made bigger news than the events they reported. The "first woman" syndrome, because it was a circulation builder, survived long after some woman had done everything except walk on the moon. The women correspondents resented it particularly when they found themselves being described as merely the "first woman" to do something no man had done before them. Irene Corbally Kuhn, for one, wanted it known that she was the first person, not the first woman, to make a radio news broadcast out of China.

One could measure the progress of women correspondents from war to war. In World War I, the U. S. Army refused to accredit women to cover American action on the Western Front, even though women had covered that war before the United States entered it. Three women denied accreditation by the Americans covered the war on the Russian front.

The depression years of the 1930s brought enthusiasm for escape, and women again made headlines, this time with their stories of royal romances and Paris fashions, thereby reinforcing the image of women as being capable of writing only about frivolous subjects.

In World War II, women won overseas assignments by agreeing that they were different from men. They argued that as they were more sensitive and more opposed to war than men, they should be sent to write "the woman's point of view." Once overseas, they took off their kid gloves, put on their helmets, and raced the men to the front and back to the cable desk. Under orders to retreat, Ann Stringer of United Press advanced through no man's land and became the first American to join forces with the Russians at the river Elbe. Her exclusive story created a sensation.

Before that war was won, at least one hundred fifty American women correspondents had covered the fighting. Numerous women covered the war in Europe and Asia before the United States entered it. After Pearl Harbor, the U.S. War Department accredited some seventeen hundred correspondents to cover American forces overseas. Of these, approximately one hundred were women, and they made a bigger splash at the front than their numbers indicated. Many of the men accredited were publishers, editors, Washington correspondents, and columnists on brief junkets to get a taste of war; most of the women were there for the duration.

When the war in Korea began, the U.S. Army ordered women correspondents out. But like General Douglas MacArthur, who declared, "I shall return!" they returned in force with his permission. Women made up a much larger proportion of the correspondents covering the Korean War than they had in World War II. Bob Considine, a famous correspondent for the Hearst newspapers, wrote, "In Korea, they landed with both feet, and if they aren't in war to stay, I'm a monkey's aunt."

The war in Vietnam, a tragedy for the men who fought it, brought triumph for women correspondents. For the first time in history, the U.S. Defense Department allowed them to cover combat on an equal footing with men, and they made the most of it. Overseas Press Club Awards, the Pulitzer Prize, the National Book Award, and the respect of their competitors attested to their newly won status.

The women took their share of casualties as well. Dickey Chapelle, a great photographer, was killed when she stepped on a land mine. Kate Webb of United Press International and Elizabeth Pond of the *Christian Science Monitor* were captured in Cambodia. From the start women had accepted the risks. In India and in Japan, women correspondents were killed in plane crashes. Women were arrested and jailed for what they wrote in Bolivia, Angola, Iran. In Moscow for United Press, Aline Mosby was drugged by the KGB, the Soviet intelligence agency. The danger attracted some to the fire.

As the jet plane made it possible for millions to become world travelers, some old-timers complained that foreign correspondence was losing its glamour. Yet the foreign correspondent was in demand as never before—world news became a life and death concern for everyone on earth. As the 1990s approached, both the total number of foreign correspondents and the proportion of women among them were increasing.

Women owed their successes in part to a small, elite minority of men who encouraged and assisted them, among them Floyd Gibbons, the one-eyed correspondent of the *Chicago Tribune*, Arthur Brisbane, the great editor of the Hearst newspapers in New York, and Fremont Older, editor of the *San Francisco Bul-*

letin. Inevitably there were love affairs and a few notable marriages among the correspondents.

From start to finish, the women were distinguished only by their individuality. Politically they covered the spectrum from Communist to right-wing radical. They were young and old, short and tall; most were friendly, a few mean. There were bleeding hearts and bloodless military strategists among them. What united them was their ambition to see for themselves, to be part of history in the making, and to inform the world.

By the 1980s, men and women were covering the same stories in much the same manner. Without a by-line, it was difficult to tell the difference between them. The growing complexity of the issues, the problems, and their solutions put a premium on intellect and a capacity to communicate far beyond the skills that sufficed when foreign correspondents were adventurers and wars were fought on battlefields.

The women correspondents changed as rapidly as the world did. Economists, linguists, specialists in Asian studies and Soviet relations have entered the field to compete with the perennials, the polished feature writer and the gold medalist of the deadline dash. As the 1990s approached, news agencies were naming women to such top jobs as London bureau chief, news editor for Asia and the Pacific, Moscow correspondent. All the television networks, all the newsmagazines, most of the specialized news agencies, and most newspapers with overseas staffs boasted women correspondents. No longer underestimated, they have achieved a place in the history they record.

2

A Man's Ambition, A Woman's Heart

THROUGHOUT THE BLOODY MONTH OF JUNE 1849, THE FRENCH forces of Louis-Napoléon brought their heavy siege guns within ever shorter range of Rome. Shells and grenades fell in every sector of the city. Margaret Fuller watched the Republican defenders of Rome reply with repeated bayonet forays. On the ramparts, her lover, the Marchese Giovanni Angelo Ossoli, fought for the Republic. Fuller found and saved a piece of bomb that burst close to him and saw blood dripping from the wall where he fought.

On the afternoon of June 30, when she realized that the Republicans could not hold out another night, she called the American envoy, Lewis Cass Jr., to her lodgings. Trembling, she gave him important papers in event of her death and confessed to the existence of her illegitimate baby, with a prayer that friends and family would care for him should she die that night. Ossoli came for her at sunset, and arm in arm they headed for the ramparts.

French President Louis-Napoléon was winning his campaign to restore Pope Pius IX as ruler of Rome, thus gaining French Catholic support and destroying potential opposition in Italy before ascending the throne as Napoléon III, emperor of France. Fuller saw it as her destiny to fall with the Republican defenders of Rome, but fate would not have it. She survived to report the catastrophe to the readers of the *New York Tribune*, and her articles created a sensation in America. She would win a place in history as America's first woman foreign correspondent and one of the world's first professional war correspondents.

Xenophon, the Greek historian, covered a war with Persia in 401 B.C. In the absence of newspapers, he wrote *Anabasis* (Upcountry march). But Xenophon was a warrior, not an unbiased reporter.

Not until the nineteenth century did William Howard Russell of the London *Times* demonstrate the imagination to describe himself as the world's first war correspondent. Until this day, most newspapers obtained their war news from the participants. As recently as 1956, Colonel Barney Oldfield, a usually reliable source, wrote, "The Danish rebellion [of 1850] was first to be covered by a professional war correspondent—William Howard Russell." Oldfield, an army information officer in World War II, had neglected to check further than Russell's epitaph in Saint Paul's Cathedral, London, which was in error.

Russell did not see action until more than a year after Fuller became a war correspondent. In her dispatches, she deplored the failure of the London *Times* to send a correspondent to cover the French attack on Rome. Correspondents based in Paris, not Rome, reported that the Romans butchered Catholic priests, cut their flesh into morsels, and threw them into the Tiber.

"I am surprised to see the air of perfect good faith with which articles from the London *Times* upon the revolutionary movements are copied into our papers," Fuller wrote the *New York Tribune*. "There exists not in Europe a paper more violently opposed to the cause of freedom than the *Times* and neither its leaders nor its foreign correspondents are to be depended upon."

Among the few disinterested observers who saw and wrote what was happening, she impressed America, and probably even the London *Times*, with the need for firsthand reporting. Whatever her influence, the *Times* decided within a year that it, too, needed war correspondents at the front.

Margaret Fuller, a brilliant woman, was regal, blessed with abundant reddish brown hair, sparkling eyes, and a captivating personality, but she was no beauty and she knew it. "I hate not to be beautiful," she wrote. At the age all ducklings dream of

developing into beautiful swans, she foresaw her destiny to be
"bright but ugly."

The eldest of nine children, Margaret Fuller was born in 1810
in Cambridgeport, Massachusetts, the daughter of a prominent
lawyer and member of Congress. Timothy Fuller stifled his disappointment when his firstborn turned out to be a girl and
promptly became a tyrannical tutor fascinated by his capacity
to develop and mold a receptive mind. By the age of six, Margaret could read Latin. She was nearsighted, and some blamed
her father for straining her eyes. Under his pressure to excel, the
child prodigy began to have nightmares and horrible headaches.
Her father realized that she needed a change and sent her, at the
age of fourteen, to boarding school, where the teachers, finding
her domineering and arrogant, undertook to make a lady of her.
She was a sweeter sixteen and dressed in silk when her father
gave a memorable party for President John Quincy Adams.

At a time when colleges still refused to admit women, Margaret Fuller became the first female allowed to use the library
at Harvard College; exceptional recognition of her remarkable
intelligence. Aware that she would not make it on her looks, she
took pains to polish her image as a conversationalist and literary
critic. At twenty-three she was devastated when her father, whose
career and health were failing, dragged the family away to life
on an isolated farm.

When he died two years later, Fuller went to work in Boston
as a teacher of languages to help support her family, a move that
liberated her. There she met Ralph Waldo Emerson and Harriet
Martineau, a British journalist, who inspired her to think and
dream. Emerson, preacher and poet, drew her into the group
that became known as the Transcendentalists, a gathering of
freethinkers united by their idealism. Martineau, who was extremely deaf, used a hearing trumpet before the advent of modern devices. In view of her handicap and her sex, her unescorted
voyages aboard sailing ships in the 1830s were indeed remarkable. She inspired Fuller to dream that she, too, could travel
and write of her adventures. For Fuller, Martineau epitomized
the liberated woman.

Fuller was teaching in Providence, Rhode Island, and earning what was then an excellent salary for a woman, $1000 a year, when the first two steamships to cross the Atlantic Ocean, the *Sirus* and the *Great Western*, arrived in New York harbor on April 23, 1838. James Gordon Bennett Sr., publisher of the *New York Herald*, sailed for Europe on the return trip of the *Sirus* and in Europe arranged the first systematic foreign coverage for an American newspaper. In the days of the sailing ship, only a few Americans wrote letters from Europe to American newspapers, and most newspapers depended for news of Europe on European newspapers delivered by ship. Bennett hired Europeans to report on their own countries rather than send Americans overseas. Events were moving Margaret Fuller's dreams from the realm of fantasy into the sphere of the possible. The next step would be for newspapers to send Americans overseas.

To widen the horizon for herself and other women, Fuller gave up the security of her teaching position and returned to Boston to earn her living conducting "Conversations," adult education classes for women who, like her, were denied a college education. By then, at Emerson's request, Fuller was serving without pay as the first editor of *The Dial*, a literary quarterly launched by the Transcendentalists as "a free organ for the expression of individual thought . . . aimed at stimulating each man to think more deeply."

No one was indifferent to Fuller. Henry David Thoreau invited her to row with him on Walden Pond; Edgar Allan Poe called her an "ill-tempered old maid" for criticizing his poetry; Nathaniel Hawthorne caricatured her as a "pretentious humbug." James Freeman Clarke, a noted theologian, and Sarah Clarke, his sister, invited her to accompany them on a trip west to visit the Indians and the settlers in Wisconsin and Illinois. The book she wrote about her first long journey, *Summer on the Lakes*, in 1843, mourned the lost majesty of Indian tribes.

Mary Youngs Cheney, a former student and enthusiastic admirer of Margaret Fuller, proudly introduced the author to her husband, Horace Greeley, a New Yorker who had founded the *New York Tribune* in 1841 and was well on his way to becoming a powerful publisher and politician. Greeley was so impressed by *Summer on the Lakes* that he arranged for publication of

Fuller's next book, *Woman in the Nineteenth Century*, which created a storm in 1845.

Fuller's call for complete equality of the sexes was hailed as a landmark manifesto in the history of feminism and condemned as an outrageous attack on the social order. She wrote,

> We would have every arbitrary barrier thrown down. We would have every path laid open to women as freely as to men. If you ask me what offices they may fill, I reply— any. I do not care what case you put; let them be sea captains, if you will.

Pirated in London, the book was issued as the first volume in M. G. Clarke's Library of Choice Reading series, and Fuller was pleased just to have an international audience.

Although Greeley was on record as opposing women's suffrage, he later called the book the "most commanding assertion yet made of the right of woman . . . to an equal voice in framing and modifying the laws she is required to obey." Now, at the suggestion of his wife, he hired Fuller to write literary criticism for the *Tribune*, making her one of the first women to serve as a member of the editorial staff of a metropolitan newspaper. In those days, a lady did not travel alone, and when she decided to move from New England to New York, where she had no family, it was a major undertaking.

As if the journey from her home in Boston to New York, unchaperoned, was not daring enough, she stopped off at the village of Sing Sing, New York, to write an exposé of conditions in the somber state prison there. Soon she was writing about the plight of prostitutes in the big city. Fuller, a passionate woman, wrote passionate love letters she lived to regret. Evident in everything she wrote was her passion for truth and justice. While establishing herself as a literary critic to be reckoned with, she also threw herself into the battle for women's rights. She exposed poverty, cruelty, and injustice wherever she found it. With Greeley's help, she scandalized the nation.

America was suffering from a split personality. Heeding Greeley's advice to "Go West, young man," men who were accompanied by their families expected their wives to join in fighting Indians if they were attacked en route. Yet ladies in New York did not go to the opera unescorted. Where there was competition for jobs, a woman's place was in the home. Serious writing was viewed as a job for men only. It was considered more than unladylike; it was scandalous for a woman to try to write like a man.

Although Greeley printed everything Fuller wrote, however outrageous, he retained an editor's right to be cranky. It took time to write as well as she did, and he was impatient for the copy; he fussed at her for missing deadlines and criticized her consumption of strong tea and coffee. He relished the chance to laugh when the stately Margaret, lorgnette in hand, swept through a door he had opened for her. "Let them be sea captains if they will," he shouted, slightly misquoting her book and ridiculing the idea that women who wanted to be sea captains should expect men to open doors for them.

At thirty-five, Fuller was passionately in love with James Nathan, a young businessman of German Jewish descent. Some said he was only using her for her connections, and he ended the romance by going to England without her. While she could scarcely have thought of following him, she thought of England and her readers there, of Harriet Martineau, and of entering a world she knew well from its literature. Early in 1846, she expressed an interest in covering Europe, and Greeley encouraged her.

To compete with the *New York Herald* and the Europeans providing it with foreign news, the *Tribune* could use an American correspondent in Europe. Besides, if the truth be known, and Greeley was not one to hide it, he was not particularly fond of Fuller. She was living with the Greeleys in their farmhouse at Turtle Bay overlooking the East River in New York City, just south of where the United Nations stands today. It is plausible to suppose that America's first woman foreign correspondent won her editor's support because he wanted her out of his house.

Greeley sent Fuller to Europe with his blessings and an advance of $125. She was able to sail only because friends, Mr. and Mrs. Marcus Spring, paid her to take care of their twelve-year-old son, Eddie, aboard ship. She was risking financial disaster, yet the deal she made was not as awful as it sounds today. In some parts of Europe, one still could get lodgings for $9.00 a month.

Her ship, the *Cambria*, reached Liverpool in ten days, sixteen hours, the fastest passage yet made across the Atlantic. In England, where she was again expected to concentrate on the literary scene, she chose to report her impression that poverty in England was even worse than among immigrants in New York. "To the horrors and sorrows of the streets in such places as Liverpool, Glasgow, and above all London, one has to grow insensible or die daily," she wrote.

At Newcastle, she descended into a coal mine in a bucket and described her distress at the sight of horses being lowered into the mine, never to be brought up again, never to see light again. She wrote a frightening account of becoming lost on the slopes of Ben Lomond in Scotland and having to spend a night on the cold mountainside before she could make her way to safety.

The warmth of her reception surprised and delighted her. In the Lake District of England, William Wordsworth recited his poems to her. Only Harriet Martineau was cool toward her, perhaps sensing that the admiring American had arrived as a rival. More traumatic was the discovery that James Nathan, her former beau, was about to marry an Englishwoman. When she asked him to return her love letters, he demanded money, which she refused to pay. Nathan did not sell her letters, but after both had died, his son made a tidy sum by selling them.

In Queen Victoria's England, Fuller's views on women's rights were applauded. Only the British *News Quarterly* rejected Fuller as "one of those he-women who, thank heavens, for the most part figure and flourish and have their fame on the other side of the Atlantic."

Professionally, she had a fateful encounter in England with the Italian patriot Giuseppe Mazzini, who even in exile devoted his life to the unification of the Italian peninsula, a land divided among warring states. Moving her base to Paris, Fuller recklessly entered into a plan to smuggle him into Italy with a false American passport. Fortunately for her own hopes of reaching

Italy, Mazzini declined the assistance. He was under death sentence in Rome, and anyone caught smuggling him into the region could expect the same fate.

In France, Fuller spent many hours in the Chamber of Deputies, observing developments under the monarchy of Louis-Philippe. In 1847, she concluded, "The need of some radical measure of reform is not less strongly felt in France than elsewhere, and the time will come before long when such will be imperatively demanded." She was among the few who predicted the Revolution of 1848.

Among her sources was her French counterpart, George Sand, a fellow woman journalist as well as novelist. The Frenchwoman shared her republican ideals with the American, and the Polish composer Frédéric Chopin played for them. Sand, born Amandine-Aurore-Lucile Dupin and married to Casimer Dudevant, collaborated with Jules Sandeau on articles for the newspaper *Figaro*, from which alliance came her by-line. The masculine pseudonym did not save her from scandal, however. While the morals of newspapermen were not subject to public scrutiny, it was open season on the private life of a woman writer who dared demand attention for her work. Fuller vigorously defended Sand and her liaison with Chopin.

By then, Fuller was fighting her own battles in Rome. Italy was in ferment when she arrived in Naples in March 1847. Before the Revolution, inevitable in Italy as well as France, she found time to explore the wonders of Saint Peter's Basilica in Rome. There, in October 1847, she became separated from friends and found an Italian, the Marchese Ossoli, to escort her to her lodgings. Ossoli was Catholic, a soldier about eight years younger than she, and by her standards poorly educated. The Catholic priest assigned to tutor him had not paid much attention. But Ossoli was handsome, and they shared a dream of freedom and democracy for Italy.

The Austrian Army occupied important centers in northern Italy, and the rest of Italy remained divided among a variety of overlords. The Revolution began in Sicily and sparked rebellion throughout the land. From Rome, the papal state, Fuller wrote on March 29, 1848,

War is everywhere. I cannot leave Rome, and the men of Rome are marching out every day into Lombardy . . . I saw the Austrian arms dragged through the streets here, and burned in the Piazza del Popolo. The Italians embraced one another, and cried, "miracolo, Providenza!" . . . When the double-headed eagle [the Vatican flag], was pulled down from the lofty portal of the Palazzo di Venezia, the people placed there, in its stead, one of white and gold, inscribed with the name, ALTA ITALIA; and instantly the news followed that Milan, Venice, Modena and Parma were driving out their tyrants. These news were received in Rome with indescribable rapture. Men danced, and women wept with joy along the street.

As Fuller foresaw, Rome would be the prize fought for by the revolutionary movement and its opponents. Mazzini at last returned to Rome after seventeen years in exile, and Fuller covered his first address to the constituent assembly. "After the Rome of the emperors, after the Rome of the Popes, will come the Rome of the people," she quoted his declaration.

In the midst of covering these traumatic events, Fuller discovered she was pregnant. Ossoli would need a dispensation from the Catholic church to marry a Protestant, but beyond that, he stood to lose his small family inheritance if he married her. They needed every penny they could get to care for the baby. Fuller told no one of her pregnancy, and the styles of the day enabled her to keep it secret. Until the moment of her confinement, she continued to report to the *New York Tribune*. Abandoning neutrality, she appealed for American aid to the Italian revolutionary movement.

During her pregnancy, Fuller suffered moments of deep depression and wrote her friend Emerson about it without revealing the cause. Her baby, a boy she called Angelino for his father, was born in the mountain village of Rieti on September 5, 1848. She returned to Rome in November without the baby and resumed her coverage of the news. The Pope's unpopular prime minister, Count Pellegrino Rossi, was assassinated on November 15, and Fuller described the scene.

Yesterday, as he descended from his carriage to enter the Chamber, the crowd howled and hissed, then pushed him, and, as he turned his head in consequence, a sure hand stabbed him in the back. He said no word, but died almost instantly in the arms of a cardinal. The act was undoubtedly the result of the combination of many, from the dexterity with which it was accomplished, and the silence which ensued. Those who had not abetted before hand seemed entirely to approve when done. The troops on the line, on whom he had relied, remained at their posts and looked coolly on.

The pope fled to Gaeta in the kingdom of Naples. In the eye of the storm, Fuller managed to visit her baby in Rieti in December. To her horror, she discovered that the village physician had failed to vaccinate little Angelino as promised, saying he had no vaccine. Ossoli sent the vaccine from Rome. Again Fuller left her baby, this time in the care of an Italian woman who had a baby the same age.

Between Rieti and Rome, Fuller traveled by public stagecoach, which could be a dangerous journey in peaceful times. A coach she almost boarded in November was swept away by mountain torrents; the coach she did take almost did not make it through the flood. This time, at an inn on the way to Rome, they encountered the menacing troops of Giuseppe Garibaldi, the warrior of the Revolution. Garibaldi's troops had to live off the land, and the people had cause to expect the worst, rape and robbery. As short of funds as anyone at the inn, Fuller demonstrated the wit to announce that she was buying lunch for the troops. Thus flattered, the soldiers graciously accepted what they otherwise would have grabbed and later escorted the lady to her carriage.

It took her special awareness to survive as a newspaper correspondent at a time when ships spent six weeks delivering news dispatches to readers. From Rome in January, she wrote, "The Romans go on as if nothing were pending. Yet it seems very probable that the French will soon be at Cevita Vecchia [the port of Rome] and with hostile intentions. Monstrous are the treacheries of our times.'' The Roman Republic was proclaimed on February 8, 1849. Twelve thousand troops sent by Louis-Napoléon seized Cevita Vecchia in April, their goal to restore Pius IX to his temporal throne.

The first assault on Rome came on April 30. That day Princess Cristina Trivulzio of Belgiojoso, impressed by Fuller's competence, put her in charge of the second of the military hospitals she had established for the war wounded. By night, Fuller comforted the wounded, assisted when they underwent amputations, and watched men die. By day she wrote. "It was a terrible battle fought here . . . I could see all its progress from my balcony. The Italians fought like lions. It was a truly heroic spirit that animates them. They made a stand here for honor and their rights, with little ground for hope they can resist now that they are betrayed by France.''

Absentee journalists throughout Europe, encouraged by clerical parties, accused the Republicans of barbarities. Fuller was there, and she observed, "Both in France and in England the grossest falsehoods have been circulated.'' There were stories about red flags being raised in Rome as evidence that the people were thirsty for blood. As she reported, those flags were raised as a signal to coachmen and horsemen that they could pass.

In response to the public interest aroused by her articles, the U.S. State Department sent a representative to Rome, but he died almost the day he arrived. So the State Department sent another, Lewis Cass Jr., who was under orders to withhold recognition from the Republic. Reporting the irritation brought about because Cass was not authorized to recognize either the papal or the republican government, Fuller argued that the only legitimate ground for a republican government, such as that of the United States, was to recognize for any nation the government it chose.

The bombardment, the bloodshed, and the anguish, every painful detail reported by Margaret Fuller, mounted daily. "The dead and dying were around her in every form of pain and horror,'' Lewis Cass remembered. "But she never shrank from the duty she has assumed. All was done that woman could do to comfort them in their suffering.''

Only when Fuller saw that the French were about to overrun the city did she make the decision to face death on the ramparts with her husband. She hastily scribbled a note summoning Lewis Cass. His regard for her as well as her newly won prestige made it seem natural for the envoy to answer the correspondent's summons on the eve of Rome's defeat, a courtesy beyond even nineteenth-century gallantry. He scarcely anticipated her news of a son to be safeguarded in the event of her death.

With Ossoli, she joined the defenders on Pincian Hill, the highest and most exposed position in Rome. To their surprise, the cannonade was not renewed. The French, too, knew that they had won. The Roman Republic was dead. Fuller survived to record Garibaldi's retreat.

> They had all put on the beautiful dress of the Garibaldi legion, the tunic of bright red cloth, the Greek cap. . . . Their long hair was blown back from resolute faces. . . . They had counted the cost before they entered on this perilous struggle; they had weighed life and all its material advantages against liberty and made their election; . . . I saw the wounded, all that could go, laden upon their baggage cases. . . . The women were ready, their eyes too resolved, if sad. The wife of Garibaldi followed him on horseback.

As they left, she endured the sense of individual helplessness one feels when faced with vast events beyond personal control, envisioning her own son dead in twenty years. As soon as the road to Rieti was reopened, she rushed to retrieve Angelino, only to find the baby emaciated, surviving on a diet of bread and wine. She had done her best to send money for his support from Rome, but not enough had gotten through. For two months the baby hovered between life and death, and as she nursed him back to health, she swore never again to be separated from her child, a fateful decision.

News of the baby's existence spread as fast as news of the fall of Rome. Fuller never wrote another story for the *Tribune*, and those who speculated that Greeley had fired her because of the scandal caused by the child's illegitimacy were wrong. As long as her articles sold newspapers, Greeley played and displayed them to the hilt. Her reportage was unique, and the international scandal she created was the equivalent in publicity to being banned in Boston; it increased public interest in what she wrote. But before her story of the fall of Rome reached the *Tribune*, Greeley's only son, Pickie, died of cholera on July 12. Pickie had been a favorite of Fuller, who had sent him presents and endearments from Rome. His death reinforced her concern for her own son. Her preoccupation with Angelino diverted her from writing for the *Tribune*, and the distraught father was in no condition to suggest new assignments for her.

With Ossoli and Angelino, Fuller moved to Florence, where she concentrated on writing a history of the Revolution in Italy. Apparently the couple was legally married in Florence; absence of proof is ascribed to her family's compulsion to destroy the evidence that they were not married until after the baby was born.

Short of funds and anxious to arrange publication of her new book, Fuller sought to bring her small family to America. Using the good name of her friend Marcus Spring, she managed to borrow the money for passage home on a freighter. A ship she planned to take was lost at sea. "I am absurdly fearful," she admitted. "In case of mishap, however, I shall perish with my husband and my child, and we may be transferred to some happier state."

They sailed aboard the barque *Elizabeth* on May 17, 1850. In midocean, the captain came down with smallpox, and Angelino apparently caught the disease from him. While the baby recovered, the captain died. Henry Bangs, the first mate, in charge of the ship, was so unsure of himself that he had to call on the captain's widow to help navigate. (If only women *had* been trained to be sea captains.) At 4:00 A.M. on July 19, the ship Bangs thought he had safely steered to New Jersey waters struck a sandbar off Fire Island, New York.

From the sinking ship, the passengers could see men gathering on shore, but they had come to loot, not to launch a rescue mission. Some passengers plunged into the water, but Fuller refused to be separated from her son, and Ossoli stood by them both. Finally, a steward took the baby, assuring the mother he would sacrifice his own life to save the child, but the steward and baby drowned. A massive wave crashed against the ship; the foremast gave way, and all remaining aboard were lost. Fuller and Ossoli went down with the ship. Also lost was the manuscript Fuller viewed as her best work. She was only forty years old when she died. As she had written, "Tis an evil lot, to have a man's ambition and a woman's heart."

Greeley, of course, had the last word. "While she demanded absolute equality for women, she exacted a deference and courtesy from men to women, as women, which was entirely inconsistent with that requirement," he wrote. But he had to be fair, and he added, "One characteristic of her writings I feel bound to comment upon—their absolute truthfulness."

For the next twenty years, American women foreign correspondents were more notable than their male counterparts. Before American newspapers stationed staff correspondents overseas in the 1870s, newsmen concentrated on the Civil War, its prelude, and its aftermath. Women could go to Europe and write on space rates for newspapers that refused to hire them to cover their hometowns. While such behavior remained scandalous, there was neither a foreign news establishment to oppose them nor men competing for their jobs. Still, many women writers, like Sara Jane Clarke, used pen names to escape the epithets hurled at untraditional women—unladylike, undignified, disgraceful. Clarke started the vogue for alliterative pseudonyms by writing under the by-line Grace Greenwood. To disarm the opposition, some women went in for the diminutive—Minnie Myrtle, Jenny June. If in the process they demeaned themselves, they at least got a foot in the door. Clarke eventually came out of the closest, using her married name, Jane Lippincott, to establish a reputation as a Paris correspondent.

The most famous nineteenth-century female by-line belonged to Elizabeth Cochrane, writing as Nellie Bly. As an overseas reporter, she had the shortest and most spectacular career in history. Nellie Bly chose her pen name from the song by Stephen

Foster. When George A. Madden, editor of the *Pittsburgh Dispatch*, had the gall to write an editorial repeating the adage that woman's place was in the home, she retorted with an anonymous letter he found too inflammatory to print. But he advertised to find her, hired her, and eventually sent her to Mexico, where she managed to get expelled for writing "Mexico is a Republic in name only. It is the worst monarchy in existence."

In 1889, for the *New York World* she undertook to break the record of Phileas Fogg, the fictional hero of Jules Verne's romance *Around the World in Eighty Days*. After some reluctance, the *World*'s editors joined in the spirit of the adventure and gave her promotion exceeding any previously given a foreign correspondent.

By ship and train, ricksha and sampan, horse and burro, Nellie Bly traveled around the world in seventy-two days, six hours, and ten minutes. With time for suspense to build and an indefatigable sense of what would interest her readers, Nellie kept them excited, fascinated, amused, and horrified. She risked her record by stopping off in Amiens, France, to interview Verne about his futuristic novel. In Brindisi, Italy, she almost missed her ship to the Orient by taking time to file a cable to her newspaper. In Singapore, she bought a monkey for a mascot. In Canton, she visited the jail and reported on instruments of torture.

For her last lap, the *World* hired a private train to take her from San Francisco to New York, and brass bands serenaded her at every whistle stop. Cowboys rode for miles to get a glimpse of her, and men who had never seen her deluged her with proposals of marriage.

Nationwide applause for her courage and audacity marked a profound change in public attitudes toward women achievers. It was no longer disgraceful for a woman to compete with men, so a woman correspondent would never again feel compelled to hide behind a pseudonym.

By then it was a compliment to tell a woman "You write like a man," and the first woman to do anything only men had done before her won applause. Fanny B. Ward of the *New Orleans Picayune*, one of the first American correspondents to enter

Cuba in 1898, was there when the mysterious sinking of the American battleship *Maine* in Havana harbor resulted in the outbreak of the Spanish-American War.

Yet new barriers to women were being erected as the old came tumbling down. The idea of foreign correspondence as a career dawned late in the nineteenth century and from the day newspapers decided they could afford to put foreign correspondents on the staff, they chose to hire men. But the women refused to fade away.

3

World War I:
The Silent Treatment

"THE GERMAN LINES ARE VERY CLOSE NOW," MARY ROBERTS Rinehart wrote from the Western Front in Belgium in February 1915. "The barbed wire barrier tears my clothes. The wind is howling fiercely. . . . No man's land lies flooded—but full of dead bodies. . . . Here the stench begins." Under cover of night she got within two hundred yards of the German lines, convinced she was covering a war closer to the enemy than would ever again be possible. Of the return she wrote, "My heavy boots chafe my heel, and I limp. But I limp rapidly. I do not care to be shot in the back. . . . I have done what no woman has done before, and I am alive. But my heel hurts."

Rinehart was among the first American correspondents to reach the front in World War I. When the United States entered the war in April 1917, it acquired and exercised the power to send women correspondents to the rear. From this and from the reluctance of newsmen to acknowledge the presence of women where they risked their lives rose the myth that no women covered the war to end all wars. In fact, despite the silent treatment, several women correspondents achieved celebrity status, if only in their hometowns, for their coverage of that war.

Mary Boyle O'Reilly, the forty-one-year-old daughter of John Boyle O'Reilly, who gained prominence as publisher of the *Boston Pilot*, witnessed the German invasion of Louvain, Belgium, in August 1914. The town had been burning for two days before another American writer, Richard Harding Davis, taken prisoner by the Germans, saw it from the window of a troop train passing through. "O'Reilly beat all the male correspondents sent in from Paris and stayed on after they left," reported George Weller, a scholar as well as a journalist in World War II. "She was the envy of my jealous sex."

Rinehart, reporting to two million readers of the *Saturday Evening Post*, reached the front in Belgium before the British government authorized London-based correspondents to cross the Channel.

Lord Northcliffe, the powerful publisher of the London *Times*, told her she was the best-paid fiction writer on earth. Critics thought she was too popular to be great, and in a moment of brutal self-assessment she agreed. "I was a bad novelist, but I was a good reporter."

Born in Pittsburgh in 1876, the year Alexander Graham Bell introduced the telephone, Rinehart grew up in genteel poverty and chose nursing as one of the few careers open to her. When she entered hospital training in 1893, there were only 471 graduate nurses in all America. She married Dr. Stanley Rinehart, a physician, had three sons, and was still planning a college education when the stock market crash and financial panic of 1903 forced her to concentrate on writing to feed the family. Her traumatic experience as a nurse provided the makings of fiction, and she crafted mysteries that made her America's most popular storyteller. *Harper's* magazine rejected her first offering, but after the *Saturday Evening Post* used a humorous story she wrote, *Harper's* asked her for similar stories, apparently unaware it had missed its opportunity to discover her.

When World War I began in the summer of 1914, experienced newspaperwomen in New York tried and failed to get their editors to send them overseas. Some editors thought the war would be over before the women could file their stories; some flatly refused to employ women to cover a war. Rinehart told her *Saturday Evening Post* editors, "I do not intend to let the biggest thing in my life go by without having been a part of it." At thirty-eight, she was in a position to demand more than money from the magazine, which needed her fiction to maintain its circulation. The *Saturday Evening Post* launched her career as a foreign correspondent with full credentials, letters of introduction, and a generous expense account. Wearing a fur coat she bought with her advance, she sailed on the *Franconia* in January 1915.

In London she found newsmen at war with the military commanders. The Allies as well as the Germans had arrested as spies newsmen caught on the Continent at the outbreak of war. The British were refusing to send reporters to the front, and all had a hard time getting their copy through censorship. Rinehart was forbidden to use her last name in her cables because of its German origin. The wife of an English barrister finally sent her to the Belgian Red Cross office at the Savoy Hotel. Her nursing experience helped convince the Belgians that she could describe their plight.

The next day she was in Dunkirk, the only woman in a crowd of men at the Hôtel des Arcades when it was bombarded by eighteen German planes celebrating the kaiser's birthday. Seeking safety, she followed two bearded Russian grand dukes, later realizing she had sat out the bombardment under a glass skylight. On her way to the front, she saw an old woman killed by a German shell dropped in front of her automobile. She watched as more German shells destroyed the village that was her destination. "Across the fields," she wrote, "a line of star lights would mark the enemy trenches, and over all would be the incessant roaring of the heavy guns."

The Allies permitted correspondents to make their first official trip into no man's land in February. From the crowd waiting in London for permission to travel, six newspapermen were selected to make a twenty-four-hour tour of the Belgian front, where the first civilian they met was Rinehart. "How long have you been up here?" Ward Price of the London *Times* asked her. "Three weeks," she said cheerfully. By then she had vermin in her hair to prove it.

To go beyond the front into no man's land, she and her fellow correspondents started from the headquarters of the Third Division of the Belgian Army, left their cars just behind the advance trenches, then set out on foot in sleet and rain. Their destination was a ruined church where a lonely Capuchin monk, formerly an Army officer and now a volunteer, spied on the German trenches for the Belgians.

The correspondents made their way back to safety along a makeshift foot path of wood and straw set across a flooded field. Rinehart understood why the men wrote of their brief adventure without mentioning her presence: the news that a woman had shared the hazards of the journey would have spoiled the male macho image. What annoyed her was that she had arranged the trip to no man's land for herself, and she did not appreciate the military's decision to let the men share it. Her spirits revived at the sight of their faces when the British returned the newsmen to London after their glimpse of war, while she, with the Belgian Army's permission, remained at the front.

Marshal Ferdinand Foch helped Rinehart reach the front in France at a time when French policy prohibited all journalists from entering the battle zone. A handsome woman possessed of innate dignity tempered by a warm sense of humor, she won the confidence of generals and privates alike. She discovered the marshal, then commander of the Northern Army and later supreme commander of the Allied forces on the Western Front, praying in a church. His mood brightening when he saw her, Foch invited her to lunch and told her that the Germans were already defeated. But he added that the war would last a long time, and he was correct. Foch took for granted her right to be there and personally briefed her on the precise positions of the opposing forces before sending her forward.

From France she cabled her editors that the Germans were using poisoned gas, but fearing to inflame the public and endanger America's neutrality, the *Post* declined to use her eyewitness account. The *New York Tribune*, with no such compunctions, printed the story filed by its correspondent, Will Irwin, who won credit for an exclusive. The *Post* did, however, print her exclusive interview with King Albert of Belgium, in which he accused the Germans of using Belgian civilians to shield their advance. To this the American public paid scant attention.

"America at large had no conception of the importance of those statements . . . or that I had at last secured an interview for which almost any European correspondent would have given a good eyetooth,'' Rinehart complained. She endured what every correspondent has experienced, the refusal of the desk to run her copy as she wrote it and the failure of the public to appreciate the importance of what she was allowed to say.

More disturbing to her were the appalling conditions the war wounded endured. Neither the French nor the Belgians had a system for training nurses, she reported. She found casualties left in barns and railway stations with no dressings, no anesthetics, their bodies black with vermin.

Marshal Foch arranged for Rinehart to visit the British forces at Saint-Omer, where Field Marshal Sir John French assigned Lord Claude Hamilton to escort her. ''We were just sitting down to lunch when suddenly Hamilton turned up with a lovely lady,'' an officer wrote in his diary. Rinehart was shown the entry after the officer was killed in action. She grieved for him and for a wounded German soldier who fell and lay in front of the British trenches for five days. The firing was so heavy and constant that nobody could bring him in. But the British passed him food and water and a candy called bull's-eye. At last he was rescued, and he recovered.

The gunners eagerly fired for her, and the Germans responded with amazing suddenness. She was invited to inaugurate a bridge, an honor she performed with her usual dignity while German shells came overhead. The trenches filled with mud and water; pumps had little effect. Her clothing was never dry.

On her return to London, Rinehart found the press corps up in arms over her exclusives. One was an interview Queen Mary granted her out of her special concern for the nursing of wounded soldiers. Another was an interview with Winston Churchill, then Chancellor of the Exchequer, who told her he never opened his mouth except to put his foot in it, which apparently he proceeded to do again by talking to her. The real bone of contention was that Field Marshal Sir John French had allowed her to cover the front while newsmen were barred. Parliament even took up the matter of two women who visited Sir John, one of them described as ''an American called Rinehart.'' The other woman was not named, possibly in deference to the British aristocracy. The implication was that both were lady friends.

On the battlefield, Rinehart had decided, "the place of a woman in war is service." Partly out of concern for her family, she left for the United States, vowing to return as a nurse. Although her war stories had made her an international celebrity, she held to her vow to serve as a nurse. When the United States entered the war, the American Red Cross accepted her application. Although the Army was pleading for women to serve as nurses in Europe, the War Department refused to give her permission to travel. Under no circumstances would the War Department accredit any women to cover the fighting in World War I, and apparently it feared other women would protest if it allowed Rinehart to return to France, even as a nurse. Two of her three sons went to war, and she was told that was enough for one family. She carried her case all the way to the secretary of war, only to be told that General John J. ("Black Jack") Pershing, commander of the American Expeditionary Forces, personally had rejected her.

The armed forces had other plans for her. For the Navy she spent time with the Atlantic fleet and reported on improvements needed in conditions for crewmen. She visited Army installations and reported on their needs to the War Department. With no time to worry about herself, she worried about her husband who, although he was less than a success as a physician, remained her pillar of stability. Loyally, she wrote to President Woodrow Wilson, demanding a proper military assignment for him. Wilson acknowledged her letter but did nothing to promote Dr. Rinehart from a modest role on the home front.

Their son Stanley Jr. also chafed under his assignment to the rear echelons. Toward the end of the war, the young officer was stationed at La Valbonne, near Lyons, France, disappointed at missing the real fighting. At last he mustered the courage to confront his superior. "If the general pleases, I would like to be sent to the front," he said.

"The front? What's the idea, Lieutenant?"

"I would like to see my mother, sir."

Mary Roberts Rinehart had done it again. Secretary of War

Newton D. Baker rewarded her for her reporting on conditions at training camps by sending her to France in the fall of 1918 to report to the War Department on what the troops at the front required. Within days after she reached Paris, and before her son caught up with her, the Armistice was declared on November 11, 1918. Three days later she met General Pershing, who said, "So you got here after all!"

Pershing sent her into Germany with the Third Army. She visited front-line hospitals the Germans had left and the French had not yet taken over and saw the desperately ill struggling to prepare food for themselves. On the road she passed newly released prisoners shuffling home in rags, without money or food, "often mere skeletons of men, unshaven, emaciated, listless." A special Red Cross studio was making masks for men whose faces had been destroyed in the fighting. Visiting the hospital wards where those men were confined, she confirmed that the masks were needed before escaping to vomit. One dedicated physician continued to administer X-rays though he lacked proper protection, well aware of the consequences. He lost both hands.

How anyone could read her horror stories and contemplate yet another war is the sort of mystery people do not pay to read. For Rinehart there was personal satisfaction in having the War Department act on her recommendations. Her inspection tour took her to Pentanezen Camp at Brest, where conditions for the troops were so scandalous that the War Department was facing a senatorial investigation. Asked what was needed, she first demanded delousing plants and laundry machinery. Her reports were radioed in code to the secretary of war, and within a month conditions improved enormously. Her lasting memory was of the dead. The day they buried the Unknown Soldier, she wrote, "I wandered over battle fields among rows of wooden crosses, looking for the names of boys I knew. . . . There was no glory now; only destruction and rows on rows of graves."

One of the few women to cover the disarmament conference, she cautioned her huge readership, "Peace is not a passive but an active condition, not a negation but an affirmation. It is a gesture as strong as war." During the conference, newsmen met at the Press Club, and Rinehart, excluded from their circle, recalled rather forlornly that she had no one with whom to compare notes. Her experiences as a war correspondent turned her into a belated suffragette and she marched, rather self-consciously she admitted, in parades in Chicago and Pittsburgh. The publishers of the *Ladies' Home Journal* offered her the then magnificent salary of $50,000 a year to edit it, but she declined to be confined to what men viewed as the women's market.

For all her efforts, her exclusive war stories, and her fleeting fame, Rinehart won sinfully little recognition from the press corps or its historians. She had two strikes against her: first, she was a woman, and women were easily ignored; second, newspapermen were always suspicious of correspondents who had acquired their status as fiction writers. Whatever their contribution, they were dismissed as "visiting firemen" who would return from a journalistic adventure to their fiction. Yet Rinehart not only beat most American correspondents to the front, she had more readers, earned more money, and produced more major exclusives than most of them.

When World War II came, the U.S. War Department again put obstacles in the path of women war correspondents, but made an exception of Mary Roberts Rinehart. Both the Army and the Navy offered to put a private plane at her disposal if only she would go and write again about our gallant warriors. As she was well into her sixties, she declined, explaining that war was for young men—and young women. She was strong enough (she lived to be eighty-two), but her heart was not in it.

Of all the correspondents who risked their lives to cover World War I, three of the best and the brightest, turned back by the U.S. Army, took even greater risks to cover Russia's war against Germany and then the Russian Revolution. They were Rheta Childe Dorr of the *New York Mail*, Bessie Beatty of the *San Francisco Bulletin*, and Louise Bryant of the Bell Syndicate. All three wrote books as well as news stories about those chaotic days of war and revolution. Their reports informed Americans of Russian losses in the war with Germany and of Bolshevik victories in the cities at a time when so little news of those momentous events was reaching the public that one historian, Phillip Knightley, accused newsmen of participating in a conspiracy to keep from public scrutiny events in Russia unfavorable to the Allies.

Dorr, just four years older than Rinehart, was a veteran of three European assignments before World War I began. Conservative by nature, she turned rebel the day she read a tombstone that said, "Also Harriet, wife of the above." Determined to earn a gravestone of her own, she applied for a job and was told that only men were entitled to wages. Because she persisted in pursuing a newspaper career, her husband left her with a son to care for. To collect child support in 1898, she would have had to prove that her husband was responsible for their divorce, and no one would have blamed him for opposing her career.

She was earning a precarious living as a free-lancer in New York City in 1900 when a news agency offered her $25 to arrange a picture of New York Governor Theodore Roosevelt, who was being promoted for Vice President of the United States. He agreed to pose provided she would handle all the photographers, an assignment she accomplished so well that it launched her career with the *New York Tribune*, then the *New York Post* and the *Mail*.

Dorr first went to Europe in 1906 to cover the coronation of King Haakon of Norway. On her own, she took a steamer to St. Petersburg, where a fellow correspondent introduced her to what he described mildly as a "revolutionary household." There she met a beautifully manicured young woman terrorist named Lisa. Dorr watched this creature drop another lump of sugar into her steaming glass of tea and listened while she talked. "The most boresome part of it is idleness, waiting months, sometimes years, enviously watching others achieve. . . . Often what we accomplish is a single deed. . . . Whether we succeed or fail we usually die. Or we will wish they had let us die."

Before she could do harm, Lisa was arrested, tried, stripped of her citizenship, and deported. Dorr covered the Duma, the legislative body elected to defuse rebellion in Russia, and she saw the czar dismiss it after two months of indirection and vain oratory. She criticized "impractical visionaries" for planning to give land to the peasants without knowing how to do it short of wrecking Russia financially. Even then her sources saw no solution short of revolution.

The only revolution Dorr supported was for women's rights. Twice, in 1912 and again in 1913, she visited Britain to write about the women's suffrage movement. On one occasion she carried $20,000 sewed into the stays of her corset, money raised in America for the cause. She smuggled it into Britain for the British suffrage leader, Emmeline Pankhurst, who was serving a jail sentence for inciting to violence. In 1914 she interviewed President Woodrow Wilson in Washington and questioned him about suffrage for American women. The President shut her off with "I think that it is not proper for me to stand here and be cross-examined by you."

By July 1917 she was back in St. Petersburg, which had been renamed Petrograd, where she was appalled by everything she witnessed. She arrived following the February revolution that brought moderates to power and witnessed the October Revolution by the Bolsheviks. In her hotel one night she awakened to piercing screams. Revolutionaries were "cutting a general to pieces in his bed," she wrote. As she saw it, Russia had become "a barbarous and half insane land. . . . Oratory held the stupid populace spellbound while the Germans invaded the country, boosted Lenin into power and paved the way for the treaty of Brest-Litovsk. . . . Russia was done."

The chaos the women covered cried for interpretation, and the violence they witnessed provoked violent reactions. Their responses differed wildly. What provoked Dorr's anti-communism brought out the pro-Communist sympathies of Louise Bryant and reaffirmed Bessie Beatty's dedication to un-biased reporting.

Of the three, Louise Bryant attracted the most lasting atten-tion, not because she wrote the best copy but because theater audiences long afterward so enjoyed her reasons for becoming a foreign correspondent. She fell in love, fell out of love, and fell in love again.

Louise Bryant was a free spirit, forever vivacious, forever questioning the values of society. Her father, a newspaperman, left the family when she was a baby, so he could only have contributed to her fantasies. She left her husband, a dentist in Portland, Oregon, for the brilliant and radical reporter John Reed. Both professed to believe in free love. In the summer of 1916, while Reed traveled, Bryant, on Cape Cod, was having a love affair with dramatist Eugene O'Neill. Reed then had second thoughts about free love, at least for her; Louise and John were married in November 1916.

Soon after the United States declared war on Germany, Reed confessed that he had been unfaithful; Bryant reacted by applying for a passport. She reached France in June, ahead of the first American troops. The authorities, however, frustrated her efforts to cover combat, and she returned to her husband in New York. In August they took off together for Russia.

Bryant traveled with accreditation from the Bell Syndicate, granted in return for her promise to write women's news, but her husband's radical views made it difficult for him to get accredited. His plans to write for *The Masses*, a radical magazine, were foiled when the U.S. government closed it down for printing Communist propaganda. His only outlet for the news was *The Call*, a struggling left-wing newspaper. He achieved fame not as a correspondent but for *Ten Days That Shook the World*, a dramatization of the Russian Revolution.

Three films were based on the book, the first in 1927. Warren Beatty produced and starred in *Reds* in 1982, and the Russians countered by producing their version, given the title of the book. Although Bryant was not mentioned in the book, the latter two films featured her as the love interest. Some who saw the movie *Reds* objected that it neglected to explain how the Reeds settled into Petrograd and immediately began reporting the news, in spite of having virtually no knowledge of the Russian language. They were helped by Bessie Beatty, who had arrived in Petrograd three months earlier than they and showed them the ropes.

Beatty, with fifteen years' experience as a reporter in California, was a protégée of Fremont Older, editor of the *San Francisco Bulletin* and member of a small but distinguished group of editors who actively promoted women journalists. She was in mid-

Pacific, headed for Japan, when the United States declared war on Germany. After visiting China as well as Japan, she spent twelve days on the Trans-Siberian Express to reach Petrograd in June. On the train she cultivated everyone who spoke English, among them Count Tolstoy, son of the author Leo Tolstoy. She needed no knowledge of Russian to see the poignancy of a soldier clutching a bouquet of lilies of the valley, long since dead, as they arrived in Petrograd at 2:00 A.M. only to discover that his bride was not there to greet him.

There were no hotel rooms available in all of Petrograd, Beatty was informed. Rather than spend the night at the railroad station, she started walking. At the Select Hotel she ran into Count Tolstoy again, and he managed to get her a room for one night. The czar had abdicated in March following the February revolution, and the shaky provisional government had no welcoming committee for the foreign press. Granted her first good night's sleep in twelve, Beatty vacated the room previously reserved for others and began walking again, aware of the adage that it takes more shoe leather than brains to make a foreign correspondent. The capacity to find and read a city map was, of course, essential.

Eventually she wandered into the elegant Astoria Hotel, restored after a fire during the February revolution and known as the "war hotel," reserved for high officials. On the staircase she encountered a gentleman who enjoyed practicing his English with her so much that he arranged for her to stay there. By the time she found the people whom she had been told to look up, she was nicely settled. They insisted that it was impossible for a foreign civilian to get into the Astoria, but there she was. She was enjoying one of the pleasures shared by women correspondents, the surprise they evoke by the facility with which they move from one world capital to the next. It comes with experience and awareness that for every problem there is a solution.

By overnight train, Beatty traveled south to the front with Peter Bukowski, a friendly American of Polish origin. She got within one hundred fifty yards of the German trenches, fifty yards closer than Rinehart and close enough to see two Germans foolishly stick their heads up and get shot by Russian riflemen.

"No man's land lay like a bone between two hungry dogs," she wrote.

She witnessed the July offensive against the Germans and recognized it as a colossal blunder. Russian soldiers were running out of strength to pursue the war against Germany. Most correspondents were barred from the front, which helps explain why the *New York Times* kept reporting that the Russians were winning.

The one Russian victory Beatty witnessed was scored by the Women's Death Battalion. At the front, she found and interviewed Marie Bachkarova, leader of the all-female force. When Bachkarova's husband was killed by the Germans, the big peasant woman picked up his gun and joined a men's regiment. Wounded, she was taken to a hospital with a hole in her back. Told that men were refusing to fight, she retorted, "Women will fight. Women have the courage, the endurance, even the strength for fighting." To prove it, Bachkarova organized the Women's Death Battalion.

Beatty and Dorr together covered the women soldiers at the front. Some Russian soldiers broke into the women's barracks and tried to rape them, but the women drove them off with guns. The Death Battalion routed the Germans on its section of the front, but at tremendous cost. Dorr reported that half the women were killed or wounded. Prime Minister Alexander Kerensky honored the survivors by assigning them to guard his headquarters at the Winter Palace in Petrograd, where Louise Bryant took up their story.

The Reeds arrived in Petrograd on the crest of a counterrevolution. Kerensky, on September 9, dismissed the reactionary General L. G. Kornilov as commander in chief of the armed forces, and Kornilov's forces fought back. Kerensky's moderate government was obliged to call on the forces of the left to defeat the right. Bryant covered a victory address by Kerensky and watched as he received an ovation—his last. On November 7, Bryant, Reed, and Albert Rhys Williams, an American clergyman and socialist, went to the Winter Palace to see Kerensky, only to be told he had fled. It was the first of those ten days that shook the world. By the old-style calendar used in Russia until 1918, the date was October 25, hence the October Revolution.

From the Winter Palace the Americans walked through streets filling with soldiers to the Smolny Institute, a former girls' school, where the All-Russian Congress of Soviets was convening. Beatty met them there, and they watched as the Bolsheviks took charge and Kerensky's followers withdrew. Not through yet, Kerensky was at the front marshaling his forces to fight the Bolsheviks.

Bryant reported that Bolshevik soldiers seeking to take the Winter Palace feared they would be accused of killing the women guards of the Death Battalion. Worse, they were accused of rape. Some of the horror stories were circulated by Dorr, who admittedly was not there when it happened. Having seen Russian soldiers attempt rape, Dorr could believe the rumors about the Bolsheviks. Beatty, who covered the Death Battalion both at the front and in Petrograd, observed that the Bolsheviks behaved with moderation.

Bryant ate cabbage soup and black bread with the Bolshevik Red Guards and watched them go out to battle in twenty-five-below-zero weather. She described them as a people's army of men, women, and children, comparable to George Washington's ragged revolutionary band at Valley Forge.

The unbearable conditions for children concerned her most. Mainly because of a shortage of medical supplies, 85 percent of the children in charitable institutions died, she reported.

I came to realize with horror that everybody in Russia is grown up. Those young in years, whom we still called children, had old and sad faces; large, hungry eyes burned forth from pale countenances, wretched, worn-out shoes, sagging, ragged little garments accentuated their so apparent misery.

"In our eagerness to aid the small nations," she remarked, "we have almost overlooked great Russia." It must have hurt to write that line, for she knew that the United States was not overlooking Russia; it was simply refusing to send aid through the Bolsheviks.

In a mighty effort to be temperate and persuasive, Bryant permitted herself only a brief statement of the truth: "The Soviet Republic will not fall from inside pressure. Only outside, foreign hostile intervention can destroy it." By then, the *New York Times*, without missing an edition, had moved from predicting a Russian victory over the Germans to predicting a Bolshevik defeat.

Striving for balance, Beatty observed that a reporter can be too close to the facts to see the truth. But in those days before the dictatorship of Joseph Stalin, she punctured the worst of the atrocity stories written about the Bolsheviks. "Whenever the death penalty was inflicted, it was done by mobs with no official sanction," she reported. Although never swayed by Communist ideology, she added, "To have failed to see the hope in the Russian Revolution is to be as a blind man looking at the sunrise." The impressive reporting she did in Russia won her the position of editor of *McCall's* magazine when she returned to the United States.

Bryant returned to the United States in January 1918, leaving her husband in Russia. Acquaintances suspected that she was rushing home to beat her husband into print, but the Reeds were not in competition. Her rival was Beatty, whose book, *The Red Heart of Russia*, came out in 1918, as did Bryant's *Six Red Months in Russia*. When Reed's volume finally appeared in April 1919, Charles E. Russell, the *New York Times* reviewer, commented, "It cannot be said that he adds anything to the essentials of the narrative already told by his talented wife."

Nor did he try. Reed's book was a fictionalized account of events, replete with scenes he could not have witnessed and conversations he could not have overheard. His book created a sensation without dwarfing Bryant's contribution. The only sour note to spoil Bryant's day was the refusal of the anti-Communist Dorr to appear on the same lecture platform with her.

For a while the Reeds were together in New York. Reed, although he was refused a passport by the State Department, returned to Russia illegally in December 1919. Trying to get home, he was arrested and jailed in Finland, where he became desperately ill. When he was finally released, he returned to Russia. He faced arrest if he returned to the United States. The State Department refused to issue Bryant a passport to join him, so she obtained forged papers and traveled disguised as a seaman. The movie *Reds* was wrong on one important score. It showed Bryant clashing with Finnish authorities. Having had the sense to avoid Finland, she paid the price of a hardship-filled trip through the Arctic Ocean, enduring bitter cold, storms at sea, and miserable food. The Reeds were finally reunited in Moscow in September 1920. By mid-October John was dead of typhus. Although in his last days Reed had been disillusioned by excesses committed in the name of the Revolution, the Soviet government buried him beneath the Kremlin Wall.

The legend that Reed's death caused Louise Bryant to fall apart and fade away is nonsense. Afterward she did some of her best work as a correspondent for the Hearst newspapers in Europe. Among her scoops was an exclusive interview with Benito Mussolini, the future fascist dictator of Italy. Her second book, *Mirrors of Moscow*, a penetrating study of the revolutionary leader Lenin and his subordinates, appeared in 1923. Sobered, she observed, "No practical politician is above intrigue." The revolutionary leaders seemed to be supermen. "But in truth," she wrote, "behind the screen of smoke and flame they are like other men; no larger and no smaller, no better and no worse, all creatures of the same incessant passions, hungers, vanities and fears."

In Paris, Bryant married and divorced William C. Bullitt before he became United States ambassador to the Soviet Union. After that marriage crumbled, she became an alcoholic and died in 1936 at the age of forty-nine.

Dorr, too, covered Europe during and after World War I. From Petrograd she went to Paris and cited her experience on the Russian front as a reason for being allowed to cover the Western Front, but that cut no ice. Denied permission to cover the fighting, Dorr managed to get to the training camps in France by joining the staff of the YMCA and offering to lecture to the troops on the Russian Revolution.

At Aix-les-Bains, she was reunited with her son, Julian, a soldier in France. "Mother!" he called in surprise when she entered his mess hall. Whereupon a whole roomful of soldiers sprang to their feet and never sat down until she found a chair. Women correspondents may not have received any respect, but mothers did.

"I think the greatest thing my generation of women accomplished was the freeing of younger women to go farther than ourselves," Dorr wrote in her autobiography, *A Woman of Fifty*.

The trio who covered Russia made a special mark. It was the first time American women correspondents worked in competition with each other as well as with men. Foreign correspondence was becoming a group endeavor for women, as it had always been for men. Politically, they disagreed, as correspondents always would, but as eyewitnesses to history, they wrote the truth as they saw it.

4

They Were Survivors

FROM WORLD WAR I THROUGH WORLD WAR II, THE CAREERS OF Irene Corbally Kuhn and her friend Peggy Hull spanned two epochs, one recorded as history, another still unfolding.

Kuhn contributed to history when she made the first radio broadcast from China on December 15, 1924. Peggy Hull made history in 1918, when she became the first woman correspondent accredited by the U.S. War Department to cover a war zone. Never mind that the U.S. Army sent her to Siberia or that the war was over by the time she arrived. By then she had acquired sufficient notoriety in two war zones to qualify for a brass star.

As Irene Kuhn described her, "Peggy was as feminine as a kitten, and she had a will of iron, a woman all men loved and no woman ever disliked." Born Henrietta Eleanor Goodnough on a farm near Bennington, Kansas, on December 30, 1889, Peggy worked as a typesetter on the *Junction City*, Kansas, *Sentinel* before her marriage, at the age of twenty-one, to George Hull, a handsome man born in Kalapuhr, India, who shared her enthusiasm for faraway places.

The Hulls went to work in Hawaii, he as a reporter for the *Honolulu Star*, she as a feature writer and women's page editor for the *Pacific Commercial Advertiser*. George Hull drank, and after four years of marriage, on the day he tried to climb a flagpole naked, his wife left him.

She was writing an advertising column for the *Cleveland Plain Dealer* when the Ohio National Guard was mobilized in 1916 and sent to El Paso, Texas, to join General John J. Pershing's punitive expedition into Mexico, its mission to capture Pancho

Villa, the Mexican revolutionary and border raider. Denied permission by her editor to travel with the guardsmen, Peggy quit, went to Texas, and worked first for the *El Paso Herald*, then the *El Paso Morning Times*.

Pershing never captured Pancho Villa and Peggy never got near the front, but she was allowed to accompany the troops on a grueling ninety-mile, two-week training march from El Paso to Las Cruces, New Mexico. In the field, she pulled a poncho around her and slept on the ground like the men. Caught in a sandstorm and separated from the troops, she stumbled onto a tiny shack, where an Indian family gave her shelter, then guided her back to the military forces.

The *El Paso Morning Times* of February 6, 1917, headlined her story of the return of the ten thousand members of the punitive expedition. She wrote,

> It wasn't the triumphal return of a victorious army or the dejected retreat of the defeated. It was a stoical, silent, unenthusiastic organization which marched through the border gate. . . . Eleven months in Mexico had sent them back an efficient, unsentimental, hardened fighting machine.

The expedition had accomplished something more important than its purpose, the preparation of American troops for U.S. entry into World War I. It was Peggy Hull's training ground as well.

Peggy's story did not mention that she stole the show. Newsreel cameramen induced her to appear on horseback just as General Pershing came riding out of Mexico on horseback at the head of his troops. On cue, she trotted her horse into position alongside Pershing's. Newspapers around the world captioned the picture "American girl correspondent leads troops out of Mexico with General Pershing." The general was described as furious, but his anger soon evaporated.

When the United States entered World War I two months later, Peggy Hull went to war wearing a uniform she had designed for herself; it featured a Sam Browne belt and a daringly short skirt. With only a promise from the *El Paso Times* to use her articles if she made it, Hull paid for her own passage to France, charmed a State Department official into issuing a passport, bribed a French consular officer to get a visa, and arrived in Paris in time to see the Allied Expeditionary Forces (AEF) parade for the first time on the Fourth of July, 1917.

An attack of appendicitis prevented her from visiting military installations the U.S. Army had offered to show her. When she recovered, she called at the office of the *Chicago Tribune* in Paris and met its publisher, Robert R. McCormick, who was serving as a major in the army and commanding the battery of the First Division artillery at Le Valdahon, near Besançon. The major would be remembered in history as Colonel McCormick, a publisher so disillusioned by World War I that he seized on any argument to try to keep America out of World War II.

Joseph B. Pierson, manager of the "Army," or Paris, edition of the *Chicago Tribune*, took Peggy with him to Le Valdahon. She arrived without credentials, and the post adjutant brought her presence to the attention of General Peyton C. March, the commanding general. General Pershing, by then commander of the AEF in Europe, was there to inspect the troops. Both generals had served in the Mexican campaign and, remembering Peggy well, they invited her to tea.

Adroitly sidestepping the fact that women had been denied permission to cover the war, she told them her newspaper could not afford to have her accredited; newspapers had to post a $10,000 bond to assure the good behavior of accredited correspondents.

She said the generals told her that she mustn't leave "when the story was getting bigger all the time." Arranging to stay in a cold barracks with women working for the YMCA canteen, she wrote what she was assigned to write, the woman's angle, mainly personal experience stories, and she signed her articles simply Peggy. Her stories were good enough to be printed not only in the Paris edition but in the Chicago edition of the *Tribune*. This put her in competition with men, and they rose in resentment at what they saw as favoritism toward an unaccredited correspondent.

The newsmen, mostly confined to the Army press camp at Neufchâteau, were bored, frustrated, and angry at military censorship. The Peggy affair gave them an opportunity to explode at the special consideration granted a woman. They said it was "undignified" for a woman to write about the war, but they saw nothing undignified about YMCA girls serving them coffee.

To reach the front, Peggy asked for accreditation only to the *Paris Tribune*, not the *Chicago Tribune*. She did not get either, mainly because of the unfriendly intervention of Major Frederick Palmer, the U.S. press officer, who had once been a leading journalist but whose military title made him the meanest censor on the front.

"If the privileges which she says have been given to her have been authorized by the Commander in Chief," Palmer wrote, "then she is receiving privileges which have never been given to any individual representing any daily paper with any European army during the present war." This was blatantly false, but its irate tone worked, and she was sent back to Paris.

Word of her mother's illness caused Peggy to return to the United States in December 1917, still determined to get military accreditation and return to Paris to cover the war legitimately. While caring for her mother, she learned of something even more interesting to her—plans for an American military expedition to Siberia. Before she could apply for accreditation, she needed newspaper sponsorship. After fifty newspapers rejected her, she finally obtained the endorsement of Newspaper Enterprise Association, the Scripps-Howard press service headquartered in Cleveland.

Army accreditation officers again rejected her application to cover the troops. Happily, her friend General March was back in Washington as Army chief of staff. He wrote the accreditation officer, "If your only reason for refusing Miss Peggy Hull credentials is because she is a woman, issue them at once." His decree produced an outcry, not from men, but from women charging favoritism. If she could go, why couldn't they?

General March retorted grandly, "Any woman who can bring me a record of two years in the field benefiting the troops and causing no trouble, can get a pass at anytime." He sounded righteous enough, but how were women to get two years' experience in the field when the Army was denying them accreditation?

Even in Peggy's case, General March did not authorize a woman to cover combat. The United States sent some seven thousand troops to Siberia, not to fight but to guard the Trans-Siberian Railroad, over which supplies were being delivered to the White Army, then locked in a losing battle against the Red Army of the Bolsheviks. March had an ulterior motive in sending Peggy to cover this action. As he wrote her, "These men are likely to be lost sight of in view of the big things that are happening in France." He wanted one American reporter, even a woman if that was all he could get, to tell their story.

Peggy obtained her accreditation in September 1918 and embarked for Siberia. She was aboard a Russian steamer when the Armistice was declared and learned of it when she landed in Vladivostok on November 15. The Russian Revolution was far from over, and the hardship she witnessed matched anything reported about European wars.

Advance newspaper publicity for her built on Siberia's image as a frozen wasteland where exiles were sent to perish. Actually, the climate of the region she visited was comparable to Canada's, and she resisted the temptation to exaggerate—the truth was more compelling. Vladivostok, a pretty city, was desperately short of food and fuel. The streets were filthy and the stench of the unwashed, impoverished population a burden to breathe. "Siberia is on the threshold of its blackest period," she wrote. "Twice a victim, first to monarchy and then to anarchy—its people will die by the thousands. They are freezing to death now."

In the face of misery, Peggy Hull dropped her girlish demeanor and reported stark horror. She traveled a thousand miles on an inspection tour of the Siberian Railroad and told of masses of refugees crushed into boxcars trying to escape both the Red and the White armies.

The indifference to suffering shocked her most. Once she came upon a Russian driver beating his horse to death. A British colonel, wielding his riding crop, threatened the driver with the same fate. The horse, bleeding and shivering, escaped the clutches of his master only to tremble and die. Peggy had noticed something else, and now she asked why all the horses were blind.

"Because their drivers beat their eyes out," the colonel replied. "That I understand is one of the first things they do when they get a horse." When she wondered how they could be so cruel to animals, the colonel asked her, "Could you expect much more when men, women, and children are whipped to death, buried alive, stripped, and left to die in the snow and be eaten by wolves?"

As the headline over one of her articles put it, "Love for Yanks in Siberia Is Slight." Anti-Communists resented President Woodrow Wilson's order that Americans confine themselves to protecting the railroad, not fight the Bolsheviks, and Communists resented the occupation by foreign forces.

Peggy spent nine months in Siberia, leaving in July 1919 before the Americans departed but late enough to see that the Bolsheviks were winning the war for Russia. Historians would dismiss the American expedition to Siberia as a foolish venture, short of disaster thanks only to the decision not to fight. Yet it was a colorful page in the story of America's adventures and misadventures. Long afterward, researchers would turn to Peggy Hull's stories for one of the few firsthand accounts of what had happened there.

On her way home, Hull stopped in Shanghai, where she met C.V. Lee, publisher of the *Shanghai Gazette*, the English-language newspaper of China's revolutionary leader Sun Yat-sen. Lee offered her a job and she promised to return. She then traveled swiftly to the United States and on to Paris.

Covering Paris in 1920, Peggy Hull was recognized as a pro by the press corps that had treated her so badly during the war. She also found a friend for life in Irene Corbally, a twenty-one-year-old correspondent for the *Chicago Tribune*, who later won fame as Irene Corbally Kuhn. The two were equally small in stature, vivacious, and adventurous.

Irene, a New Yorker more sophisticated than her Kansas-bred colleague, was memorable for her wide smile and the lavish wardrobe she induced the *Tribune* to purchase for her so she would be properly attired when covering the Paris fashion shows.

Having failed to find a newspaper job in Manhattan, Irene got her start on the *Syracuse*, New York, *Herald* in 1919. Within months, she was back in Manhattan working for the brand-new *New York Daily News*, founded June 26, 1919. The *News*, dismissed by other publishers as the "servant girls' Bible," had difficulty recruiting able newsmen, so there was room for Irene. No sooner had she landed on the *Daily News* than she began plotting to get overseas.

Irene quit the paper and reached Paris by accepting the first European assignment she was offered, a job writing patent medicine advertising, without pausing to think that her employer might have had ulterior motives in hiring her. For failing to oblige the men on the staff with sexual favors, she was fired by executives who had every intention of leaving her stranded in Paris without money to buy passage back to the United States. Threatening to tell her story to the American embassy, she obtained both severance pay and a ticket home she had no intention of using.

It was time to use a letter of introduction a *Daily News* editor had written for her to Floyd Gibbons, the European director of the *Chicago Tribune*, and her timing was perfect. Rosemary Carr, the fashion editor, had resigned to marry an unknown poet, Stephen Vincent Benét. Gibbons, a man who always strove to give women a chance, was not in Paris when Irene visited the *Tribune*, but when contacted, he suggested she be given the job sight unseen.

The American correspondents in Paris worked and played together, their favorite gathering place the Left Bank Café des Deux Magots, and Irene blew her first paycheck to make a down payment on a studio near the café. The first night, when she turned off the lights, rats hopped into bed with her. Frightened and sleepless, she went to the café. The assembled newsmen rallied to move her belongings out of the rat-trap and collected enough money to stake her until the next payday.

Floyd Gibbons unwittingly got her into trouble by suggesting she pursue the famous American draft dodger, Grover Bergdoll, who had taken refuge in Germany, and bring him back to America. If she found him, how was she to manage this? "You'll hypnotize him," Gibbons said. Following Bergdoll's trail, Irene reached St. Moritz, Switzerland, just three hours after the elusive quarry had departed. There she had to wire Paris for money. In the absence of Gibbons, the *Tribune* Paris correspondent, Henry ("Hank") Wales, replied indignantly, "Return Paris immediately."

So back she went to covering what passed for the routine in Paris, the visits of such Hollywood movie stars as Charlie Chaplin, Mary Pickford, and Douglas Fairbanks, plus the Paris fashion shows. In Paris in the spring, she fell in love with a young American.

For Peggy Hull, the frivolity of postwar Paris could not compete with the lure of the Orient, and she booked passage for Shanghai on the *Inaba*, a Japanese freighter, for a six-week cruise from Marseilles to Hong Kong and Shanghai. While the Japanese were not her ideal traveling companions, the price was right. Her friends in the press corps arranged a champagne party as a farewell salute to her, and Irene arrived with her new beau, both still angry after a lovers' quarrel.

"Why don't you go?" her angry escort taunted Irene.

"I'm as good as gone," she said, and away she went.

As usual, Floyd Gibbons, who might have dissuaded her, was out of town. In his absence and feeling the effects of two glasses of champagne, Irene resigned her job that night, packed her belongings, and the next morning caught a train to Marseilles. A cancellation for the second berth in Peggy's cabin enabled her to board the fully booked *Inaba*.

Aboard ship the correspondents had to overcome the fears of fellow passengers that they were spies. Why else would women be traveling to Asia unescorted in 1921? Peggy, at thirty-two, with a secure job awaiting her on the *Shanghai Gazette*, was supposed to be the sensible member of the party. Irene, a decade younger, was traveling on impulse for a lark. They reversed roles at the first port of call.

After a month at sea, the *Inaba* reached Singapore, where Peggy learned that the *SS Nile* was also in port and decided to go calling on its skipper, a Captain Kingsley she had met in Vladivostok. She soon discovered that Kingsley had left the ship, and she met instead a dashing young British captain, John Kinley, who was entranced by her. His ship followed hers to Hong Kong, where he persuaded her to disembark and travel with him on the *Nile* to Shanghai. Peggy left most of her luggage in Irene's keeping aboard the *Inaba*—and did not see it again for close to three years.

The *Inaba* left port on schedule; the *Nile* was detained in Hong Kong by a shipping strike. After a brief but passionate courtship, Captain Kinley took Peggy to an Episcopal church, presumably to sightsee. There she found a minister and witnesses primed for a wedding, and they were married on the spot.

While the Kinleys honeymooned aboard his ship, Irene, guarding more luggage than she could handle alone, arrived in Shanghai and headed for the safest destination she knew, the Palace Hotel. After paying for three nights in advance, she discovered she had twenty-five dollars in U.S. traveler's checks between her and starvation. Again she produced a letter of introduction, and again her timing was almost perfect. It was the Chinese New Year, and she had to wait two tense days before she met Edward I. Ezra, publisher of the English-language *China Press*.

Ezra, a Levantine Jew who had made a fortune as former head of the legal Shanghai Opium Monopoly, favored Americans for his editorial staff. He had recently hired Edna Lee Booker, an American woman, and she was doing so well that he hired Irene as well. Although salaries were low, the reporters lived in splendor in an elegant house in the French concession, a bridge removed and a world away from the poverty of downtown Shanghai.

Her first day on the job, Irene attended a wedding, where she caught the bridal bouquet and met Bert L. Kuhn, a Chicago newspaperman, the man she would marry.

Irene recalled exploring the city with Margaret Sanger, the American birth control advocate, and the horror they shared at discovering emaciated babies, their bodies covered with scabs and sores, on the garbage heaps of Shanghai.

The day of her wedding, late in the spring of 1922, the ever industrious Irene accepted an assignment to visit an American destroyer in port. The crew, enjoying her company, saw no reason to let her go. "But I'm going to be married at four-thirty," she pleaded.

Eventually she managed to thumb a ride from the ship to the pier on a sampan. Along the way, she remembered she had neglected to buy a wedding gown. Happily, her "number one boy," knowing her wardrobe better than she, greeted her with a pink organdy dress she had ordered and he had arranged to have delivered in time for the ceremony.

The newlyweds soon took a year's sabbatical to have their baby in Honolulu, Hawaii, but it was scarcely a vacation. While Bert worked for the *Honolulu Star Bulletin*, Irene served as a stringer for International News Service (INS). Just days before the baby was due, Hawaii experienced five destructive tidal waves. Irene dashed to the wireless office and, pretending she was in labor, begged the operator to give her all the facts he had collected, then to file her story to INS while she waited. He obliged just to get her out of there before the baby arrived. The bonus she received for her scoop paid for the baby, René Leitani Kuhn. As soon as they dared travel with the baby, the family returned to Shanghai, where the plethora of amahs made it easier for a mother to pursue a career than in the United States.

Irene Kuhn won the distinction of making the first radio broadcast from China, partly because Roy DeLay, the Shanghai manager of the Kellogg Switchboard and Supply Company, having supplied radio transmission equipment, could not afford to pay a broadcaster. He asked her to do the honors "for the thrill" of it, and for her it was indeed a thrill. There were people living in the hinterlands of China who still did not know that the monarchy had fallen in 1911, a thirteen-year gap in news delivery.

Although it would be several years before she broadcast on a regular basis, Kuhn was probably the first woman news announcer in the radio business. She remained virtually the only woman in the game until World War II, because radio executives viewed women's voices as unsuitable for announcing the news. With a voice as clear as a bell and her tone of authority, she used the medium to achieve an international reputation in an era when radio correspondents attracted as much attention as television commentators would in a later generation.

Soon after her first broadcast, Floyd Gibbons arrived in Shanghai and sternly demanded return of the Paris wardrobe the *Chicago Tribune* had bought for her. When she actually produced the four-year-old garments, he laughed and agreed that she had earned them.

When Peggy Hull made her delayed appearance in Shanghai for a happy reunion with Irene late in 1924, both her trunks and her job on the *Shanghai Gazette* were waiting for her. After three years of traveling aboard the *Nile* with her husband, Peggy had induced him to accept the lucrative position of harbor pilot in Shanghai.

The Kinley marriage was not going well. Peggy found she had repeated the mistake of marrying a drinking man, and in the fall of 1925, she returned to the United States without her husband. Only then did she discover, to her horror, that she had lost her American citizenship by her marriage to a foreigner. Until years after the suffrage law was passed, a married woman had no personal right to citizenship; she belonged to her husband and his country. The discovery probably prolonged her married status. Not until she had regained her citizenship through a successful campaign to change the law did she return to Shanghai in 1932 to divorce Captain Kinley.

Bert Kuhn died in Shanghai in 1927 while Irene was visiting the United States with their small daughter, René. He had been involved in undercover work for United States Naval Intelligence and, although the cause of death was not determined, his wife believed he paid for his work with his life.

After her husband's death, Irene Kuhn worked for three New York newspapers, the *Mirror*, the *Daily News*, and the *World Telegram and Sun*, before joining the Mutual Broadcasting System. In 1940 she went to the National Broadcasting Company, where she made the name Irene Corbally Kuhn familiar to a generation of radio listeners.

Her friend Peggy Hull returned to overseas reporting first. While free-lancing in New York, she had fallen in love with

Harvey Deuell, the managing editor of the *New York Daily News*. She was in Shanghai arranging a divorce so she could marry him when the Japanese attacked in January 1932, and Deuell cabled, asking her to cover for the *Daily News*.

During a battle that destroyed much of the city, Peggy set out from the international zone with a Russian chauffeur to interview Japanese General Tsai Ting-kai. On the way they were caught between retreating Chinese and advancing Japanese, and the noise of bombers, artillery, and rifle fire suddenly was deafening. They took refuge in a Chinese tomb, but the chauffeur, crazed by fear, tried to escape. As he ran from the tomb, advancing Japanese troops shot and killed him. Peggy knew that, as soon as the Japanese could reach the tomb, they would level it to destroy any snipers left within.

Casting about for a way of survival, she remembered an identification badge the admiral of the Japanese fleet, Kichisaburo Nomura, had given her. But where was it? She emptied her purse without finding it before recalling that she had put it in the passport she had thrown on the floor. She pinned the badge over her heart with hairpins, then fluffed her hair to identify herself as a woman.

Just as the Japanese troops approached, she stepped into the light. The terror on their faces as they advanced to meet the Chinese gave way to bewilderment at the sight of her, and the men held their fire. The commanding officer took her to General Shirakawa, an officer she had met in Siberia. "If you do not give up your war corresponding," he told her, "you are surely going to end your life on a battlefield."

At a victory party aboard his flagship, Admiral Nomura told Peggy that Americans could not fight. This admiral would be the Japanese ambassador to the United States when his country attacked Pearl Harbor on December 7, 1941.

Peggy Hull remembered the prophecies of both the general and the admiral when she applied for accreditation to cover World War II. Her third marriage, to Harvey Deuell, had ended with his death in October 1939, just weeks after World War II began. Her efforts to cover that war were initially almost as discouraging as her Great War attempt. In view of her China experience, she asked first to join General Joseph Stilwell, commander of American forces in China. His one-word response was no; he wanted no women in his theater.

Lieutenant General Robert C. Richardson Jr., commanding general of the Central Pacific area, at last agreed to accept Hull in his area, and the War Department issued her orders on November 19, 1943. At fifty-three, she went to war wearing the uniform of the Women's Auxiliary Army Corps, sporting two campaign ribbons and accredited by the North American Newspaper Alliance and the *Cleveland Plain Dealer*, the newspaper that had refused to send her as far as the Mexican border in 1917.

Never far behind the fighting forces, she traveled to all the major Pacific islands—Guam, Saipan, Guadalcanal, the New Hebrides. On Guam, several Japanese were killed outside her tent; on Saipan, she saw thirteen hundred wounded brought in and baskets of amputated limbs. Personal danger never fazed her, but this did. "I can't take it," she said. "I couldn't write about it."

She wrote mainly about GIs—what they experienced, how they endured. Gone was the brassy "I was there" approach frequently found in the Peggy pieces of World War I. Her articles were compared favorably with those of Ernie Pyle, the great chronicler of GI experiences, who died in the Pacific theater. After the war, Peggy Hull retired to Carmel Valley, California, where she died in 1967 at the age of seventy-seven.

General Stilwell was forced to accept women correspondents in China before World War II was over, and Irene Corbally Kuhn, as a correspondent for NBC, reached his headquarters in Chungking early in 1945, after an absence from China of nearly eighteen years. As important to her as covering the war was her ambition to be the first Western radio reporter into Shanghai to make the first broadcast of the end of the war as a sequel to her 1924 Shanghai broadcast. News of the Japanese surrender on August 14, 1945, produced a rush of correspondents to get out of Chungking. An American Army public relations officer infuriated most correspondents by booking his friends on the first flight out to Japan. Fortunately, Kuhn's destination was Shanghai, and she made it.

Her first shock in Shanghai was finding the defeated Japanese still directing traffic. Without their help, she reached the radio station and undertook to broadcast. Night after night, she announced the news, ending with the message "Please relay to San Francisco," not knowing if anyone was listening. At last, after about two weeks, she received a telephone call. The aide to U.S. Admiral Thomas Kincaid called to report that the USS *Rocky Mount*, the communications ship of the U.S. Seventh Fleet, was moving up the Whangpoo River to dock in Shanghai harbor. The admiral, if nobody else, had picked up her newscasts on his high-powered communications equipment, and he offered her the facilities of the *Rocky Mount* to make the first postwar broadcast out of China to the United States.

Impulsively, she told the only other radio reporter in Shanghai, George Moorad of the Mutual Broadcasting System, but as they raced for the harbor, she had second thoughts. Why had she told him? She had jeopardized her chance to score another first. Suggesting that they toss a coin for it, he added graciously, "I hope you win." Kuhn did, and when Moorad was killed in an airplane crash in India, she was glad she had shared the news.

The mighty American ship, first to test the waterway to see if it was safe for the rest of the Seventh Fleet, anchored at number one buoy, a place traditionally reserved for the British. Out of nowhere, Chinese firecrackers, not heard for the duration of the war, exploded. "The noise, the cheers of the Chinese were not to be believed," she recalled.

In New York, Kuhn's daughter, René, who had no notion where her mother was, happened to be listening to the radio when she heard, "This is Irene Corbally Kuhn broadcasting from the USS *Rocky Mount*, the communications ship of the Seventh Fleet, in Shanghai harbor." René fell off the sofa.

In Shanghai, Kuhn discovered some old friends in the newly liberated Japanese prison camps, among them British and Americans. The correspondents visited the building where the Japanese had court-martialed three American fliers brought down and captured after they had participated in the American bombing raid on Tokyo. They were shown the place where the fliers were shot, then offered tea. While they were being served, a Japanese soldier, still on the scene, brought them two small boxes, one containing a few items taken from the pockets of one of the pilots, Captain Robert J. Meder, the other, his ashes.

Kuhn, in tears, cradled the box of ashes. She called it "a sadistic little gesture." Relatives of soldiers killed in action, unable to have the remains of their kin returned, might have appreciated that gesture. But she was thinking of the little box in which her husband's ashes had been sent to her from Shanghai eighteen years earlier, and this was not a moment for gratitude. From Shanghai, Kuhn flew on to Okinawa, then to the Philippines, where she once more made a first overseas broadcast, this time from liberated Manila.

During the 1950s, Irene Kuhn gained new audiences with her syndicated column, "The Way Things Are." The Overseas Press Club paid tribute to her career at a luncheon in 1985, where only her reminiscences revealed her age. Having arrived with the twentieth century, she conveyed confidence in her capacity to survive it.

5

The Dragon Lady
from Chicago

THREE WOMEN PROMOTED TO JOBS AS CORRESPONDENTS IN EU-
rope after World War I established their sex as permanent members of the overseas press corps and formidable competition for
fellow correspondents. Sigrid Schultz of the *Chicago Tribune*,
Anne O'Hare McCormick of the *New York Times*, and Dorothy
Thompson, who would win worldwide recognition for her syndicated column, constituted a memorable triumvirate.

Sigrid Schultz was the first of the three to win a staff position
as a foreign correspondent. John Hohenberg, in *Foreign Correspondence: The Great Reporters and Their Times*, described
her as "one of the finest of all women correspondents." The
Nazi leader Hermann Goering called her "the dragon lady from
Chicago." She was indeed "Adolf Hitler's greatest enemy,"
said Quentin Reynolds, a colorful correspondent best remembered for his articles in *Collier's* magazine. "No other American correspondent in Berlin knew so much of what was going
on behind the scene as did Sigrid Schultz," commented William L. Shirer who, as author of *The Rise and Fall of the Third
Reich*, might have advanced that claim for himself.

Without contemplating a career in journalism, Schultz acquired five languages, English, French, German, Italian, and
Norwegian. Without thought of using them, she acquired excellent connections in Berlin. She happened to be where she was
needed with the qualifications required.

Schultz was born in Chicago in 1893, the year of the first

Chicago World's Fair, where her father, Herman Schultz, an artist of Norwegian descent, had gone to paint the official portrait of Mayor Carter H. Harrison Jr. for the fair. The child managed to receive two years of schooling in Chicago before the family returned to Europe when her father received a commission to paint the portrait of the king of Wuerttemberg and stayed to paint the rich, the royal, and the famous.

Sigrid graduated from the Lycée Racine in Paris and from the Sorbonne in 1914, on the eve of World War I. The family was caught in Berlin for the duration of the war when first her mother, then her father, became too ill to travel. When the United States entered the war in 1917, the family, as enemy aliens in Germany, had to report daily to the authorities. Schultz watched as the Germans marched off to war, and although she obviously was a foreigner, friendly citizens pushed her to the front of the parade route to see the show.

Her first ambition was to be an opera singer but she could not afford the lessons, so she spent much of the war teaching French and English, mainly to wealthy Jewish families. She also studied international law at Berlin University under a Professor von Martitz, who was bold enough to tell his students that Germany would rue the day it violated Belgian neutrality.

Richard Henry Little of the *Chicago Tribune* arrived in Berlin at the end of the war and hired the twenty-six-year-old woman as his interpreter. The violently anti-British publisher of the *Tribune*, Colonel Robert R. McCormick, had assigned Little to obtain the German version of the Battle of the North Sea because McCormick thought the British claim of victory was false. He wanted proof, although with the Germans having lost the war, what battles they had won were at best of academic interest. Not even the Germans cared to talk about them.

Schultz undertook to get the German Navy to grant Little an interview, and for the assignment, he had given her his visiting card and the title "reporter." The German Navy had a rule that no women, not even those who worked in the building, could enter the Navy office by the front door. Defying authority, Schultz marched up the front steps. Less than five feet tall, weighing a bare ninety pounds, a blond Nordic doll, she launched her career on her capacity to disarm the guardians of the establishment, and it worked. Her mission was so successful that the Germans kept sending the *Tribune* veterans of the Battle of the North Sea to interview until riots erupted in Berlin, providing genuine news to cover.

"I saw a ravenous mob slaughter a starving horse where it fell," she wrote of those grim days of defeat for Germany. "I hurried through the Berlin streets under a crossfire of Red guns on one side and Republican soldiery on the other."

She toured Germany with Little, and among those they interviewed was "a sour, disagreeable little man in navy blue." He said, "You Americans need not feel proud of yourselves. Within twenty-five years at the latest, your country and my country will be at war again." She would meet this man again as Grand Admiral Dr. Erich Raeder, commander of the Nazi Navy.

Working out of an office at the Hotel Adlon, Berlin, she discovered the whereabouts of General Erich von Ludendorff, the commander mainly responsible for military policy and strategy against the Allied powers late in the war. Allied diplomats staying at the Adlon did not know that Ludendorff, who had the use of a private entrance, also resided there.

"His brain," Schultz wrote, "conceived the nightmare now known as total war." As she witnessed history, Adolf Hitler was Ludendorff's creation, his protégé, his pupil. Even before the Versailles treaty existed, Ludendorff was preparing for World War II, she said. In reply to those who said that the treaty was unfair to Germany and caused the destruction of the German economy, Schultz wrote, "Our alleged unkindness at Versailles had nothing whatever to do with Germany's dedication to another war." That dedication she found in the mindless ambition of the militarists. She accused them of engineering the devastating inflation that followed the war in Germany. As she saw it, they wiped out Germany's internal war debt and made fortunes for themselves at the expense of the people.

On March 17, 1920, Schultz witnessed what history would record as the first stirring of the Nazi movement, the Kapp putsch, an effort by Junkers, militarists, and others to smash the republic. A German newsman and tipster, Dr. Johann, burst into her apartment in search of a hiding place. While the telephone company was not completing ordinary calls, Schultz got through to her sources by playing the role of a nurse and insisting on speaking to a succession of "Herr Doctors."

While she was finding out what was happening, her informant disappeared. After she filed her story, she found him hiding in the bathtub, buried beneath piles of papers and newspapers. By then, the putsch had been aborted. "You Americans can laugh," he said. "You don't know how ruthless these putschists are. If you stay long enough in Germany, you'll find out why we are scared." She later said, "His was the truest forecast ever made."

The Kapp putsch was a dress rehearsal for the Munich beer hall putsch of November 8, 1923, Adolf Hitler's unsuccessful effort to unseat the Bavarian government. By then Schultz had won the confidence of Germany's chancellor and foreign minister, Gustav Stresemann, and one memorable evening he stopped by her office in the Hotel Adlon and talked at great length about the threat of Hitler's National Socialism. He was not the only leader who found her a good listener. As she recalled, prominent men frequently dropped in on her after attending meetings and banquets at the Adlon. With such help, she said, "I was able to forecast the development of the most sinister of all political regimes."

Richard Little was succeeded as Berlin bureau chief for the *Chicago Tribune* by Parke Brown, who was Schultz's boss when Friedrich Ebert, first president of the Weimar Republic, was admitted to a private clinic in Berlin in February 1925. Schultz arranged to be admitted there as a patient as well, and when she made it to the president's floor she could see the anxiety in the eyes of the president's wife. As a patient she had to undergo an examination, during which the physician found her heart acting strangely. When she confessed that she was there to get a news story, he suggested a pact: if she would rest, he would get her the facts about Ebert. Thus did she learn that Ebert had delayed the removal of his appendix too long. He had declined to go to the hospital so he could be available as a witness in a case in which he was accused of treason for his part in a 1918 ammunition workers' strike. She phoned in the story of the president's

impending death while officials were still belittling the serious-
ness of his illness.

Her initiative was rewarded when McCormick decided he no
longer needed Brown in Berlin and sent him to Rome in the fall
of 1925. As Schultz told the story, "My predecessor protested
so violently against his removal from this post to Rome that it
took until the end of the year for Colonel McCormick to order
me to take over the post." But in due time she won the title
correspondent in chief of the *Chicago Tribune* for the German
capital and all of Central Europe, becoming the first woman
foreign bureau chief for a major American newspaper.

McCormick, who had given Peggy Hull assignments in
France during World War I, and Floyd Gibbons shared the credit
for promoting a woman to a management post. Gibbons, a fa-
bled war correspondent who had lost an eye in the 1918 battle
of Belleau Wood, was commissioned by McCormick to build a
foreign service. Schultz had met him when she was sent to Paris
to meet Brown's wife and escort her to Berlin. "Gibbons was
impressed by my knowledge of history and languages and helped
me cover stories which were usually assigned to men," Schultz
said.

Gibbons was also impressed by her ability to hold her liquor.
When Schultz entered the profession, ladies did not enter a bar
unless a father or husband came along as protector. Schultz
quickly discovered that the male reporters came across many
stories in the Adlon bar, so in she went, pausing only to negotiate a deal with the bartender whereby he would serve her non-
alcoholic drinks that looked like the real thing. When Gibbons
visited Berlin, she attended a party in his honor at the hotel bar.

"I could see his one eye almost falling out of his face as I
joined in one round of drinks after the other," she wrote. "When
I was called to the telephone, Floyd jumped up as if expecting
me to fall. To his intense surprise, I reached the phone booth in
perfect harmony." Gibbons, she remembered, "worked very
hard to help me become a full-fledged foreign correspondent."

Until Schultz was named bureau chief in Berlin, reporters for
the Paris edition of the *Chicago Tribune* were constantly after
her job. The competition was fierce because men thought a

woman in the position was vulnerable, but she preferred to dwell on the advantages of being a woman. Dorothy Thompson arrived in Berlin in 1925 as a correspondent for the *Philadelphia Public Ledger*, and Schultz included her in the recollection. "We had no trouble securing the attention of famous Germans who were curious about the new invaders of the profession."

Once Schultz arrived late for a banquet of important economic leaders and, though she showed her invitation, women secretaries refused to let her pass on the grounds that no women were allowed. "I made them take a visiting card to the press chief after I wrote on it, 'Are two hundred men scared of one woman?' He came out laughing and took me in. One big boss after the other came over to interview the strange woman," Schultz said, "and from then on I never had any trouble seeing world leaders."

So little was expected of women at the time that whatever she did won admirers, particularly since she did not break with the tradition of professional beauties, the women who won acceptance in European society on the basis of their looks and their social graces. Schultz in her youth was among the best-dressed women in Germany. A gourmet chef, she used the art to establish her own small salon, inviting diverse personalities to confront one another over caviar on potato pancakes, fondue bubbling on a hot brick, or marrow bones, the marrow dropped on hot melba toast.

Until the Nazis scored their first victory in the Reichstag in 1930, she retained hope that the German people would control their own destiny. No longer so sure, she sent her assistant, Alexander von Schimpff, whose British mother was a relative of the queen of England, to find a deputy "whose manners were good enough to invite him to lunch."

Von Schimpff snagged Nazi Captain Hermann Goering, a rotund ace pilot, who would rise to be chief of the German Luftwaffe and eventually the designated successor to Adolf Hitler. Goering introduced Schultz to Hitler in the lobby of the Hotel Kaiserhof. "As was his habit," she recalled, "Hitler grabbed my hand in both of his hands and tried to look soulfully into my eyes, which made me shudder, and Hitler sensed it."

The next time Schultz saw Hitler she interviewed him with a group of British and French colleagues. "He gave that same handholding treatment to them. But he gave me only a quick handshake, showing he had realized how I had resented his effort to mesmerize me the first time we had met."

She encountered Hitler again at the Berlin Auto Show, and he remarked on the arrival of the machine age. "Man must act automatically," he said. "There is no time to think. The number of people who think for themselves is dwindling. That makes it possible for the men who know what they want to lead the masses more easily than ever before."

On June 30, 1933, Adolf Hitler became chancellor of Germany legally, not by revolution. The event raised a question democrats had neglected to face. Granted freedom, would man choose democracy or a dictator? Goering remarked to Schultz, "You people try to understand with your heads. We must be understood with the heart." Her heart was not in it. Her contempt for Hitler was matched by her low regard for those who brought him to power.

At her home, Goering gorged himself on the delicacies Schultz served. Then he turned on the assembled guests, including Katherine Anne Porter, the American novelist, and accused them of his sin: "You gorge yourself while the masses starve." His comment was Schultz's cornerstone for a carefully constructed edifice of evidence that the Nazis had not arrived to save capitalism but were indeed on their way toward an alliance with communism.

In 1935, Goering, as chief of the secret police, adopted the idea of seducing correspondents into reporting military secrets, whereupon he proposed to arrest them and stage spectacular espionage trials. Correspondents alert to the threat pooled information and warned each other. On a balmy day in April, a man went to Schultz's home and entrusted a large, sealed envelope to her mother. Schultz raced home and burned the contents, so sure was she that Goering was out to get her. As she left home, she found the man who had delivered the envelope coming to arrest her. She told him not to bother, she had destroyed his evidence. Then she stepped into a taxi and commanded, "The American embassy."

On another occasion, a man who identified himself as Dr. Richard Sallet of Chicago, a teacher at Northwestern University, called on her to ask about Nazi war plans. She took the precaution of taking him to a public lounge where she knew there were no listening devices before assuring him the Nazis did plan war.

Within hours, a friendly diplomat informed her that the Nazis knew everything she had told Dr. Sallet and proposed to put her on trial. She figured it was Dr. Sallet's word versus hers, so she told all her press and government contacts about a visitor who behaved like an agent provocateur. She asked whether they thought he was trying to get a job in their ministries or on their newspapers by cooking up fake stories about her. Germans accepted the opportunity to "expose" the incompetence of the newcomer Sallet.

At a gala luncheon in the Hotel Adlon on May 2, 1935, Schultz seized her opportunity to confront Goering about the men sent to entrap her. The party honored Goering and his bride, whom Schultz described as "gentle, shy, blonde former actress Emmy Sonnemann." Schultz recalled speaking "as if exchanging chitchat about the opera." But she made it clear she did not intend to be intimidated. She stressed that correspondents were not foolish enough to buy or send information meant for spies. She said agents who, judging by their seedy looks, were obviously underpaid posed the danger of concocting lies about the press.

"Schultz, I've always suspected it," Goering said. "You'll never learn to show proper respect for state authorities. I suppose that is one of the characteristics of people from that crime-ridden city of Chicago."

"Naturally, the Nazis thought up other ways to intimidate us," Schultz wrote, "but for many a month no obvious agent descended upon us, and I felt as proud as if I had scored a scoop and netted gratifying headlines."

The Nazis could have sent her packing. They did evict a succession of correspondents, but each time world reaction was so adverse they regretted it. Besides, the Nazis viewed her publisher, Colonel McCormick, and his friends as potential supporters to be wooed, not alienated.

When Charles A. Lindbergh, the American air ace famed for his dramatic solo flight across the Atlantic in 1927, visited German air centers in 1936, Schultz was scandalized to discover that a U.S. embassy attaché, a colonel, was working hard to win Lindbergh's support for the Nazi cause. She wrote the story but was dissuaded from sending it by an attaché who was not pro-Nazi. "As we travel along with Lindbergh," he explained, "and the Germans try to show how efficient they are, we get to see far more than our secret service men."

Schultz faulted American diplomats of the 1930s for failure to recognize the evil nature of the Nazi regime and for blindness to Hitler's plans for global conquest. "Once Hitler had come to power, I had no doubt that the Germans would carry out the war for which they had been preparing secretly and with immense success, thanks to the credulity of American diplomats and officers," she wrote me in a letter about her career. "The pro-German element among our ministry attachés worked very hard."

Chicago was the center for pro-German elements in the United States, and Schultz's articles about the Nazis provoked them to mount a campaign against her. When Schultz visited Chicago on leave, they called her a liar and said she had not even been born in Chicago. *Tribune* reporters found the portrait her father had painted of Carter Harrison hanging behind the desk of the mayor, and she had her picture taken beside it, which ended the campaign against her for a while.

Remarkably, Colonel McCormick, the leading isolationist publisher in America, continued to support and depend on Schultz throughout the 1930s, even as his readers accused her of being anti-German as well as anti-Nazi. To save money in the depression year of 1932, he drastically cut his foreign staff, firing, among others, his Vienna correspondent, William L. Shirer. Yet Schultz escaped the ax.

"I got into the habit of writing to him personally, giving him explanations about the background of the political situation in Germany, and I continued to do this until I came home in 1941," she said. "This special relationship with the colonel was further supported by our meetings when I was home on short vacations and when he summoned all overseas correspondents to confer with him in Paris and London on his trips to Europe."

McCormick took no notice of her disagreement with his friend Lindbergh until her 1941 visit to Chicago. Even then, although he trusted Lindbergh, he did not fire her but simply stopped consulting her. While McCormick's views alienated many Americans, his newspaper continued to thrive mainly because he did not allow his personal bias to interfere with putting out a first-rate newspaper.

Forever a factualist, Schultz, of course, took care not to editorialize in the news columns. She could report damaging facts and recalled that "I succeeded in revealing a great number of terrible crimes the Nazis were committing. In 1938, I sent my mother and my dog home to America, knowing that war was inescapable."

When the Nazis seized Austria on March 13, 1938, Schultz hired Canadian-born Madeline Cummins Meyer as her Vienna correspondent. Meyer's first impression of her new boss was dominated by the discovery that Schultz smoked a pipe, which went with the image she cultivated. As small as ever, Schultz had long since discarded the doll-like qualities of her youth. At the age of forty-five, she was an elegant, silver-haired woman with a commanding presence. Since she had never married, there were the inevitable rumors, possibly started by discarded suitors, that she was a lesbian. William Shirer, who had become the Columbia Broadcasting System (CBS) correspondent in Berlin, had the feeling she would have liked to marry "but that the luck of life was against her on that." As Shirer said, she had a passion for politics, and she thoroughly enjoyed her position in Berlin. Remarking that Berlin correspondents were accepted as members of the elite, Schultz said she never wanted to cover the United States, where reporters had so little access to the authorities.

Meyer soon learned that women correspondents no longer had access to Adolf Hitler, who had seen all he wanted of the likes of Sigrid Schultz. With a correspondent for the *New York*

Times, Meyer went to Klagenfurt, Austria, in February 1939, because Hitler was going there to attend the funeral of an obscure *Gauleiter*, Hubert Klausner. The two correspondents were standing at the top of a stairway when the tolling bells announced the arrival of Hitler. With him came all the top Nazi leaders—Joseph Goebbels, Rudolf Hess, and four generals, among them Erwin Rommel. Everyone except the journalists raised their arms in a rigid salute. Hitler looked directly at Meyer, then turned and whispered to Goebbels. The correspondents were told that the man could stay; the woman would have to leave. "Der Fuehrer wuenscht keine Frauen Journalisten." (The Fuehrer doesn't want any women journalists.)

As she passed Hitler on her way out, she saw his cold blue eyes flash with anger. Most observers concluded that the brass had congregated in Klagenfurt to make final arrangements for the takeover of Czechoslovakia, which the Germans put into operation on March 15.

From Berlin, Schultz covered the inexorable march toward World War II. Of all her achievements, her proudest boast was that she scooped the world on the signing of a ten-year non-aggression treaty between Nazi Germany and the Soviet Union on August 24, 1939. This was the infamous Berlin-Moscow Pact announced on the eve of Germany's invasion of Poland. Schultz saw it coming as early as April 1939, and she radiocast the news of the signing via Mutual Broadcasting System on August 24. Ironically, the *Chicago Tribune* used the Associated Press copy reporting the pact on August 25; Schultz was relegated to writing Berlin reaction. In a sidebar, the *Tribune* did mention that she had reported the news on radio the day before. The scoop belonged to her.

Shirer learned of Germany's invasion of Poland when Schultz woke him with the news at 6:00 A.M. on Friday, September 1. All she said—all she needed to say—was "It happened." Britain declared war on Germany in time for her weekly Mutual network broadcast Sunday. For the first year of the war, Schultz continued to cover the German capital in spite of enormous difficulties. When Germany invaded Norway on April 9, 1940, the Nazis moved to evict her for writing in her article about "big

Germany" and "little Norway." The expulsion order was "reconsidered," but censorship made reporting a nightmare. Four censors read each radio script she wrote. In August 1940, wounded by shrapnel during a British air raid, she insisted on doing her weekly broadcast—only to learn that technical difficulties had knocked her off the air.

It was time to go home, and she tried. In Spain she contracted what she called Rocky Mountain typhoid fever. This was a long way from the Rockies, and others have described her illness as typhus. Whatever it was, she nearly died. She got home by ship from Portugal. Yet, by August 1941, she was applying for readmission to Nazi Germany. Denied a visa, she undertook to write a book, *Germany Will Try It Again*. They would do it, she said, "at the first sign of weakness on our part."

The view she shared with others accounted for President Franklin D. Roosevelt's insistence on "total surrender" by the Germans in World War II. After his death, Roosevelt would be criticized for prolonging the war by failing to make a deal with those Germans weary of war and wanting only to save face. But everything Schultz wrote suggested that if the Allied powers had spared the Germans total surrender, they would have risen to fight again.

It was agony for Schultz to sit at her desk in New York while American troops invaded France, and by early 1945 she was back in Europe for the *Tribune*, *McCall's* magazine, and Mutual Broadcasting. Assigned to the First Army, she advanced into Germany with the troops from Belgium. While other women correspondents had difficulty getting permission to reach the front, she was admitted to a select group of correspondents the Air Force flew to important battle zones.

"We were the first pressmen who landed near Weimar and entered the corpse-strewn concentration camp of Buchenwald. When our plane flew into Leipzig where the battle was raging, we nearly got trapped by SS guards in a big building we examined," she recalled. Fortunately, they did not go into the basement where, they later learned, SS guards stood ready to shoot them. They were in Nuremberg the day of victory in Europe; from there, she raced back to Berlin. The Western world remained dubious of reports that Hitler had actually committed suicide in his bunker until she found a dental assistant, Frau Kaethe Haeursemann, to identify two of Hitler's dental bridges found in the remains of the bunker. After the war she covered the Nuremberg war crime trials.

Schultz quit the *Chicago Tribune* in 1945, continuing to work for the Mutual Broadcasting System and write for *McCall's*. Indeed, her personal prestige soared with her recognition as a commentator after World War II. Until late in the 1950s, she frequently traveled to Europe to gather ammunition for her commentaries and did not like what she saw.

"The similarity between events that took place in 1919 and 1945 is truly shocking, because we allowed ourselves to become scared of the Communists and went in for the Cold War instead of concentrating on the need to reconcile opposing forces," she wrote me more than three decades later. "Germany's first postwar Chancellor, Konrad Adenauer, and his friends exploited our fear of Communism with extraordinary dexterity. If we have the courage to study events closely, it will be possible to prevent a new international conflagration. Hatred will not do it, but the effort to face reality squarely without hysteria can do it."

A woman who set high standards for herself and for others to live by, Schultz was frequently disappointed by the actions of the U.S. government and by the behavior of her fellow women. After World War II, she complained, "thousands of agents and spies trained in Nazi organizations secured jobs with Eastern and Western intelligence outfits regardless and often because of shady pasts."

As for her fellow women, she was convinced that Hitler could never have come to power without the acquiescence of German women. As she saw it, the downtrodden German women were not striving for equality. They embraced Hitler because he promised to elevate them to the status of heroines simply for producing the master race. Some German women she encountered resented the evidence she presented that a woman could aspire to equality.

Schultz demonstrated her willingness to give women a chance when she hired Madeline Meyer fresh out of college because she was fluent in German and answered pointed questions to Schultz's satisfaction. But she would not compromise in her insistence on excellence. At the age of eighty-seven, she wrote, "The number of women who tried to become full-time correspondents grew slowly because most of them lacked the knowledge of languages and history needed to do a good job. Feminists like to claim that editors are often unfair to women correspondents. I don't share that view, because I'm sure there is the same kind of competition among men."

If Schultz was harsh in her judgment of women, she could be equally acerbic on the subject of men in the profession. She held war correspondents in low esteem because so many were reduced to the role of cheerleaders for their armed forces. The correspondents she met after the war left her with the impression that "the efficiency of male reporters [had] been decreasing in recent years."

The Overseas Press Club honored Sigrid Schultz with a copper plaque on November 21, 1969. It was inscribed in part, "To a tough competitor, staunch friend, honest reporter, she worked like a newspaperman." The last phrase annoyed some feminist members of the club with its implication that you had to work like a man to work well. Schultz enjoyed it all.

In a letter dated May 13, 1980, she answered many questions. The last paragraph said, "Yes, I certainly believe in the rights of the female, but I insist that the only thing that counts is efficiency, which is a fact that leading newspapermen believe, and therefore I am grateful to the Overseas Press Club for the copper plaque." And she reproduced the entire inscription.

The letter was not signed. A note, dated May 14, 1980, read, "Sigrid passed away in the night before she was able to sign this. But I am sure she would want you to have it. It was important to her." The note was signed simply "Lynne G. Nieller (helper)." Schultz was dean of the overseas press corps when she died at the age of eighty-seven.

After women had won the abrasive fight for suffrage, Schultz launched an era of reconciliation. Her own success inspired her hope that women were on their way to full equality. Rather than blame men for failing to promote women, she exhorted women to demonstrate their ability. Her special contribution was the evidence that a woman can report as well as any man the intricacies of diplomacy, international economics, and military power.

6

Anne O'Hare McCormick and the Changing Times

IN A TIME OF CATACLYSMIC CHANGE, ANNE O'HARE MCCORMICK of the *New York Times* established a new standard for commentary on world affairs. Displacing generations of armchair pundits, she explored a world in conflict to answer the question "Why?"

Benito Mussolini confided in her. Joseph Stalin granted her an unprecedented six-hour interview. When Adolf Hitler was not on speaking terms with the press, he was willing to talk to her. President Franklin D. Roosevelt broke his rule against exclusive interviews for her and spent hours listening to her views.

McCormick held the same fascination for her audience as for world leaders, and the nation rewarded her with honors galore, the first of which were perhaps the best. In 1935, Carrie Chapman Catt, the pioneer suffrage leader, chose her as one of the ten outstanding women of the country. In 1937, she became the first woman journalist to win a Pulitzer Prize, the highest accolade of her profession. The New York Newspaper Women's Club followed with its prize for best feature article. The Overseas Press Club presented her with a gold watch for best interpretation of foreign affairs. At college commencement time in 1941, *Time* magazine counted the honorary degrees awarded the eminent. Wendell Willkie, the Republican candidate for President in 1940, and China's Ambassador Hu Shih, symbol of resistance to Japanese aggression, shared the championship with Anne O'Hare McCormick, each receiving four. Hers were bestowed by New York University, Columbia, Ohio State, and Rollins College.

She won such fame that everyone jumped on her bandwagon, including the hosiery manufacturer who gave an elegant luncheon at the Plaza Hotel in New York during World War II to present her with a dozen pairs of rare nylon stockings.

A generation growing up without her columns well might wonder what all the excitement was about. What was it about her that fascinated world leaders? At first encounter, she was more disarming than impressive—five feet two inches tall with an Irish twinkle in her blue eyes, a smile on her face, and a chuckle in her voice. When she was young, she had reddish ginger hair and was so slender that she scarcely impressed the scales. As she grew older, her hair darkened and her figure thickened. Her fanciful hats betrayed an impish nature, but she dressed conservatively, never smoked, and only sipped old fashioneds. Her contemporaries said she was so quiet that she often slipped in and out of European capitals unnoticed by fellow correspondents.

Anne O'Hare was born on May 16, 1882, of American parents in Yorkshire, England, and grew up in Ohio. Rebellion, so often an essential first step for women achievers of her generation, played no part in her youth. The eldest of three girls, she attended Catholic schools and graduated from Saint Mary's College in Columbus, Ohio. Her mother, Teresa Beatrice O'Hare, was a poet who became women's page editor of the *Catholic Universe Bulletin*, a weekly published in Cleveland. After graduation, daughter joined mother on the staff and later was named associate editor. In 1910, Anne married Francis J. McCormick, an engineer and importer of industrial equipment, and moved with him to Dayton, Ohio. Through World War I, she made a home for him, writing poetry, fiction, and an occasional article for Catholic publications.

Anne O'Hare McCormick was thirty-nine years old in 1921, when she wrote Carr V. Van Anda, managing editor of the *New York Times*, that she was going to Europe with her husband and asked if she could submit articles to the *Times*. Her query, described as "a timid note," took some courage to mail under the prevailing circumstances. From the day he became publisher of the *New York Times* in 1896, Adolph S. Ochs, a Southern conservative, fought to deny women the vote and keep them out of the newsroom. (The *Times* did not hire a woman general assignment reporter until his final illness in 1934.)

During World War I, when other editors were hiring women to replace men going off to war, Ochs wrote a fellow publisher, "We have almost a prohibition against the employment of women in our editorial staff."

When a woman job applicant denied employment at the *Times* asked the managing editor how single women were supposed to survive without jobs, Van Anda retorted, "If I had my way about it, all unmarried men would be taxed to support indigent women."

But change was in the wind. Although Ochs did not know it, some of his own money went to aid the cause of women's suffrage during World War I. His daughter, Iphigene, was secretly supporting the Suffrage Committee at Barnard College out of her allowance. Ochs appointed his daughter to the board of directors of the *Times*, giving her a vote at least as powerful as one in a national election, but he may have seen it simply as a vote he could control. Then, at the end of the war, Ochs collapsed of emotional exhaustion, and it was Iphigene who kept the board from replacing him. Ochs was still ill and it remained uncertain whether he would ever return to his desk when McCormick applied to the *Times* as a stringer.

Van Anda was more receptive than he might have been had Ochs been at the helm. As long as McCormick would be neither underfoot nor on the payroll, he was willing to see her cards. "Try it," he wrote her.

In Rome, Arnaldo Cortesi of the Associated Press helped McCormick get into the Italian Chamber of Deputies to hear an address by King Victor Emmanuel II on June 21, 1921. Her article, published July 24 in the *New York Times Magazine*, reported:

> More interesting than the speech of the King was the sudden emergence of the new party of the Extreme Right, the

small group of Fascisti. Benito Mussolini, founder and leader of the Fascisti, was among the parliamentary debutantes and, in one of the best political speeches I have heard, a little swaggering, but caustic, powerful and telling.

Italy, she said, "has heard its master's voice." Her Catholic training in Latin helped her understand much of what he said. More than those who spoke Italian fluently, she grasped his power to sway the masses.

Mussolini and thirty-five other Fascisti had won election as deputies only because the Liberal Party included them among candidates of the government coalition. Correspondents knew him as a fellow reporter covering news events for his newspaper, *Il Populo d'Italia*, and paid no attention to him. McCormick was first to predict the rise to power of the future Duce and to alert the American public to the menace of fascism.

For her first interview with Mussolini, McCormick prepared carefully, as she always did. Mussolini met her jutting the fierce bulldog jaw with which he faced the world. She began by asking his opinion of a new and heavy book, *The Law of Corporations*, a legal volume about law for a corporate state. He asked if she had read it, and she said she had. Mussolini finally smiled and said, "My congratulations. You and I are the only ones who have." From then on she had no difficulty seeing him.

Her access mattered to the *Times* after the Fascisti made their October 28, 1922, March on Rome, encountering virtually no opposition, and the king invited Mussolini to form his first cabinet. On one occasion Mussolini told McCormick he detested "society" because it was dominated by women, but as time went on his friendliness demonstrated that he did not put her in the same category as other women. For her part, she observed and wrote about the contrast between Mussolini's reasonable manner in an interview and the arrogant posture he assumed on the podium. To explain his appeal, she wrote,

It is impossible to blink the fact that all over Europe there is growing up a generation tired of old men's wisdom, of the fumbling of Parliaments, of the cautious formulas of statesmanship. That is what the Fascisti movement in Italy really amounts to. . . . It is a ruthless movement as youth is ruthless. It substitutes swift and decisive action for the slow processes of legislation and experiment.

Harold Callender, a *New York Times* correspondent in the 1920s and later an editor, recalled he often heard it said that McCormick combined a masculine mind with a woman's intuition. Her intellect combined with her sensitive perception inspired him to express his doubt that the traits were gender related.

Appreciation from the men who edited her copy was not so easily won. In those days, she filed her stories to Lester Markel, the brilliant but irascible Sunday editor of the *Times*. Notoriously uncivil, he was especially hard on her, never accepting a first draft of an article, often making her rewrite it three or four times. Once, after failing to please him in three attempts, she resubmitted her first draft, and this time he accepted it without question. The copy desk was the next hurdle. In the early days, the men on the desk called her "Verbose Annie." But she honed her skills so carefully that eventually her columns went to press untouched.

The *Times* gave McCormick status as a regular contributor in 1922. For three years, she wrote for the *Atlantic Monthly* as well. From 1925 until her death, she wrote exclusively for the *Times*, except for one series of articles in the *Ladies' Home Journal*. Her husband's export-import business and her career meshed splendidly. She traveled with him until her assignments became too demanding for her to be the follower, whereupon he retired and traveled with her, handling all their arrangements.

McCormick prepared exhaustively for every interview, every event she attended. The knowledge of complex issues she brought to an international conference on balance of payments astounded the assembled economists. Wherever she went, she walked, turning off the boulevards to explore winding cobblestone alleys, browse at bookstalls, and strike up conversations with people. By the time she met a chief of state, she frequently had information he needed about what his people thought and wanted of him and about the reasoning of his enemies and allies.

Joseph Stalin was still struggling to consolidate his power over the Soviet Union when McCormick went to Moscow in 1927. Even the dean of the diplomatic corps, during all his years in Moscow, had never obtained a private audience with Stalin, according to Dorothy Thompson, who had tried and failed to get an interview with the dictator for the *Philadelphia Public Ledger*. Yet Stalin not only agreed to see McCormick, he allowed the questions and answers to flow for six hours. It was understandable that, granted something to say to the Western world, he would choose the prestigious *New York Times* as his outlet. For the normally taciturn chief of state to carry on any conversation so long was a tribute to McCormick's magic.

Stalin was "affable, self-possessed, almost gentle" toward her. Recalling that Lenin had complained of Stalin's rudeness, she found the reason in the roughness of his "steam-roller" tactics. "Lacking brilliance, Stalin gives an impression of craft and suppleness. He is the shrewd manipulator, quietly obstinate, ruthless without passion," she wrote in another early warning to the world.

Her only book, *The Hammer and the Scythe*, published in 1928, described the Communist regime in depth. Abjuring the polemics of the radicals and reactionaries drawn to the subject, she wrote that "nothing in Russia is fixed enough to hang a judgment on." A decade later, after she had interviewed Adolf Hitler, she wrote,

> Mussolini runs the whole show in Italy and does it extraordinarily well. Hitler is the whole show in Germany; he makes the big decisions but the business of government he leaves to others. Stalin is not a show piece at all; he acts behind the scenes to control the party which controls Russia, as completely under the new constitution as under the old. They all act alone. . . . They make their own rules, change them when inconvenient, interpret all laws to suit their own improvised notions.

McCormick seldom took notes during her interviews for fear of distracting her subjects. She managed without complaints, thanks to her capacity to recall verbatim quotes. Besides, she never reached for a front page by-line with quotations of startling declarations. Her goal was to capture the essence of the man and to reveal how his mind worked. Her personality as well as her mind contributed to her success at getting the great and the near great to open up to her. As Iphigene Ochs later wrote, "Anne had the map of Ireland on her face, but what stood out most was her innate charm, her femininity, her dynamic personality."

Iphigene married Arthur Hays Sulzberger, who became publisher of the *Times* when Adolph Ochs died in 1935. Her husband, an independent thinker, was making changes at the *Times*. Iphigene and McCormick were close friends, and on the subject of McCormick, the Sulzbergers thought alike. Sulzberger's first important official act was to name Anne O'Hare McCormick as the only woman to serve on the editorial board, the group that decided policy for the *Times*. Sulzberger told her, "You are to be the freedom editor. It will be your job to stand up and shout whenever freedom is interfered with in any part of the world." And she did just that.

Sulzberger gave McCormick her own column on the op-ed page, alternating with the Washington correspondent, Arthur Krock. Her assignment was to write three columns a week on world affairs. Her column, appearing on February 1, 1937, was called at first "In Europe," then "Affairs in Europe," and finally simply "Abroad," as she covered the Far East as well as Europe. The *Herald Tribune* had hired Dorothy Thompson to write a column on world affairs the year before, and its partisans cried "copycat." The *Herald Tribune* had long been ahead of the *Times* in promoting women, but in this instance there was merely the form, no substance, to support the boast.

The era between the world wars produced four great political columnists—Walter Lippmann and Arthur Krock, writing on national affairs, Anne O'Hare McCormick and Dorothy Thompson, writing on world affairs. Both women got their start in Europe in 1921 without any experience on the staff of a daily newspaper. While Thompson covered the news, McCormick was writing political commentary for the *Times* a year before the *New York World* hired Walter Lippmann, eleven years before the *Times* gave Arthur Krock a column, and fifteen years before the *Herald Tribune* hired Thompson. The first of the four to write commentary became the last to get a column of her own. But her style, her substance, and her by-line were well established long before she was given a space to fill thrice weekly.

In a column published June 21, 1936, she had already felt the "seismic disturbance" of "a world-wide storm":

> All the rules of Europe have shriveled or aged during the past few years. On the faces of Mussolini, Hitler, Stanley Baldwin, even the rotating governors of France, strain and worry have etched indelible lines. Caught off-guard, when they are alone they are tired and baffled men who have paid a heavy price for power.
>
> The face of the world has changed. You walk familiar streets and they are strange. People everywhere are like houses with the shutters down, withdrawn and waiting, as if life were held in suspense; or they are quarreling within their houses, hating one another because long-drawn-out uncertainty has rasped their nerves to the breaking point.

McCormick foresaw the repercussion in the United States and added, "In another four years we may face a division on principles as fundamental as the issues of the Civil War." Within four years, the United States was indeed deeply divided between the isolationists and those who wanted to help Britain and France in their war with Germany. Her feeling for the mood of the people was as remarkable as her knowledge of the conflicts consuming their leaders.

Few prophets have been so honored in their own time. Her 1937 Pulitzer Prize was the award for correspondence. Only one award was given then for the best of both national and international reporting, and she won it for the general excellence of her reportage.

At the height of her fame, she was described as "one of

America's most modest women.'' She never wrote about herself, never provided the personal anecdotes others loved to write about women correspondents, and for years refused even to be listed in *Who's Who*. When she was named woman of the year 1939 by the National Federation of Business and Professional Women, she remarked that the emphasis was on the year rather than the person. ''I have been moving around among thunderous events, and I have stolen some of the thunder.''

That disastrous year began for her with a five-month journey through thirteen countries of Europe on the eve of World War II. On March 14, 1939, at the time of the second partition of Czechoslovakia, she witnessed a courageous act of defiance by the people of Ruthenia in eastern Czechoslovakia. As the Germans strengthened their hold on Czechoslovakia, Father Augustin Voloshyn, head of the autonomous Ruthenian government, proclaimed the independence of Ruthenia and renamed it Carpatho-Ukraine. From the capital city of Huszt, McCormick, who almost never wrote straight news stories, cabled hourly reports and captured world headlines with the Ruthenian people's cry for freedom. Within twenty-seven hours, three flags flew over the city. Independence lasted only one day before the Germans authorized Hungary to occupy and annex the little nation. After World War II, Czechoslovakia ceded Ruthenia to the Soviet Union.

McCormick was in Rome when Neville Chamberlain, the British prime minister, went to see Mussolini, and she was in the British Parliament when Chamberlain cast aside his policy of appeasement. When World War II began with Hitler's invasion of Poland on September 1, 1939, she went immediately to Romania, where refugees were pouring across the border that country shared with Poland. ''It is a story of crackling frontiers and of people literally worried to death,'' she reported. After interviewing Grigore Gafencu, the foreign minister of Romania, she wrote, he ''told me that in daytime it isn't so bad to be foreign minister. . . . It is the nights that wear you down, nights when you are tortured by thoughts of the horrors to come.'' They came—Nazi, then Communist domination. The partition of Poland after World War II left Romania with only the Soviet Union, including Ruthenia, as its northern neighbor.

The nights were just as bad in Berlin, she discovered by visiting the source of the horror and walking the streets during a blackout. "Groping along the tunnel-like streets, you almost never hear a voice. Other gropers are shadows and footsteps," she wrote.

In British-occupied Palestine, she had tea with the British commissioner of Jerusalem. Afterward, they stood chatting on a stone wall outside his headquarters. Within twenty minutes of their departure, the wall was blown up by a time bomb that had been ticking away as they talked. The bombing was blamed on Jewish terrorists.

Danger never fazed her. When finally the Allied forces invaded France, she insisted on going to the front to interview the controversial American General George S. Patton, although night had descended and the roads were pockmarked with bomb craters. Military vehicles were not moving. Yet the sixty-two-year-old correspondent's prestige sufficed to cow fearful men, and they pushed through the black night. Patton was indeed surprised by his late dinner guest.

As always, McCormick interviewed everyone high and low, probed beneath the exterior of GIs as well as generals, and related what she learned to what she knew.

> Behind their gay and casual front they are about the angriest army which ever went to war. This anger is general. The prevailing mood of the country is irritation at the waste, the upset, the stupidity, the agony, the destruction, the obscenity and arrogance of war.

Before the war, isolationists had criticized McCormick for her support of the League of Nations. In the midst of war, she used her columns to impress on Americans the need for an international organization to maintain the peace once the war was won. As she observed, America's hatred of war had produced the isolationists who "thought war could not come to the United States unless we went out to meet it." The attack on Pearl Harbor, without diminishing the hatred of war, prepared the people "to try almost anything that will guarantee a peaceful world," she said. Recalling the stampede to "normalcy" following World War I, she warned it could happen again "if there are shabby compromises in the peace and the ordinary citizen sees the principles he is fighting for scuttled to serve the ambitions of great powers."

Before the war in Europe ended, she returned to the United States and interviewed President Franklin D. Roosevelt just three weeks before he died on April 12, 1945. Like other world leaders, Roosevelt relied on her to brief him about conditions in Italy, the political outlook in France, popular feeling in England toward America, the mood of liberated people. Both were preparing for the forty-six-nation conference to be held in San Francisco on April 25, 1945, toward establishing the United Nations.

A week spent watching the sparring of the Soviet Union and the Western powers at San Franciso compelled McCormick to write,

> The struggle to maintain peace is immeasurably more difficult than any military operation. . . . Here is . . . where the desperation of the peoples of the world beats upon the Golden Gate. For if the forum does not take the place of the battlefield this war is lost and the next begins.

After the war, she rode with Secretary of State James F. Byrnes from Berlin to Stuttgart, Germany, in what had been Hitler's private railroad car, then crossed the countryside to Nuremberg to hear the German war criminals sentenced by the international tribunal.

She was chosen as a delegate to the United Nations Educational Scientific and Cultural Organization (UNESCO), an effort she hoped would bind wounds. Although she dreamed of one world made by men who did not have to think in terms of boundaries and national prestige, it came as no surprise to her that delegates persisted in thinking in nationalistic terms. In her words, "As soon as the war partners begin to think in terms of peace, they tend to think separately."

Perhaps in part because of her UNESCO service, she was described as "America's ambassador to the world," a title she found less than flattering because of her low regard for diplomats. Anthony Eden, when he was British foreign secretary, remarked to her in a condescending manner that American reporters as well as diplomats realized the menace of dictators. McCormick, fiercely proud of her fellow correspondents and equally contemptuous of diplomatic blunders in dealing with Hitler, retorted, "As a matter of fact, they were ahead of the diplomats. After all, Mr. Secretary, diplomats are only badly trained reporters."

By 1949, at the age of sixty-seven, she was covering the guerrilla war in Greece, scrambling up and down mountains with soldiers less than half her age. On her return to Athens by military plane, she was thrown to the floor of the plane and hurt her knee. Flora Lewis, who eventually followed in McCormick's footsteps as a *New York Times* columnist, remembered her arrival in Athens: McCormick was "very cheerful and clinical about the injury, but so vivid in recounting just what happened that I nearly fainted."

McCormick's jovial equanimity in the face of adversity was matched by her compassion for others. Her tall, hawk-faced husband, eight years her senior, continued to travel with her even after he needed more care than she could give, and those who met them remembered her gentle way with him. The railroad station in Yugoslavia confused him, and while trying to collect the luggage, he turned and asked, in front of a welcoming newspaperman, "Who's king here now?" In reply, she smiled. "Don't tease the boy, dear. You know Yugoslavia has a president."

Her sense of humor sustained her and her audience. She arrived at the Republican National Convention in 1952 wearing a lovely white dress printed with tiny Democratic donkeys, and she next appeared at the Democratic Convention in another white dress decorated with little blue Republican elephants. She remained on equally good terms with Democratic President Harry Truman and his Republican successor, Dwight D. Eisenhower, if not with Eisenhower's secretary of state, John Foster Dulles.

Dulles received a standing ovation when he announced his policy of "massive retaliation"—his threat to use the atom bomb before the Russians had it—at the 1953 annual dinner of the Overseas Press Club. At a time of virtually no dissent, McCormick had the nerve to say "I've watched Dulles's performance at a number of international conferences, and in my opinion he's demonstrated a complete lack of sensitivity and understanding." Most historians would come to see it her way a generation after her death.

When McCormick chose to disagree, she carried more impact than constant dissenters. Although she never shied from controversy, her style was never confrontational. Her way was to study the motivations of those with whom she disagreed, as with the isolationists, find some common ground, and build her argument from that base. While she held strong opinions, she never saw her column as a forum for self-expression. Her contribution was to explain and interpret the news, to make world events understandable.

McCormick was writing at a time when editors were making a valiant but faltering effort to separate the news from opinion, placing the news on page one, opinion on the editorial page. When it came to national politics, the editorial writers usually knew what they were talking about. But in foreign correspondence, the effort to separate fact from opinion produced a long line of editorial writers who sat in New York offices, tore the wire service copy off the teletype, and specialized in instantaneous opinion.

McCormick and Dorothy Thompson broke new ground. Working overseas, they specialized in collecting the facts they interpreted. They were the pioneers of the modern column on world affairs. Thompson, controversial, emotional, and enormously successful in appealing to a mass audience, was one of a kind. McCormick started a trend.

McCormick's success demonstrated the need for commentators who could explain what was happening abroad and help readers understand the complex issues generating the action. The sort of columns she wrote later would appear frequently on page one, sometimes labeled "commentary," sometimes "news analysis," sometimes not labeled. Her style and her methods set the standard for the next generation of columnists specializing in international relations, among them Flora Lewis of the *Times* and syndicated columnist Georgie Anne Geyer.

Publishers deluged McCormick with requests to write books, but after writing only one she found herself too busy researching and writing for the *Times* to produce another. Two collections of her columns, *The World at Home* and *Vatican Journal*, both edited by Marion Turner Sheehan, were published after her death.

It is doubtful that she ever counted the number of countries she visited or chiefs of state she interviewed. There is no doubt that she remembered the first names of all the leaders she knew—Churchill, Baldwin, Blum, Dollfuss, Schuschnigg, Beneš, De Valera, De Gasperi, Venizélos, the men who made the history of her time.

The citation given her with the 1950 Roosevelt Medal of Honor noted that she had "over the past quarter of a century done more for enlightenment of the American public in international affairs than most secretaries of state."

When she died in 1954, the *Times* ran black borders around her column and a tribute by her colleague Robert Duffus.

> She had a great tenderness for people. She had great compassion for those who suffered. War to her was not something abstract that destroyed nations. War was the thing which destroyed individuals.

On the op-ed page, the *Times* maintained the tradition McCormick had established with such first-rate columnists as James Reston. Of her, he wrote,

> She had all the qualities of a good reporter—vitality, curiosity, intelligence, courage and something more, a rare gift of sympathy for all sorts of people . . . a religious conviction which enabled her to see things in the ultimate perspective of life itself.

McCormick's religious conviction emerged in her writing when she said, "Women have the soul of the nation in their keeping, a special obligation to preserve and manifest spiritual values in an age of skepticism."

7

The Blue-eyed Tornado

IN WORLD WAR I, AMERICAN SOLDIERS WENT TO WAR WAVING the flag and singing patriotic songs. Why the slaughter had to take place was never properly explained. If the soldiers marching off to World War II knew the nature of the enemy, Adolf Hitler and the Nazi drive toward world domination, much of the credit for preparing them belonged to Dorothy Thompson.

At the height of her career, her column, "On the Record," appeared in two hundred newspapers with a circulation of more than eight million. At a time when more people reached their conclusions from what they read in the newspapers than from any other source, a statistic that will probably never recur, her sway over public opinion was unrivaled. She may not have done as much as Walter Lippmann, her fellow columnist on the *New York Herald Tribune*, to inform his elite audience. She was too controversial, too emotional, to win the respect in her lifetime accorded Anne O'Hare McCormick of the *New York Times*. Her contribution was to brace the nation for war.

Radio news reached its zenith with the outbreak of war in Europe, and five million Americans listened to Dorothy Thompson's NBC broadcasts. The pecking order was reflected in a note Edward R. Murrow of CBS received from the British Broadcasting Corporation confirming a 1940 broadcast date—"unless the Prime Minister or his Cabinet, Dorothy Thompson or Quentin Reynolds need the air." Reynolds was beloved in Britain; Thompson was the star to beat in the competition for American audiences.

John Gunther, a celebrated journalist, described her as "a

blue-eyed tornado." *Time* magazine, in a 1940 cover story, rated her second only to Eleanor Roosevelt in power and prestige. Both women were the butt of jokes by enemies trying to laugh them off the stage. Ridicule was the last resort of right-wingers finally losing the argument that women should not be taken seriously.

One analyst estimated that of 238,000 words Thompson wrote on world affairs in her column between 1938 and 1940, three-fifths were devoted to attacking Adolf Hitler and his mad ambitions. She knew whereof she spoke, and from her coverage of Nazi Germany she brought home to a would-be isolationist nation the imperative of intervention.

The flamboyant Thompson was in many ways the antithesis of her fellow columnist Anne O'Hare McCormick. Both dug deeply for their facts, but McCormick was ruled by her head, Thompson by her heart. McCormick mastered in-depth analysis of world trends; Thompson broke the news and predicted the consequences.

Thompson, like Sigrid Schultz, was born in 1893. Her father, a Methodist minister in Lancaster, New York, remarried after her mother's death, providing his first offspring with her first enemy, her stepmother. Differences developed into a feud, and the child was sent to live with an aunt in Chicago, the city being another bond with Schultz. When Thompson graduated from Syracuse University, she went to work for $8.00 a week as an organizer for women's suffrage. Like many other women, she tried and failed to get overseas in World War I.

At the age of twenty-seven, Thompson set sail for Europe in 1920 with $150 she had saved from her job as a social worker in Cincinnati, Ohio. Her first coup was selling a series of articles about the Irish rebellion to International News Service. In Italy, she interviewed the left-wing leader of the maritime union, Captain Giuseppe Giuletti. A revealing entry in her diary would have been more worthy of an adolescent. "He wasn't touching me, but I might have been in his arms. . . . We said another adio in the street, and we kissed each other with our eyes."

Although a feminist, Thompson blamed only herself for what she saw as her slow progress as a journalist: "Oh why, why haven't I talent. . . . It is horrible to be intelligent but uncreative." Her luck changed when she talked Whythe Williams, the chief of the *Philadelphia Public Ledger* bureau in Paris, into agreeing to read articles she submitted on a free-lance basis. She earned money working for the American Red Cross, and her two jobs fit together neatly when she went to Hungary. The Red Cross commissioner, Captain James Pedlow, introduced her to Marcel Fodor, the Hungarian-born correspondent of the *Manchester Guardian*, and a fruitful collaboration began.

Her first two major scoops were interviews with Emperor Karl, last of the Hapsburg rulers of the Austro-Hungarian Empire. After World War I, Austria and Hungary emerged as separate republics. In March 1921, Karl returned to Hungary from exile in Switzerland in an effort to regain the throne, and Fodor and Thompson met him at the border. For Americans, she broke the news of a plot to restore him to the throne. It failed and Karl and his empress, Zita, went into seclusion in Budapest. Although reporters were not allowed to visit them, Thompson, as a Red Cross worker, got in for her second interview.

She also went to Czechoslovakia and, again with Fodor's help, visited President Tomáš G. Masaryk at his home. Fodor's efforts would be amply repaid as she learned the ropes and shared her sources with him. In appreciation, Whythe Williams put her on staff as Vienna correspondent at a salary of $50 a week. Although she was making that much as a free-lancer, the appointment allowed her to file her stories by collect cable.

Thompson has been described as a "blonde Brunnhilde." In 1922, she still had dark brown hair and she was overweight. She would become truly handsome only when her hair turned prematurely silver and her face acquired more character with age. Among the assets she possessed from the start were a pink and white complexion and an effervescent personality.

Early in 1922, she married the most handsome man she had ever seen, Josef Bard, a romantic Hungarian writer, and, like Peggy Hull, she lost her American citizenship. For a while, only her work and her marriage mattered.

She was so successful at her work that she was named chief of the Berlin bureau for both the *Philadelphia Public Ledger* and the *New York Post* in 1925, scarcely a step behind Sigrid Schultz, the *Chicago Tribune* competition. Talk about which deserved credit for a "first" may have provoked Thompson to write an article for the *Nation* magazine ridiculing women's magazines for the childish jubilation they displayed "every time a woman becomes for the first time an iceman," and so on. She made the point that women should be accepted as part of the mainstream of society, not set apart and treated as freaks for doing what they could have done all along but for the barriers society erected. As she saw it, firsts were only the means to the end of full equality, not the end itself. Her editors all but spoiled her purpose by describing her, erroneously, as "the only American woman in such a position."

Through her friends Edgar Ansel Mowrer of the *Chicago Daily News* and his wife, Lillian, Thompson acquired a large and lavish apartment in the house where they lived, and she began to compete with Schultz as a hostess as well as reporter. Josef Bard, who did not come from Vienna to share in the festivities, was, according to loyal Lillian Mowrer, a philanderer whom Dorothy could no longer afford to support. But the other side of the story was revealed in a letter Bard wrote his wife, reminding her she had said she wanted a simple life. "You are drunken with life. You would grab everything, live in a wild flush. . . . Something is wrong with us."

In England, Thompson obtained a two-week renewal of her passport, granted for the purpose of going home to spend a year renewing her citizenship. Instead, she took the valid passport back to Berlin, and a U.S. consular officer thoughtlessly extended it. He violated the law but he didn't know that he had. She did.

While she always wrote the truth as she saw it in the news columns, Thompson was not above embellishing anecdotes about herself. She made many friends, and they joined in the game. Separating truth from tales she told so lightheartedly in her youth would become an ordeal for her biographers.

One of the better stories began with her presence at the opera in Vienna in May 1926, when she learned that right-wing General Józef Pilsudski was marching on Warsaw in a military coup.

Borrowing money from the only man in sight with cash, her friend Sigmund Freud, off to war she went. It has been said that she departed in her evening gown and tramped through the mud of Poland in dancing slippers, that she escaped death by renting an old Ford to drive into Warsaw, rather than hiring an expensive Daimler limousine, which arrived in Warsaw filled with bullet holes.

Don't believe it. According to her biographer, Marion K. Sanders, Thompson had the sense to change into sensible shoes and a suit before catching the train to Warsaw, and she took a bus into town with other correspondents. It overturned en route, but no one was hurt, and the correspondents made it safely into town together. If Thompson did not tell the story that way, it could be that she never enjoyed being just one of the boys. Brash, competitive, and sexy, she invented the genre of anecdotes about the antics of women correspondents.

Romance and excitement were two things she could not resist, and she clung to romantic notions about love and marriage despite endless heartache. Her Methodist background accounted for her delaying the divorce Bard wanted, but it went through in 1927.

Possibly because she enjoyed dramatic coincidences, Thompson said she met Sinclair Lewis, already America's leading novelist, the day her divorce became final and promptly invited him to her birthday party on July 9, 1927. At 3:00 A.M. the next morning, she called Lillian Mowrer and awakened her to say that Lewis had proposed marriage and asked if she should say yes. Lewis was the last man Lillian would have married, and she threw cold water on the idea.

When Sinclair Lewis looked in the mirror, he saw a gaunt, ugly man, his face scarred by acne lesions, the reason, his friends said, that he drank. It did not stop him from pursuing Thompson across Europe and writing her outrageous love letters. Lewis, who possessed a brilliant mind and fascinated almost everyone, could be wonderfully funny. To please her, he wrote that he found Sigrid Schultz dull and provincial, when in reality Schultz had the international background Thompson might have envied.

Thompson and Lewis were in love but unmarried when she

went to the Soviet Union for the tenth anniversary of the Russian Revolution in November 1927. In Moscow, she told her friend Vincent Sheean, a journalist who wrote *Dorothy and Red*, "Every day I change my mind about everything I've made it up about the day before. And all the time I am excited." Her capacity to convey her excitement would help her achieve a vast audience, but her habit of changing her mind would get her into trouble. Although she would not have described herself as a woman with an open mind, she constantly advanced new ideas, which she discarded when new facts convinced her they were wanting.

Although she did not get to meet Stalin personally, she interviewed everyone who could tell her about him. She described him as "a man with a long standing grudge; a man who loves power and who feels that he never got his just deserts." Both Thompson and McCormick used the words *machine politician* to characterize Stalin. Thompson lacked McCormick's style, but she was livelier, including talk of vodka and sex as well as politics. Together, the two women did much to shape the American conception of the Soviet regime.

Thompson wrote about Russia for the *Saturday Evening Post*, and in 1928 she produced a book, *The New Russia*. At about the same time, Theodore Dreiser, the noted novelist, came out with a book about Russia containing whole sentences, even paragraphs, identical to Thompson's copy. Sinclair Lewis, furious, accused his fellow novelist of plagiarism. Thompson calmly concluded that a young editor assigned to convert Dreiser's newspaper columns into a book had flushed it out with her reportage, but she may have been too forgiving. Dreiser was also caught lifting a page describing a traveling salesman from a book by George Ade.

Thompson's human warmth was demonstrated in Moscow by her concern for Rayna Prohme, a young leftist intellectual who went to China with her husband, William Prohme, an editor from San Francisco, in 1922. They edited two newspapers and ran the Nationalist News Agency for the Kuomintang Party in China. After the death of the revolutionary leader Sun Yat-sen in 1925, the Nationalists broke with the Communists. Rayna, siding with the leftists, escaped to Moscow in 1927, when the Kuomintang drove out the leftist forces.

Vincent Sheean fell madly in love with Rayna and was horrified when she decided to enter the Lenin School for training as an agent of the Communist International. Before she could do so, she fell ill and died of encephalitis. Thompson and Madame Sun Yat-sen both attended the funeral and, in the Russian manner, walked the distance to the cemetery wearing similar blue capes unsuitable for the cold climate and shoes unsuitable for the march, though each had an automobile waiting for her.

Sinclair Lewis and Dorothy Thompson were married in 1928, and she quit her job to return with him to the United States. The marriage was marked by heartache from the start, for Lewis did not stop drinking. Their son, Michael, was born in June 1930, when Dorothy was thirty-six. Determined to be the perfect mother, she started by breast-feeding the baby. Although he was usually happy, he cried, as babies will. Lewis could not stand the noise, and she had to separate them. They had acquired an estate in Vermont, Twin Farms, with two houses on it, so Dorothy and her husband occupied the main house while the baby and his nurse were assigned to a cottage.

That year, Sinclair Lewis became the first American to win the Nobel Prize for literature. He had rejected the Pulitzer Prize because he did not like the company he was asked to keep, but the Nobel Prize delighted him, and he managed to remain sober through the ceremony.

Thompson returned to Germany in 1931 for *Cosmopolitan* magazine and interviewed Adolf Hitler. In her book *I Saw Hitler*, she wrote, "When I walked into Hitler's salon I was convinced I was meeting the future dictator of Germany. In less than fifty seconds, I was sure I was not. It took me just that time to measure the startling insignificance of the man who had set the world agog." Her contempt for him caused her miscalculation; she could not believe the German people would let this horrible little man come to power. The Reichstag fire of February 27, 1933, changed her mind. Hitler pronounced it a Communist plot, and his Nazi storm troopers went on a rampage.

Thompson was among the first and loudest to condemn him for his anti-Semitic campaign.

In July 1934, Hitler expelled her from Germany. Later the rising dictators of Europe would expel many correspondents, but she was among the first to go, creating an international cause célèbre. Almost the entire press corps went to the Berlin Bahnhof to see her off by train and presented her with roses. "My offense was to think that Hitler is just an ordinary man," she commented. "This is a crime against the reigning cult in Germany which says that Mr. Hitler is a Messiah sent of God to save the German people—an old Jewish idea." Her capacity to infuriate him had survived unscathed.

Helen Rogers Reid, a suffragist and zealous champion of her sex, persuaded her husband, Ogden Reid, publisher of the *New York Herald Tribune*, to hire Thompson. Her column, "On the Record," first appeared in 1936, a year before Anne O'Hare McCormick's did, and broke the male monopoly on column writing. It ran thrice weekly, alternating with Walter Lippmann's column, and within a year was syndicated in one hundred thirty newspapers.

As her popularity soared, she was invited to address businessmen and other all-male audiences. The *Ladies' Home Journal* paid her $1000 a column to write for the magazine. Thompson also possessed a fine voice, and she was recruited by NBC to cover the 1936 Republican presidential convention. By 1937, she had achieved stardom with her own nationwide radio newscasts. Almost overnight, she was earning $100,000 a year, an unprecedented sum for any journalist in the depression-ridden 1930s.

Sinclair Lewis had married her because she was exciting and had done everything in his power to advance her career. He wanted her to shine, but when the incredible happened, he could not endure it. He could not live with her success while his own career was on the skids. Lewis went to their New York apartment in April 1937, found a young writer with her, and accused them of being lovers. She told him, "You have built up the idea about being a tail to an ascending comet." It was the beginning of the end for that marriage.

The tears she suppressed found release in her writing about the tragedy of people imprisoned and refugees fleeing Nazi Germany. Her column of March 9, 1938, was devoted to the concentration camps and prisons of Germany. She also broadcast the story in German to the German people via shortwave. Her broadcasts were worth remembering when Germans later said they knew nothing about the concentration camps before World War II.

President Franklin D. Roosevelt, influenced by her columns on refugees, convened the conference of thirty nations at Evian, France, in July 1938, its purpose to establish a worldwide emigration and resettlement program for the Jews in Germany. Serious observers were convinced that Hitler would have allowed the democracies to take the Jews off his hands at that time, but virtually nothing came of the conference. No nation, not even the United States, opened its door to the unwanted.

American isolationists still wanted no part of Europe's problems, and Thompson went after them with a vengeance. In two brief, devastating columns, she destroyed the political ambitions of the most admired isolationist, Colonel Charles Lindbergh. Lindbergh, old acquaintances recalled with glee, had in his youth pulled what he thought was a practical joke, pouring Listerine into a bottle of priceless Burgundy served at a dinner party Thompson attended. Thompson could hold a grudge, and her enemies could expect to get their comeuppance eventually. Only if she felt their political views warranted it, however, did she attack them publicly.

Another isolationist, the Catholic Father Charles Coughlin, referred to her demeaningly as "Dottie." When she wrote of him thereafter, she called him "Chuck." She even relished making a spectacle of herself for her cause. In New York, she was expelled from a meeting of the pro-Nazi German-American Bund for laughing and shouting "Bunk."

She came down hard on all involved in the signing of the Munich Pact—Britain, Germany, France, and Italy—in September 1938. As a novice in Europe, she had written with hope of the young republic of Czechoslovakia. Sixteen years later she suffered to see the Allied powers agree to its dismemberment as the price of postponing war with Germany for one short year.

Six months after World War II began, but while Italy remained neutral, she went to Rome in March 1940 and pleaded with Pope Pius XII to keep Benito Mussolini out of the war. "Now I know you are a Protestant, my child," he said, "because you have such faith in the limitless power of the Catholic Church." She also visited the Maginot Line in France and fired three shells from a French artillery battery at the German lines, for which she was criticized. After all, the United States remained neutral.

Her celebrity status combined with her explosive personality invited attack. Alice Roosevelt Longworth, the sharp-tongued Washington dowager, was not above remarking, "Dorothy is the only woman in history who has had her menopause in public and made it pay." Britain's Sir Wilmot Lewis quipped, "She had discovered the secret of perpetual emotion." John Chamberlain, a conservative critic, commented, "Her emotional zeal runs away with her intellectual analysis."

She was fair game, too, for Edward R. Murrow, covering the blitz in London for CBS and hearing her one night broadcast a message of courage to the British people in which she quoted the poets of the world. "That must have helped a lot as they grabbed their blankets and headed for the shelters," he grumbled. Murrow did an imitation of her his friends said caught her style to perfection. But brickbats among the bouquets came with the fame.

Her power at its peak, she threw her support to Wendell Willkie, who was seeking the Republican nomination for President, mainly because she saw him as an internationalist and feared the Republicans might otherwise choose an isolationist candidate. Then, in October 1940, she dismayed the Republican *Herald Tribune* by switching her allegiance and calling for the reelection of Democratic President Franklin D. Roosevelt on the theory that the nation needed his experience. It exemplified Sinclair Lewis's pet nickname for her, "Waffle." This time she waffled beyond the pale. Her contract with the *Herald Tribune*, which expired in March 1941, was not renewed.

Her sponsors had already canceled her radio program, with what her fans saw as less justification. The war in Europe was confirming her direst predictions, but it was also producing enormous pressure to maintain America's neutrality. Her violent attacks on Adolf Hitler and his brief alliance with Joseph Stalin upset the sponsors, and they did not renew their contract. As Thompson once remarked ruefully, she was applauded when she was wrong and hissed for being right.

Thompson landed on her feet, switching her column to the Bell Syndicate and acquiring the *New York Post* as her New York outlet. Her radio appearances resumed, and she later broadcast for the Mutual Broadcasting System. I found out in the spring of 1942 that, as further vindication, she would dearly have loved to win the Pulitzer Prize for 1941. As a student at the Columbia University School of Journalism, I was commissioned to phone and ask her to address the group and instructed to identify myself as representing the "Pulitzer" School of Journalism, the name of the great publisher and sponsor being calculated to appeal.

Thompson's secretary apparently caught only the word *Pulitzer* and quickly passed the phone to her boss. When she understood the request, Thompson could not contain her rage. "You know my lecture fee is five hundred dollars," she screamed, and she slammed down the receiver. It took me several minutes to realize that she had thought the Pulitzer Prize committee was calling to offer her an award. Columbia University had awarded her an honorary degree in 1939 and saw no harm in asking her to lecture. At the time, though, she was getting seven thousand requests a year for personal appearances and depended on three secretaries she called Madeline to reject most of them. Thompson would never win a Pulitzer Prize. But then, Sinclair Lewis had rejected one, and she scarcely needed it.

In her personal life, Thompson needed more than Sinclair Lewis gave her. She finally divorced him and in 1943 married an Austrian painter, Maxim Kopf, a robust man who was right for her. Her commitment to her column, with its global perspective, rather than her marriage, kept Thompson from following American forces into action during World War II. As victory approached, she worried about how the Allied powers would behave without an enemy to keep them united.

A week before victory in Europe was declared in April 1945, she flew to Germany, where she visited the death camps and reported that the victims had descended to cannibalism, then returned to Berlin for the first time since 1934. No sooner was Hitler found dead in his bunker than she found an enemy to replace him, the Soviet Union. She had treated the Russians gently enough while they were Allies in the war against Nazism, but now she lashed out at their brutality and intransigence. In contrast to Sigrid Schultz, she showed compassion for the German people and opposed the Morgenthau plan to reduce Germany to an agricultural society.

Her brief, safe journey in the mainstream of American political thinking ended with her visit to the Holy Land in May 1945. She had fought for the Jews as hard as anyone using a typewriter for a weapon could, and she had a large, loyal Jewish audience, but she was appalled by Jewish extremist attacks on the Arabs. Worse, she foresaw that the creation of Israel as a Jewish state would cause endless friction and lead to bloodshed in the Middle East. History would prove her right about that, but her editors and her audience thought it was wrong to say so.

Zionists reacted to criticism of their politics by accusing her of anti-Semitism. After all her efforts to save the Jews from the Holocaust, this cut her to the quick. Forever an emotionalist, she overreacted, and friends said that years later she admitted it. The *New York Post*, with its large Jewish audience, dropped her column in 1947, but the Bell Syndicate continued to run it.

Nobody retained better credentials. President Roosevelt had written her in 1944, "I know it took courage and a resolute spirit to oppose the powerful interests in declaring your confidence in the Administration's policies and purposes." Britain's Prime Minister Winston Churchill wrote, "You have rendered services to both our countries which it would not be easy to overestimate." She still could reach presidents and prime ministers just by making a phone call.

Sinclair Lewis died in January 1951, and that saddened her, although she was happily remarried. Also in 1951, she helped to found and became the head of American Friends of the Middle East, which started as a prestige peace group but over the years degenerated into an Arab propaganda organization.

Thompson made numerous trips overseas to report world events for her column and for Mutual Broadcasting. Perhaps her most memorable trip began in 1956, when she visited President Gamal Abdel Nasser of Egypt at the time he announced the nationalization of the Suez Canal. In Greece, she was the guest of honor at a dinner given by King Paul and Queen Frederika. In Saudi Arabia, its ruler, Ibn Saud, entertained her lavishly.

While she was overseas, Benjamin McKelway, the respected editor of the *Washington Star*, protested to John Wheeler, her editor at Bell Syndicate, that she should not try to be both a newspaperwoman and president of American Friends of the Middle East. John Wheeler ordered her to make up her mind whether she wanted to be a newswoman or a propagandist. She resigned from the AFME.

Her book *The Courage to Be Happy*, published in 1957, contained some of the old excitement. She complained about loyalty oaths as a requirement for government office. It was not enough to be anti-Communist, she saw. People were asked to say what they were against when they should have been asked to say what they were for. A sign she was getting tired was the space she devoted to the joys of being a housewife. At the age of sixty-four, she was preaching what she had never found time to practice.

More typical of Thompson in her prime was a feminist statement in total conflict with the efforts of Sigrid Schultz and others to play down their problems with male competitors. Of the working woman, Thompson wrote, "She can be sure that if she is chaste, men will call her cold; if she is brilliant, men will call her 'like a man'; if she is witty they will suspect her virtue; if she is beautiful they will try to annex her as an asset to their own position; if she has executive abilities they will fear her dominance."

After fifteen years of marital happiness, Maxim Kopf died in July 1958. She wrote her farewell column in August, after more than two decades of constant exposure. Her son, Michael, pleased her by giving her two grandchildren but disappointed her by divorcing his wife. For Christmas 1960, Dorothy Thompson went to Lisbon to visit her former daughter-in-law and her grandchildren. She died there in January 1961, at the age of sixty-seven. If not the "first" of her breed, a distinction she ridiculed, she would live in history as one of a kind. Historians would be hard put to find another journalist who created as much controversy and attracted as much attention as she did by speaking her mind.

8

The World at War

FOR A GENERATION OF AMERICANS, THE SINGLE QUESTION CERtain to evoke a flood of memories was "Where were you the day the Japanese bombed Pearl Harbor?" It changed their lives, but the day that changed the lives of war correspondents in Europe came sooner. For them the question was "Where were you the day the Germans invaded Poland?"

Mary Marvin Breckinridge was in Switzerland photographing the Lucerne Music Festival for *Town and Country* magazine. An established photojournalist at thirty-four, she had photographed a Nazi rally in Nuremberg for *Life* magazine before arriving in Lucerne. Tears were rolling down the cheeks of the waiter who brought her breakfast on September 1, 1939. "They have just gone into Poland," he told her.

Breckinridge reached London before Britain declared war on Germany on September 3. That night the Germans bombed London, and she took the first wartime pictures in an air raid shelter.

In the midst of frantic mobilization for war, she focused her camera on the countryside for a picture story she called "An English Village Prepares for War." Edward R. Murrow of CBS, an old friend, asked her to come on the air and talk about it. Also at his request, she spent a night in a firehouse with newly recruited women coordinating the firefighting. On her own, she went to Ireland for a story about Irish neutrality, a stance that seemed strange to her. In Dublin she received word that Murrow wanted her to go to Sweden the next day. By ship and train, sleeping in her clothes, she reached London only to learn that her destination had been changed to Holland. Boarding a blacked-out plane for an intended weekend assignment, she stayed six months.

Tall and statuesque, Breckinridge possessed an authoritative voice. When Murrow put her on the payroll, she became the first woman foreign correspondent on the staff of a radio network. She dropped the Mary from her name, using the signature Marvin Breckinridge for her radio work. Breckinridge broadcast from Berlin during January to March 1940, filling in for William L. Shirer, the CBS Berlin bureau chief. In February, the airwaves crackled with charges and countercharges concerning the British capture of the German vessel *Altmark* in the neutral waters of Norway, where both the British and the Germans were operating illegally. The *Altmark* was carrying 303 British merchant seamen rescued from ships sunk by the German battleship *Graf Spee*, when the British boarded her to retrieve them. The nervous boarding party killed six unarmed German sailors, and the Germans felt they had a case against the British.

The Germans, aware that the world was more likely to believe an American than a German, sent Breckinridge to Norway aboard a plane emblazoned with a huge swastika. She visited the *Altmark* in Jessingfjord, Norway, then spent twelve hours traveling thirty miles in a blizzard to broadcast from Stavanger, Norway. She covered the funeral of the German sailors and found it "more ominous than sad." Half the funeral oration by the German minister to Norway was a warning to that country against allowing British incursions. The British would again be accused of violating Norwegian neutrality when they mined Norwegian waters on April 8 in an effort to keep German supply ships from reaching Sweden. In retaliation, the Germans invaded Norway the next day, a move they had of course been planning for months.

That action convinced the people of Holland that the Germans would attack them next. In mid-April, CBS sent Breckinridge from Berlin to Amsterdam, where she sought out the leader of the Dutch Nazi movement, a man named Mussert, and asked him, "In the case of a possible attack on Holland by Germany, would the Dutch Nazis use German help to achieve their aims in Holland, or would they fight for their queen?'' Mussert replied that the Dutch Nazis would do absolutely nothing but sit with their arms folded. That entire broadcast, scheduled for April 20, 1940, was censored by Dutch authorities, but the government that censored it took note. Forty years later, Eric Sevareid of CBS recalled that her report created a diplomatic incident and an uproar in the Parliament of the Netherlands over the audacity of Dutch Nazis declaring they would refuse to defend their country.

Jefferson Patterson, a diplomat serving as secretary of the American embassy in Berlin, drove to Amsterdam on May 5, a beautiful day, to see Breckinridge. Having fallen in love with her while she was in Berlin, he came to tell her that separation was too painful. They became engaged and celebrated by walking in the tulip fields. They would soon be safe, except for British bombs in Berlin. The Dutch were smiling, oblivious to the preparations for invasion Patterson had seen along the way. Five days later, May 10, the German blitzkrieg on Holland began.

Breckinridge and Patterson were married in Berlin on June 20, and she was forced to resign from CBS because the State Department refused to waive a rule allowing it to censor anything a diplomat's wife wrote for publication. Its four censors rejected everything she tried to write, no matter how innocuous. She even provoked a letter from J. Edgar Hoover, director of the Federal Bureau of Investigation, warning that anything she wrote could be extremely damaging to her husband's career. The damage a diplomat could do to his wife's career was not a consideration in those days.

No correspondent covering World War II achieved a more spectacular combination of headlines and by-lines than Helen Kirkpatrick, reporting for the *Chicago Daily News* foreign service and its one hundred member newspapers. Like the wire service reporters, she frequently covered the ''headquarters'' story. Communiqués, briefings, and press conferences provided the substance for the major news story of the day and the newspapers' banner headlines. Most newspapers depended on the wire services for this official account of what was happening as their own correspondents specialized in covering the action at the front. Kirkpatrick covered both: she collected headlines covering the historic pronouncements of the Allied powers and won by-lines for her exclusive articles on military strategy and diplomacy and her eyewitness accounts of the fighting.

Kirkpatrick encountered little of the hostility experienced by other women in World War II, her appearance as much as her expertise commanding respect. Having inherited the features of her Scottish ancestors, she was a distinguished-looking woman, as tall as Breckinridge, with high cheekbones and blue eyes that seemed small set in a memorable face. As a fellow correspondent remarked, she was tall enough to overlook insults. By the time the war correspondents arrived, she had acquired five years' experience in Europe. At the age of thirty, she knew all the leaders of Britain and France, and they respected her.

At war, she escaped the restrictions the U.S. armed forces placed on American women correspondents by traveling with the Free French forces. Instinctively, she avoided offending. For instance, when she arrived in Algiers she did not go to the press center where other women encountered hostility. She went to the billeting office and accepted what she described as "a terrible room overlooking the casbah." Kirkpatrick was shocked to learn, forty years later, that fellow correspondents who saw little of her described her as "a loner." As she remembered it, she just went her way, doing what she saw she had to do for positive and plausible reasons. Because she knew her way around so well, she did not have to depend as much as others on fellow correspondents and press officers.

Thanks to an outstanding academic background—Smith College, University of Geneva—Kirkpatrick was hired in 1935 as a researcher and editor for the Geneva Research Center, sponsored by the Foreign Policy Association. John Elliott, *New York Herald Tribune* correspondent in Switzerland, took her on as a stringer. In 1937, she went to London and filled in as a diplomatic correspondent for the London *Sunday Times*. What the editors did to her copy convinced her the British press did not wish to face the truth, the inevitability of war with Germany.

Kirkpatrick and two British correspondents, Victor Gordon

Maddox of the London *Daily Telegraph* and Graham Hutton of the *Economist*, started the *Whitehall News* to warn Western leaders that Adolf Hitler would attempt to take over all of Europe. The newsletter was soon being read by members of the House of Commons and by Winston Churchill, Anthony Eden, and the king of Sweden. As the men who worked for the letter were moonlighters, Kirkpatrick and her secretary were the only full-time members of the staff. Of the 1938 Munich Pact between Hitler and the Western powers, she wrote, "This truce may well induce rather than prevent war."

Early in 1939, she produced a book for British audience, *This Terrible Peace*, again predicting war. Some Britishers were furious that an American would presume to predict their future. Appeasement remained the policy of Prime Minister Neville Chamberlain, and his staff managed to ban the sale of the book at railroad kiosks in London.

As World War II approached, Kirkpatrick was hired by William Stoneman, chief of the *Chicago Daily News* London bureau, because he recognized her ability and needed her help. During World War II, bureau chiefs in Europe loved to hate the women their editors sent to work for them, but the women the bureau chiefs hired themselves endured no such friction. Kirkpatrick's ordeal was to win acceptance in the home office.

Editors in Chicago gave Stoneman permission to hire Kirkpatrick apparently without realizing that she would be writing for the newspaper. For her first assignment, she suggested she interview the Duke of Windsor, the former Edward VIII of England. The male staff members hooted at this, knowing that he had refused to be interviewed by his best friends. But Kirkpatrick knew the people with whom the Windsors were staying in Paris and went to see them. The duke explained that he had sworn not to give any interviews, but he saw no reason that he could not interview her. Thus her first contribution to the *Chicago Daily News* was the duke's interview with her.

With the outbreak of World War II, Bill Stoneman went to France, and Leland Stowe came to London for the *Chicago Daily News*. Stowe soon went off to cover the Soviet invasion of Finland in November 1939 and left Kirkpatrick in charge of the

London bureau. "But how will I know I am writing the right story?" she asked. "You will know," he assured her. "I began dreaming in cableese," she said.

On a brief trip to the States in January 1940 to promote her second book, *Under the British Umbrella*, Kirkpatrick had to face the editors of the *Chicago Daily News*. Although the book was universally acclaimed—the *Washington Post* credited her with "balance and calm and good analytic reporting, not the impassioned pleading of Dorothy Thompson"—the *Daily News* editors were divided about her. Carroll Binder, the foreign editor, wanted her on the staff. Unmoved, Paul Scott Mowrer, the editor, was both formidable and taciturn when they were introduced. A note that Colonel Frank Knox, the publisher, wished to see her rescued her from Mowrer's austere presence. Knox was hearty and warm, but he explained, "We don't have women on the staff."

"I can't change my sex. But you can change your policy," she told him.

He made no comment, and there the matter rested until she made a speech before the Council on Foreign Relations at the Palmer House, then Chicago's leading hotel. The whole *Daily News* hierarchy was in attendance, and she won them over. Binder helped by telling Knox that the United Press wanted to hire her, a blatant fantasy. Knox, soon to be named secretary of the Navy by President Franklin D. Roosevelt, did not change his policy; he simply made an exception for her.

Kirkpatrick, having sounded like the voice of doom on the eve of World War II, became the voice of hope when Britain faced its darkest hour. "The Germans cannot win even though the war will be a long one," she told her audiences in January 1940. Days before Adolf Hitler's blitzkrieg on Western Europe in the spring of 1940, she cabled that the king of Belgium expected his country to be the next victim of Germany. As usual, she was right.

As she recalled it, her frustrations were as memorable as her scoops. In March 1941, she sailed from a Scottish port for Iceland, where the United States, in violation of its neutrality, was establishing a naval base. It was black and bitterly cold as the convoy moved out, the only light supplied by searchlights sweeping the sky for enemy planes. The wireless was sealed and signals were banned because of enemy aircraft in the vicinity. They had scarcely cleared the harbor when Kirkpatrick heard the impact of steel on steel. Several ships were sunk by German submarines. Two British ships collided. The Icelandic crew of her ship wanted no more and returned to port. Before the ship could sail again, she received an urgent message to return to London. The Germans had invaded Greece. Had her trip not been aborted, she could have been stuck in Iceland without a story she would be allowed to file. Secretary of the Navy Knox had alerted his newspaper to the Iceland story, but he never paused to consider how to get it through censorship.

In June 1941, she was driving into the English countryside when British police stopped her. The *Daily News* bureau had managed to deliver an SOS. Germany had attacked Russia, and she was to go straight to the airport and take the first plane to Moscow. Blessed with a competent housekeeper, Kirkpatrick called her to pack a suitcase and meet her at the airport. At the last moment, she was not allowed to board the plane because U.S. Ambassador Laurence Steinhardt, convinced the Russians could not hold out for more than a few weeks, wanted no women in Moscow.

In World War I, women correspondents had covered the Russian front, and Russian women had fought in the war. In World War II, few Western correspondents got near the Russian front. Kirkpatrick was angry about not even getting to Moscow, but there were bigger headlines to be had in London and more trouble for those who wrote the news.

The U.S. State Department took offense when Kirkpatrick wrote stories favorable to General Charles de Gaulle, the French resistance leader, whom President Roosevelt disliked. The Americans smuggled General Henri-Honoré Giraud out of France and installed him as French high commissioner in North Africa. Still, it took de Gaulle to achieve unity among the anti-Nazi French.

In Chicago, a subscriber objected to the paper's allowing a woman to cover military strategy. This sparked considerable controversy both in the letters to the editor column and among editors at the *Daily News*, but in the end the newspaper stood by her.

For light relief during the Nazi blitz on London, there was the article in the New York newspaper *P.M.* describing Kirkpatrick as among the six bravest women in the world, along with Queen Elizabeth and a chambermaid named Maude. At least Kirkpatrick laughed. She appreciated *P.M.*'s way of saluting the bravery of British women. As for herself, she reported the global proportions of the tragedy and dismissed the risks she took as "details of no real interest, I'm sure." Correspondents who saw far less of the war than she dramatized their close encounters and narrow escapes. Kirkpatrick could tell as good a war story as anyone, but hers was always factual, with a humorous twist. *P.M.* had a point. Most people were victims of war, but the correspondents didn't have to be there. Indeed, the women correspondents had to battle the authorities to get there.

At a high-level conference in London, objections were raised to allowing a woman to cover any part of the war in France. Generals who thought they could defeat the Germans could see no way of providing latrines for women. After a long, boring hour of listening to this discussion, George Lyon, a public information officer, put a five-pound note on the table and offered to wager that "Helen Kirkpatrick could dig a latrine faster than anyone in this room." There were no takers. (She was in her thirties then. I saw her at the age of seventy-three lift a suitcase so heavy a skycap could barely budge it. Kirkpatrick moved with a manner that brooked no nonsense.)

Early in 1943, she went to Algiers and spent six months covering the North African campaign, where it seemed that objections to women correspondents came more from higher headquarters than from front-line forces. Her presence, she discovered, somehow boosted the men's morale. If a woman was there, things could not be all that bad.

Free French Forces joined the struggle to liberate the island of Corsica from the Germans on September 20, 1943, and Kirkpatrick boarded a French destroyer traveling with Moroccan troops to the port of Ajaccio on the south of Corsica. As they arrived, the Germans were attempting to retreat from the island via Bastia to the north. In Ajaccio she could find no transportation—until she encountered three Americans, members of the Office of Strategic Services, who took her with them to Bastia, up to the point of the fighting. High on a hill, they walked around the rim of the city and were sitting on a wall when shooting began. The Germans were at the other end of the town; these marksmen were trigger-happy and equally dangerous Corsicans. The Americans ducked behind the wall, and when the coast seemed clear, they crawled across the square and knocked on a door. A man admitted them and eventually guided them into the town, which had been heavily bombed, to the police station. The police were occupying a former nightclub, replete with red velvet drapes and bedrooms upstairs the Germans had just vacated. There was no water. The Germans had left the place a mess.

"What makes you think this place hasn't been mined?" Kirkpatrick thought to ask. "It probably has been," she was told. The Germans had mined many buildings as they retreated. She was too tired to move. "We all woke up alive, so we knew it hadn't been mined," she recalled. The Germans were too busy pulling out to inflict more casualties. This was the first liberated department of metropolitan France, and she was there to see de Gaulle receive a tumultuous welcome.

To view the surrender of Italian forces in North Africa, she flew aboard a one-seater P-38, wedged into a narrow space behind the pilot's seat. The pilot obligingly took risks to show her everything. She also flew to Malta to see the surrender of the Italian Fleet. There Kirkpatrick was exposed to "sandfly fever," an illness marked by high fever and diarrhea, which she caught. She was flown back to Algiers and hospitalized by medics who saw no reason to let her go. General Robert McClure, the U.S. Army public relations officer who initially had shown fierce hostility toward women correspondents, came to her rescue and obtained her release after she had spent five days in the hospital.

By October 31, 1943, Kirkpatrick was in Naples to cover the war in Italy. At a field hospital a mile from the front, she watched surgeons operate on casualties too critically wounded to be moved. In one night, while loud and insistent guns pounded away, she witnessed twenty major operations performed by surgeons standing on a slippery mud floor.

Despite their successful coverage of the war in Africa and Italy, the U.S. War Department ruled that no women correspondents would be allowed to accompany the armed forces during the invasion of France. Nevertheless, Helen Kirkpatrick was chosen to represent all newspapers on a committee assigned to arrange coverage of the landings in Normandy. Edward R. Murrow served as the radio representative on the committee, which included a representative for magazines and another for wire services, as well as representatives of the American, British, and Canadian armed forces. From January to May 1944, she participated in the decisions on how the newspapermen would cover the invasion, working out the logistics about how many would go where and what facilities were required.

The important question was not who was first to reach the front but who did the best job of reporting the war, she observed. By more or less illicit means, several women correspondents did reach the front within days of the Allied invasion on June 6, 1944. Kirkpatrick concentrated first on obtaining an interview with General Dwight D. Eisenhower, the supreme allied commander. As she entered the room, his aide whispered, "Remember, the boss doesn't like complaints." She simply remarked on the bombing of Britain and said, "It is too damned dangerous here. I want to go to France." Eisenhower laughed at the idea that she would be safer in France, but he appreciated her point that confinement to Britain was no protection and directed his aides to cut her orders for France.

The French requested her presence, and Kirkpatrick became the first correspondent assigned to the headquarters of Brigadier General Pierre-Joseph Koenig, commander of the French forces of the interior, the Free French Forces operating inside France. The Second French Armored Division took Argentan, in Normandy, on August 9. As its members rolled out of Argentan to participate in the liberation of Paris, Kirkpatrick went with them. One of the first correspondents to enter Paris on Liberation Day,

August 25, she was with Free French leaders when they entered Notre Dame Cathedral to give thanks to God. Then, as she cabled the *Daily News*,

> Suddenly an automatic opened up from behind us. It came from behind the pipes in Notre Dame's organ. . . . Other shots rang out, and I saw a man ducking behind the pillar above. Beside me, Free Frenchmen and the police were shooting. For one flashing instant, it seemed a great massacre was bound to take place as the Cathedral reverberated with the sound of guns. . . . There was a sudden blaze, and machine guns sprayed the center aisle, chipping tiles to my left. Time seemed to have no meaning. Spontaneously, a crowd of widows and bereaved burst forth into the Te Deum as the generals bravely stood before the altar.

This one last gasp perpetrated by French fascists the Nazis had trained failed because people who had already endured too much refused to panic.

On that Liberation Day, the people of Paris poured out of their homes and lined the boulevards to watch the Germans pulling out. The first French out on the sidewalks stayed and held their seats to watch their liberators moving in, the French, the Americans, and the British all converging at once from different directions on the Arc de Triomphe. No sharpshooters hiding in Notre Dame Cathedral could spoil the event.

Kirkpatrick went into Frankfurt, Germany, with the first Allied tanks, on the day the mayor of that city killed his wife and children, then committed suicide. Germans bombed out of their homes were living in tunnels beneath the railroad station, and there was little left to eat. She had seen so many of their victims, she did not want to feel sorry for the Germans, but she did.

She reached the Berghof, "Eagle's Nest," Hitler's famous retreat high on a mountain above Berchtesgaden in Bavaria ahead of some Allied forces. She swiped a skillet from the kitchen to cook field rations. The nest was destroyed by advancing forces soon after she left.

Stationed in Paris after the war, Kirkpatrick went to Nuremberg to cover the first and major war crimes trials. American and Russian women shared one bathroom. The Russians, seven to nine at a time, usually reached the bathroom first and left it a mess. The Americans began setting their alarms to beat the Russians to the bath.

As much as she loved her work, Kirkpatrick faced it with increasing heartache. Colonel Knox died in 1944, and John S. Knight bought the *Daily News*, installing Basil L. ("Stuffy") Walters as executive editor. The new owners chose to emphasize local coverage at the expense of the foreign service.

In March 1947, Kirkpatrick traveled to Moscow to cover the meeting of the Council of Foreign Ministers. Ensconced in a new hotel close to the Kremlin, she marveled at the white bread served for breakfast. Every morning she took Russian lessons, sharing the bread with her teacher, who had seen nothing like that bread since before World War II. She was so grateful that she refused to accept payment for the lessons. For a while, international understanding and appreciation seemed possible.

Then came a cable from Stuffy Walters, asking Kirkpatrick to concentrate on "the Chicago angle," and she was furious. What Chicago angle? Wasn't it angle enough to make peace or perish? She wrote her resignation and put it in a drawer, to be delivered as soon as she cooled off. Her loyalty to the *Daily News* foreign news service and to such men as Stoneman and Stowe caused her to delay her resignation, but the foreign service soon fell apart and Paul Scott Mowrer left the *Daily News* to join the *New York Post*.

Dorothy Schiff, publisher of the *Post*, and her husband, Ted O. Thackrey, the editor, saw their chance to take over the neglected *Daily News* foreign service, and they offered fabulous contracts to its staff, Kirkpatrick recalled. Although Bill Stoneman declined, Kirkpatrick accepted the job of roving correspondent for the *Post*.

Among memorable assignments was her interview in New Delhi with Jawaharlal Nehru, the first prime minister of independent India. Nehru arranged for her to visit Kashmir in the north, territory claimed by both Pakistan and India. After obtaining India's side of the dispute, she went to Pakistan and into the part of Kashmir Pakistan controlled. She was driving by jeep through the mountains along dirt roads, looking down on sheer drops of thousands of feet, when it occurred to her that she had not told anybody where she was and could have disappeared without a trace. But luck was a lady, and she made it back to New Delhi. When Nehru made the mistake of asking her opinion about the Kashmir dispute, she told him she thought Moslem Kashmir belonged with Moslem Pakistan rather than Hindu India. Nehru was enraged, and India retained control of most of Kashmir. The incident demonstrated that chiefs of state could expect a straight answer, however undiplomatic, from Kirkpatrick.

What happened to her copy never ceased to concern a correspondent with integrity. Kirkpatrick quit the *Post* when she concluded that Thackrey was following the Communist Party line. Dorothy Schiff ordered an investigation when dissatisfaction with her husband among members of the staff was brought to her attention. Neither the *Post*'s foreign news service nor the marriage of Schiff and Thackrey survived the dispute.

Kirkpatrick landed on her feet as chief of information for the French mission, Economic Cooperation Administration, Paris, where her work contributed to the success of the Marshall Plan for the rehabilitation of war-torn Europe. For her many contributions, she won the French Legion of Honor, the French Medaille de la Reconnaissance, the U.S. Medal of Freedom, a Nieman Fellowship to Harvard University she did not use, and the Rockefeller Public Service Award.

During the Depression, Kirkpatrick had been married briefly, against her parents' wishes. In 1954, at the age of forty-four, she married Robbins Milbank, member of a prominent and philanthropic New England family. For thirty years, the Milbanks maintained homes in California and New Hampshire. In both states, she achieved prominence as a civic leader, serving on innumerable committees, boards, and commissions in the fields of higher education, conservation, crime prevention, and world affairs. After her husband's death, Kirkpatrick settled in Williamsburg, Virginia.

9

Asking for Trouble

FOR A YEAR AFTER THE ATTACK ON PEARL HARBOR, THE U.S. War Department refused to send women correspondents overseas in uniform with America's fighting forces, which left the impression that women saw little of World War II. As it happened, no newsman covered more of World War II than Sonia Tomara of the *New York Herald Tribune* or Martha Gellhorn of *Collier's* magazine.

Martha Gellhorn was credited with covering four wars in a row—the Civil War in Spain, the Russian invasion of Finland, the Japanese invasion of China, and finally the American invasion of Europe. As she saw it, this fighting was all one war, her first. By her count, the Vietnam War was her second, and the fighting that began with the Six-Day War in Israel in 1967 and resumed in Lebanon, her third.

Sonia Tomara and Richard Mowrer of the *Chicago Daily News* (son of Paul Scott Mowrer and nephew of Edgar Ansel Mowrer) shared the horror of hearing the first bomb explode in World War II. They were among the small band of Western correspondents in Warsaw on September 1, 1939, the day Germany invaded Poland and German bombers began their air attacks on unprotected cities. Tomara went on to cover the collapse of France, the China-India-Burma theater, the North African campaign, the liberation of Paris, and the final defeat of Germany.

In her Warsaw hotel room the day the war began, Tomara heard first the rumbling of planes overhead, then the air raid sirens, and seconds later, the explosions. Tenements and a Jewish orphanage were hit. Soon bombs were falling around the bridges and near the main railway station. German armies converged on Warsaw from the north, the west, and the southwest. Part of the agony for her was that she could not get her stories through censorship and the telegraph office to the *Herald Tribune*.

When France and Great Britain declared war on Germany on September 3, jubilant Poles felt victory was theirs. They did not foresee the devastating impact of high-speed armored warfare. By September 8, the Germans were on the outskirts of Warsaw. Americans in Warsaw, as neutrals, could expect to survive Nazi occupation. Tomara, Russian by origin and American by adoption, carried a French passport and could expect the doom awaiting declared enemies. But it was too late for her to panic. At the age of forty-two, she had survived World War I, the Russian Revolution, and a sentence to die at dawn, and she had to wonder how many lives God had given her.

Born into the Russian aristocracy in 1897, Tomara vividly recalled wearing a green velvet dress with rose coral buttons to a family party in December 1916, where a friend of her father, the former minister of agriculture, Alexander Krivosheine, announced, "We are racing toward an abyss, and little can be done about it." After two and a half years in World War I, the Russian people had lost the will to fight the Germans, and revolution was in the wind.

A tall brunette with fine features and a patrician's style, Tomara arrived in Petrograd for a visit on February 26, 1917, the day the Russian Revolution began. The elegant Astoria Hotel went up in flames. There was shooting in the streets, and strangers as well as friends took refuge in the apartment where she stayed. Yet in the end the newspapers called this "the great bloodless revolution." When the extremists seized power from the moderates, in the October Revolution, Tomara was in Moscow. The house where she lived with her aunt was in the line of fire. For days they heard continuous gunfire and exploding shells. When she could venture into the street, "blood was still running in the gutter and dead men lay in grotesque positions."

Civil war was still raging in the spring of 1919 between the Red Communists and the White Russians seeking to preserve what was left of old Russia. Unwilling to endure the misery of Moscow another season, Tomara, with her younger sister, Irina, headed south toward Sukhumi, their family home on the Black Sea, deep in the republic of Georgia. Finding no other way, they undertook to cross the battlefield on horseback. The Reds intercepted and arrested them, and Sonia was sentenced to be shot. "I sat alone in a cell that afternoon, trying to imagine how I would behave on the way to death," she recalled.

With the help of a sympathetic Red Guard, the sisters escaped. Their elder brother, fighting for the White Russians, died of pneumonia and typhus. After delivering Irina safely to Sukhumi, Sonia traveled to Rostov, in the center of White Army territory, and worked as an interpreter with the British military mission. She was not spared the sight of wounded men freezing to death unattended in open railroad cars or of women carrying dead children wrapped in their shawls.

Eventually, she made her way to the Black Sea port of Novorossisk. On March 20, 1920, while fire was enveloping the town in smoke, she sailed into exile and an uncertain future aboard a former Austrian collier, *Buergermeister Schroeder*, with four thousand refugees. After nearly starving to death in Constantinople, she found refuge there with a British colonel, Archie Walker, and his wife, but safety was not for her. Tomara, finding herself falling in love with Walker, fled back to her family in Sukhumi. When the colonel heard of fighting in the region of Sukhumi, he commandeered a British destroyer, the *Sportive*, and went to her rescue. What should have been the ending of a novel was only the beginning of her career in journalism.

Walker's wife, also a Russian, refused to give him a divorce, and the romance ended, but not their friendship. Tomara went to Paris and worked for six years as a secretary to the foreign editor of the Paris newspaper *Le Matin* before Leland Stowe, then Paris editor of the *Herald Tribune*, hired her for his news staff. Promoted to Rome correspondent in 1935, she broke the news to the world of the forging of the Rome-Berlin Axis in October 1936, an alliance that was to be Mussolini's undoing. She learned about it from the German ambassador, Ulrich von

Hassel, a gentleman later hanged for participating in an attempt on the life of Adolf Hitler.

Mussolini's foolish dream of empire, his war on Ethiopia, had brought higher prices and taxes, and foreign trade and tourism declined. As Tomara wrote, "The Roman empire began sliding down the slope while Mussolini, blinded by the Fuehrer's promises of victory over the democracies, traveled up and down the Brenner Pass."

Her success in Rome won Tomara an invitation to join the *Herald Tribune* staff in New York late in 1937. As war approached, she obtained permission to return to Europe as a roving correspondent for the *Herald Tribune*. But in the absence of a bureau opening for her, she was traveling at her own expense when she witnessed the eruption of World War II.

British correspondents, as vulnerable as she in Warsaw, squeezed her into their automobile, and they struck out for the Romanian border, not just to flee from danger but to file their stories. They drove south to a small health resort called Nalenchow, where swans still glided on the ponds. Americans, Chinese, Romanians, the automobiles of the whole diplomatic corps, arrived and lined up with them to wait for gasoline as a yellow moon rose over the blacked-out countryside. The Germans were scarcely thirty miles away. "The feeling of disaster was with us all."

Polish government vehicles clogging the route were headed for the Polish town of Kremenetz. The correspondents drove south, traveling night and day until they reached Bucharest, the Romanian capital, on September 9, four days after leaving Warsaw. There they stopped just long enough to file their stories and fill up on gasoline, then turned around and headed back toward the Polish border. Wilbur Forrest of the *London News Chronicle* and Richard Mowrer made it to their destination, only to be arrested as spies and detained briefly. Tomara was among those who made their headquarters at Czernowitz, the capital of Bukovina. Austrian before World War I, it was then part of Romania and was later claimed by the Soviet Union. There were two fair hotels in the town, as well as a Jewish population clad in black and peasants from Ukrainian villages dressed in gaily embroidered white linen garments.

On September 17, Tomara and Forrest hired a car to cross the Polish border, taking with them two Polish women, wives of members of the Polish Ministry of Foreign Affairs. But when they reached the bridge separating Poland from Romania they saw a strange procession of cars, buses, wagons, trucks, vans, and a mob on foot moving over the bridge out of Poland and into Romania. Delivering a stab in the back, the Russians had invaded Poland from the east, and the Polish government was departing. It had taken exactly seventeen days to destroy the "free and reunited" Polish state created after World War I. This time Tomara managed to report the news immediately by telephone from Czernowitz to New York.

The *New York Times* soon had a correspondent in every capital of southeastern Europe, but for the *Herald Tribune*, Tomara covered them all—Bucharest, Budapest, Belgrade, on to Athens, Ankara, Syria, and Palestine. In the still neutral capitals, the French, the British, the Germans, and the Italians mingled with correspondents of every nationality.

On another trip to the Polish border, Tomara learned that the Jews were being rounded up and sent to Lublin, her first inkling of the Holocaust, the extermination of the Jews. Yet in Romania and Hungary the lights were still blazing, the Gypsies playing, the food plentiful. At the Athenée Palace Hotel in Bucharest, an enormous portion of caviar cost fifty cents. While spies consorted in the bar, the correspondents took off for a fancy-dress ball to celebrate New Year's Eve 1940 at the home of the American military attaché. Romania was to remain neutral until it entered the war on the side of Germany in 1941.

In the face of warnings that she might be trapped, Tomara flew to Paris on May 20, 1940, to report the fall of France. German panzers were deep in France, only a hundred miles from Paris, when she arrived. On June 3, German bombers attacked Paris for the first time, and caravans of cars began to file out of the capital, headed south.

"I knew by then that France had been defeated," Tomara said. "In Warsaw I had been a spectator afraid of war and sorry for the Poles. Here I felt a part of my heart was being torn out of my breast.''

Tomara waited until June 10 to join the exodus. Once more, as on her departure from Moscow twenty years earlier, she was accompanied by her sister, Irina. They were less than fifteen miles from Paris when their old car broke down, and they spent the night in a ditch. Millions of French people were fleeing before the enemy, and the roads were so clogged with traffic that some who walked made better time than those who rode. The Tomara sisters abandoned their car and, with typewriter and heavy packs, thumbed rides on trucks that crawled with the traffic through the night. It took them four days to reach Montbazon, a small town seven miles south of Tours—in better times it was less than a half-day's journey from Paris.

The news traveled faster. On Friday, June 14, as the Germans were entering Paris, Tomara, to cable her story, picked up her typewriter and pack, left her sister, and began hiking back toward Tours against the current of humanity fleeing south. Getting a lift on a truck, she reached the press wireless office in Tours just as the censor and the operator were preparing to join the exodus for Bordeaux. As a siren howled for an air raid, she began to type. ''We heard the ack-ack and the sound of bombs,'' she recalled, ''but I did not have time to take shelter. . . . Never did I write a long story so fast and probably so well.''

Tomara returned to the city square in Montbazon only to see big Navy vans moving out, and her heart fell for fear that her sister was gone. But no, Irina was sitting on a pile of luggage, still waiting for her. They traveled by truck to Bordeaux with French sailors whose despair convinced Sonia they would not willingly leave France to fight on the side of Britain. Officers might, but these men were through with war. The elderly Marshal Pétain announced the end over the radio: ''We have asked the enemy to cease hostilities.''

With her French passport, Sonia got out through Spain. Irina, stateless, had to be left behind, but they found a cousin on the streets of Bordeaux, so Irina was not abandoned. In Portugal, Sonia boarded the Greek steamer *Hellas*, bound for New York.

The *Herald Tribune* was loath to let a woman return to a war zone. Restricted to the city staff, Tomara watched the German invasion of the Soviet Union in June 1941, the Japanese attack on Pearl Harbor in December. On her own, she obtained a British affidavit of identity and visas to enter India. The State Department gave Herbert Matthews of the *New York Times* priority to travel to India, although she had been on the list ahead of him. The War Department said she would have to wait and threatened that if she asked once more, she would never get overseas.

Tomara was one of several women who had already covered the war in Europe and in Asia but were sidelined by a government reluctant to allow women to go overseas in wartime. Mary Welsh, an American married to an Australian journalist, was hired in London by *Time* magazine in July 1940 and covered the London blitz. But on a 1942 visit to *Time*'s headquarters, she was stranded in New York for months by the State Department's refusal to let her go home to her husband and her job in London.

The State Department, which issued passports, and the War Department, which accredited correspondents, joined forces to perpetuate the World War I policy of forbidding women to cover combat. The War Department first bent its rule to send Margaret Bourke-White, a *Life* magazine photographer, to London in the spring of 1942, under an agreement with Time Inc., publisher of *Life*, to undertake assignments for both *Life* and the department. Author Eve Curie and Clare Boothe Luce, the wife of *Time* publisher Henry Luce, were allowed to visit India.

Helen Rogers Reid, who had succeeded her husband, Ogden Reid, as publisher of the *Herald Tribune*, went to bat for Tomara and in one hour in Washington obtained War Department accreditation for her. Five months before women were authorized to cover combat, she was assigned to the China-Burma-India (CBI) theater, which appeared to make her the first woman newspaper correspondent allowed to cover the war.

Flying out of Miami in a bucket seat on a C-47 Army plane, Tomara went for the duration. It took ten days to fly over Africa and into Asia. She arrived in India on August 27, 1942, in time to report on riots, revolt, and, worse, a devastating hurricane in Bengal. The white man had lost face for suffering defeats at the hands of the Japanese, rekindling Indian nationalism. The British response was to jail Nationalist leaders; Mahatma Gandhi, the symbol of passive resistance to British rule, had been arrested on August 9.

Tomara crossed the easternmost province of Assam to an American air base on the Burma border. Thousands of refugees fleeing the Japanese in Burma died on the mountainous footpaths leading into Assam. "I saw their skeletons, cleaned by wild beasts and ants, being quickly covered up by the jungle," she recalled. New Year's Day 1943 was made bearable when a pilot took off in a small pursuit trainer plane and rescued a pilot downed in the Burma jungle.

In 1943, Tomara moved her base to Chungking, the wartime capital of China. At a press conference, she delivered her request to go on a bombing mission directly to General Joseph W. Stilwell, commander of U.S. forces in the China-Burma-India theater. "Nope!" he said. The male correspondents, all of whom were authorized to make such trips, burst out laughing. Tomara was outraged. Why should the *Herald Tribune* be denied a story for sending a woman overseas?

Short of ammunition, Tomara threw the sugar bowl. When Stilwell made a trip to Washington, she wrote an article about what a great job he had done in the CBI. Forty years later, she confessed that, while she admired him, this was a bit of a puff piece. When they next met, at a dinner party in Chungking, the General said, "What are those lies you have written about me? Come and collect the pay some day." That was precisely what she had intended to do.

Before leaving Chungking to spend a month with the Fourteenth Air Force in southern China, Tomara again went to Stilwell to ask permission to fly on a bombing mission. This time he said, "I would hate to see you shot down." For once, he had not said no. She went to K'un-ming and won permission to fly from General Claire Chennault, U.S. air commander in China. Chennault sent her to Kweilin, a town renowned for its superb landscapes, the headquarters of the forward echelon, and she was assigned to the first bombing mission against the Japanese in Hangchow.

The American air base had no concrete runways, only gravel ground by rollers pushed by Chinese coolies. For an 8:00 A.M. takeoff, Tomara climbed aboard a bomber, its instructions to follow the lead ship piloted by Lieutenant Colonel Mory Taber. "The planes fell into formation, flying like cranes in a triangle," she recalled. "I could see Taber's plane in front of us and the second wing ship on our left, then only the shadows of the others way down on the ground. . . . Bombers are not comfortable means of transportation. I sat on my heels behind the pilots and looked at the country through the windshield."

They were so high that the bombardier beside her reached for his oxygen mask. With only one between them, they took turns using it. She was aboard one of nine B-25s, medium-size bombers, expecting to rendezvous with seven larger B-24s, but the B-24s did not show up. Fortunately, Japanese fighters also failed to show, and the pilots were accepting her word that she was a good-luck talisman. Suddenly, long black objects began to drop from under the plane ahead, and she saw the bombardier next to her press his bomb release. She did not look down at the destruction.

Back on the ground in Kweilin, she learned that there had been a battle over Hangchow after all. The B-24s had arrived early, only to be overtaken by a force of fifty Japanese Zeros. American P-40 pursuit planes coming to the rescue attacked the Zeros, thirty-five of which were downed. Twenty Americans on two planes were lost, and more were killed and wounded on others.

While her newspaper congratulated her, an irate public relations officer ordered Tomara back to Chungking and gave her hell for going without Stilwell's authorization. Unable to get an appointment with Stilwell, she wrote a note telling him she did not mean to violate his orders. Back came a note scribbled in his hand. "Let us forget about it, Sonia. We all think that you are a good newspaperman, and we like you."

For the correspondents, Chungking was like living in the trenches. "Nowhere have I been so dirty; nowhere have I walked so much, jumping over open-air sewers and heaps of garbage," she recalled. The air smelled of human fertilizer used on vegetable fields nearby. Rain came through the wall of the room she occupied at the press hotel. Rats ate her soap, and mosquitoes formed clouds around the netting over her bed. Yet there was camaraderie among the press. They saluted their hostel with raw gin: "We may damn you, we may slam you, but we love you nonetheless."

In China death was considered just bad luck, and the people were capable of laughing when they saw somebody dying. Tomara watched women and children laughing at the deathbed of a Chinese prostitute in an opium den. They could laugh because they were alive.

Tomara was transferred to North Africa in October 1943. She was in Cairo when Prime Minister Winston Churchill of Britain and President Franklin D. Roosevelt of the United States arrived en route to the Tehran Conference with Joseph Stalin of the Soviet Union to plan for the opening of a second front in Europe. The correspondents were not allowed to go to Tehran, and the news of that conference was broken by a neutral correspondent who flew to Portugal and filed it free of censorship.

By Easter 1944, Tomara was with the Fifth Army, composed of American and French troops, fighting on the Garigliano River, halfway between Naples and Rome. The Easter Sunday services she attended were held within two hundred yards of the German foxholes. In German, the pastor wished the enemy, "Ein fröhlichs Osterfest," a joyous Easter. Most of the Americans put their helmets on the ground but held their rifles. The Easter truce lasted through a Protestant, then a Catholic service, but soon the big guns were going full blast again, and shells whizzed over their heads as they left the place of worship.

Tomara knew that the story of Europe's liberation would be written from France, not Italy, so in the second week of June, just after the first wave of Allied troops landed on the coast of Normandy, she flew to England, then traveled by ship to France. As Paris was about to be freed from the Germans, the driver of a weapons carrier offered her a ride. When they arrived, there were Allied tanks in the Bois de Boulogne, but Paris still had not been liberated. Tomara made her way to the apartment she had occupied before the war for a joyous reunion with Irina and

French friends who were living there because it was safer than their homes.

"Let's go to the Ritz and celebrate," she cried.

"You can't go there," she was told. "That's Gestapo headquarters."

The Germans were moving out as fast as they could, but not as fast as she had thought. Her sister knew it was not yet safe to go to the Ritz.

At the end of the war, Tomara married Colonel William Clark, a legal officer on the staff of General Eisenhower. A bride for the first time at the age of forty-eight, she acquired a new reason to travel, her husband. During the occupation of Germany, General Lucius D. Clay, the American military governor, hired the former colonel, by then Judge Clark, to reform the German courts. While the Clarks lived in Germany from 1948 to 1954, Tomara continued to write for the *Herald Tribune*, but not as a member of the staff. Judge Clark died in 1957.

Irina was living with Tomara in Princeton, New Jersey, in a lovely house with a blossoming pink magnolia tree on the lawn and the river beyond when I visited them in the spring of 1982. Tomara showed me unpublished memoirs she said she had not looked at in thirty years. I urged her to complete them and offer them to a publisher.

She laughed. "Oh, I shall never live so long."

She died of a stroke within six weeks, at the age of eighty-five.

Martha Gellhorn's first experience as a war reporter led to her marriage to the novelist Ernest Hemingway. His second marriage, to Pauline Pfeiffer, was breaking up when Gellhorn met him in Madrid, where both were covering the Spanish Civil War. The Catholic revolutionary Francisco Franco, fighting for restoration of the rightists, was a rebel in name only; Gellhorn was a rebel to the core. While she was lovely to look at, her special attraction for Hemingway was her passionate concern for the underdog—and her spirit of adventure. In some ways, she took after her mother.

Edna Fishel Gellhorn, a leader in the suffrage movement,

reared three sons and her daughter, Martha, to be achievers. As a naval officer, a law professor, a medical educator, and an author-journalist, they all won distinction in their own right. Born in 1908 and reared in St. Louis, Missouri, Martha rode streetcars as a child and imagined they were taking her to far-away places like Peking or Katmandu. At the age of twenty, she set out for Europe.

Paris in 1928 was a place of romance. Not only gossip columnists but biographers married Martha off to a French journalist, Marquis Bertrand de Jouvenal. Gellhorn corrected the record. "I was never married to Bertrand de Jouvenal. The press married us at some point due to hotel registration. Long ago you could not get a room unless Mr. and Mrs., and we had no money for two rooms."

She added, "For some years in France, I wrote about anything which would bring in a few francs." She also wrote two well-received books of fiction. Between trips to Europe, she worked as a reporter on an Albany, New York, newspaper. She met the Nazis in Berlin in 1934, and the experience changed her from a pacifist into a defender of liberty.

Spain was a shattering experience for her. Sent there as a special correspondent for *Collier's* magazine, she sought not to write in global clichés but to portray the tragedy of war, looking at it from the bottom up. Of the wounded children she wrote, "Sometimes the child is so small you think the white crib is empty."

She was at her best portraying the bewildered. "I love my friend very much," a wounded soldier told her. "But he should not have cut off my leg." The amateur surgeon had had no choice.

Only a woman reared to wave the flag could have been so disillusioned by America's slowness to respond to the suffering she saw. "We were guilty of the dishonest abandonment of Spain and the quick cheap betrayal of Czechoslovakia," she wrote. "We niggled and refused asylum to doomed Jews. We inspected and rejected anti-Fascists fleeing for their lives from Hitler. We were full of shame and ugly expediencies."

Gellhorn covered the war in Finland alone before she and

Hemingway were finally married in Cheyenne, Wyoming, on November 21, 1940. Together they went to Asia early in 1941. When later she wrote a book about her experiences, she referred to him only as ''the unwilling companion'' and denied her publishers permission to identify him. Because cheap gossips credited her marriage to Hemingway for much of her success, she developed a fixation against having her name linked with his. Hemingway could afford to be more generous. Gellhorn was identified as the inspiration for his play, *The Fifth Column*, and he dedicated his most successful novel, *For Whom the Bell Tolls*, to her.

Gellhorn was impulsive, and she could be reckless, which she demonstrated on their trip to Asia. Leaving Hemingway in Hong Kong, she flew with the China National Aviation Corporation, a commercial airline operated by American pilots, from Hong Kong into China, across territory held by the Japanese. In three days she covered fifteen hundred miles, to the terminus of the Burma Road and back. When K'un-ming was bombed at one o'clock, it meant to them that they could return and land at 5:30.

Hemingway joined her on a short flight from Hong Kong to Shao-kuan, China, their objective to reach the Canton front, where the Chinese were fighting the Japanese. From Shao-kuan, they traveled by truck, on horseback, by motor boat, and sampan. The whole trip was one long disaster, unrelieved by news worth cabling. Hemingway ended up carrying the sick little horse he was given to ride. When Gellhorn at last latched on to a bottle of wine, she took a sip and discovered a dead snake in the jug. After several weeks, they reached Chinese headquarters at Chungking, a city where lepers abounded and the streets were as filthy as Tomara found them two years later.

What was supposed to be the highlight of the trip was lunch with China's chief of state and his wife, Generalissimo and Madame Chiang Kai-shek. The encounter, a terrible letdown for Gellhorn, convinced her that the Nationalist rulers cared nothing for the miserable hordes. The Communist leader, Chou En-lai, was also in Chungking, in hiding. For a visit to him, she was blindfolded and taken by a circuitous route. Chou En-lai impressed her as the one good man they had met in China, and she foresaw that the Communists would take over. For predicting in 1941 what others could not see because they did not wish to, Gellhorn was branded a fellow traveler.

She later demonstrated that she was no such thing. In Italy in 1944, she covered the Carpathian Lancers, a Polish force fighting the Germans. For *Collier's*, she reported that the Poles feared the Russians as much as they feared the Germans, but the magazine did not print the story because, she believed, the editors felt it was too critical of our Russian allies.

For the invasion of Normandy, June 6, 1944, Gellhorn stowed away on a hospital ship in violation of a U.S. Army order that women were not to cover the invasion. Hers was the first hospital ship to arrive off the beach at Normandy, and she saw the first wounded German prisoners, for whom she had no sympathy, brought aboard. For the Americans, her heart bled. "His face was fairly good," she wrote of a wounded GI. "But the sides of his head had been burned flat, and a head is strange without ears."

U.S. Army press officers punished her for defying orders not to go to Normandy by refusing to take her when others were finally allowed to go, and for a while she was confined to covering secondary fronts with foreign commanders not fussy about travel orders.

Gellhorn's marriage to Hemingway came to an end at about this time. To his publisher Hemingway wrote, "Have a new housemaid named Martha and it certainly is a pleasure to give her orders. Marty was a lovely girl though. I wish she hadn't been quite so ambitious and war crazy." Gellhorn left it to his next wife to describe how difficult he was to live with.

The charge that she was war crazy would stick. During the Battle of the Bulge, on a freezing night in January 1945, she climbed into a Black Widow night fighter and flew off to Germany with a pilot searching for a dogfight with Nazi war planes.

The first hazard was an ill-fitting oxygen mask. "They didn't make these for ladies," said the enlisted man supplying it apologetically. Holding the oxygen mask with one hand and holding on to a steel shelf with the other, she experienced the hideous sensation of climbing rapidly to eleven thousand, then twenty-two thousand feet. "One's body turned to iron and was crushed down, feeling as if an enormous weight were pressing on something that would not yield. . . . I thought my stomach was going to be flattened against my backbone, that I was going to strangle," she wrote.

It was thirty degrees below zero up there. Her nose flowed and produced a frozen river on her face. She could see flashes of flak from the guns shooting at them. On the trail of an enemy plane, they were brought down by winds on top of it instead of under it where they wanted to be and thus were being shot at instead of doing the shooting. Somehow they landed safely. Not even Hemingway, who envisioned himself as a daredevil, surpassed that stunt.

As Allied forces advanced toward Germany, Gellhorn made her headquarters at the Scribe Hotel in Paris, the "press camp" for American correspondents. She could charm most men, especially Frenchmen, into doing her bidding; after years in Paris, she was French at heart. Fellow correspondents recalled that while she came and went, the management always reserved the most desirable accommodations for her. Patricia Lockridge, a writer for the *Woman's Home Companion*, and others attributed the attention she received to the world's admiration for Hemingway. But by then, everyone in Paris knew he was living at the Ritz with Mary Welsh of *Time* magazine; both had to be divorced before they could marry in 1946.

Hemingway had not lost his love for women with brains as well as beauty. Welsh, a blonde with a heart-shaped face, was best remembered for a story she could not print. Early in 1944, aware that the invasion of France was coming, she bought an almanac in London and observed that June 4, 5, and 6 would be high tide dates. With this intelligence, she went to the British Admiralty, where an officer reacted to her information by announcing, "Mary, you are under arrest." She had pinpointed the dates for the invasion. They let her go when she promised not to tell.

Gellhorn, as much as she enjoyed her freedom, wanted something, and in Italy in 1948, she adopted a ten-month-old orphan, whom she named George Alexander Gellhorn. "You might say he is entirely mine because I adopted him and was unmarried," she wrote me. "I learned to change diapers in an airplane over the Alps; he had diarrhea and cried constantly, poor little brute, and when he stopped crying I thought he had died and spent my time then on my knees beside the seat listening to his heart."

It was a daring thing to do at that time. "I adopted him against the combined efforts of the church and the state," she recalled. "Italy had nothing in excess except orphans but did not believe in letting them leave. I used skullduggery and a few powerful friends."

Then the United States refused to let her bring her baby into the country, citing the immigration quota, so they lived in Mexico until she obtained U.S. citizenship for her boy by unanimous vote of both houses of Congress. In 1953 she acquired more family by marrying T.S. Matthews, editor of *Time*. They were later divorced, but she remained close to her stepsons.

While building her reputation as an author, Gellhorn continued to cover troubling world events. A war she wanted to forget was Indonesia's battle for independence against the Netherlands, a scene she described in one word, *disgusting*. Gellhorn despised colonialism and deplored the effort to perpetuate it. She was in Israel for that nation's birth in 1948 and later for its conflicts with Arab neighbors.

In 1966 she went to Saigon to cover the war in Vietnam for the *Guardian* of England. She also wrote a series of five articles for her hometown newspaper, the *St. Louis Post-Dispatch*. They were so inflammatory that the *Post-Dispatch* printed only the two mildest, but she would have her say, and in her book *Travels with Myself and Another*, she struck out at American military leaders.

> I told them they were inhuman. We were destroying a country and a whole innocent peasant population while proclaiming that we were saving them from Communism. Had they any idea how children looked and sounded when half flayed by napalm? Could they picture an old woman screaming with a piece of white phosphorous burning in

World War II correspondents in France gather outside their tents at a U.S. Army evacuation hospital subjected to nightly bombings by the Germans in violation of the rules of war. *Left to right:* Ruth Cowan, Associated Press; Sonia Tomara, *New York Herald Tribune;* Rosette Hargrove, Newspaper Enterprise Association; Betty Knox, London *Evening Standard;* Iris Carpenter, *Boston Globe;* Erika Mann, *Liberty* magazine. *(U.S. Army photo, National Archives)*

Margaret Fuller, idealized in this portrayal, actually despaired of her looks and, to compensate, cultivated a formidable intellect.

Mary Roberts Rinehart, compensating for hardships she had endured, including life at the front in World War I, spent a fortune on clothes. *(Library of Congress)*

Peggy Hull, wearing the World War I uniform she designed for herself. *(Kansas Collection, University of Kansas Libraries)*

Irene Corbally Kuhn arrives by dugout canoe at a village of the Djukas, bush Negroes, on the Marowijne River in Surinam. *(Courtesy Irene Corbally Kuhn)*

Sigrid Schultz, Berlin correspondent for the *Chicago Tribune*, warns a 1941 American audience to prepare for war with Germany.

Anne O'Hare McCormick of the *New York Times* with Wendell Willkie, the 1940 Republican candidate for president. The two were frequent award winners.

Helen Kirkpatrick, *Chicago Daily News* correspondent in England during the spring of 1944, participates in a rehearsal for D-Day, the Allied invasion of France, but was not allowed to cover the real event. (*U.S. Army photo. Courtesy Helen Kirkpatrick*)

Dorothy Thompson in the 1920s, before she achieved fame as a syndicated columnist. *(Library of Congress)*

Martha Gellhorn, aboard the *SS Rex* in January 1940, returns from her coverage of the war in Finland for *Collier's*. *(UPI/Bettmann Newsphotos)*

◄

Sonia Tomara of the *New York Herald Tribune*, with Captain James A. Murray, U.S. Army Air Force, arrives in New Delhi, India, after a trip to U.S. air bases in the eastern province of Assam during World War II. *(New York Herald Tribune photo. Courtesy Jean E. Collins)*

Margaret Bourke-White, in England during World War II, is photographed by fellow photographer Lee Miller of *Vogue* magazine beside
the Flying Flit Gun, a U.S. Army Air Force bomber whose crew named
an engine Peggy in in her honor. *(Photo by Lee Miller. Courtesy George
Arents Research Library for Special Collections at Syracuse University)*

Ruth Cowan as a Washington correspondent for the Associated Press. (*Washington Press Club Archive, National Press Club, Washington, D.C.*)

Iris Carpenter, at her home in Virginia, reflects on her Americanization as a British correspondent covering American forces during World War II. (*Courtesy Colonel Rozwell Rosengren*)

In 1945, Ann Stringer drew wolf whistles from GIs and warnings from military authorities at the front in France. *(Photo by Allan Jackson)*

Marguerite Higgins, rushing from battle to typewriter, did not pause to wash her face before a photographer shot this candid picture of her during the Korean War. (*Keystone photo. Courtesy George Arents Research Library for Special Collections at Syracuse University*)

◄
Esther Van Wagoner Tufty, known as "the duchess," as president of the Women's National Press Club in Washington, D.C. She appears to be wearing a crown, an effect produced by the light fixture behind her and befitting her stature in the press corps. (*Washington Press Club Archive, National Press Club, Washington, D.C.*)

Dickey Chapelle chose this unflattering picture taken in 1959 as her favorite photograph of herself at work. She was photographing her favorite subject, the U.S. Marines, an Operation Inland Seas, a salute to the opening of the Saint Lawrence Seaway. (*U.S. Marine Corps photo by Master Sergeant Lew Lowery. Courtesy State Historical Society of Wisconsin*)

Kathleen McLaughlin of the *New York Times* interviews Irish delegates at the United Nations in New York in 1955 after covering the occupation of Germany. (*Reprinted by permission of The New York Times Company. All rights reserved.*)

Flora Lewis, *New York Times* Paris bureau chief in 1972, interviews Xuan Thuy, North Vietnam's delegate to the Paris peace talks, about prospects for ending the Vietnam War.

Aline Mosby, granted her choice of assignments after hazardous duty in Moscow and Peking, chose Paris, where she pauses outside Notre Dame Cathedral in the summer of 1987. *(Copyright © by Helen Marcus, 1987)*

Gloria Emerson of the *New York Times* is photographed after parachuting from a plane in New York in 1959, a training exercise that proved useful to her during the Vietnam War. *(Reprinted by permission of The New York Times Company. All rights reserved.)*

Elizabeth Becker in the city room of the Washington Post in 1974. (*Courtesy the Washington Post*)

Georgie Anne Geyer interviews Guatemalan guerrilla chief Cesar Montes for the *Chicago Daily News* during a dangerous journey to the rebel stronghold in Guatemala in 1966. (*Photo by Henry Herr Gill*)

her thigh? We had uprooted and turned into refugees millions of helpless people by unopposed bombing of their villages. We were hated in Vietnam and rightly.

Gellhorn was one of the few correspondents who so angered the American military that she was denied a visa to return to Vietnam. There were other things to do, of course—trips to the Soviet Union and Africa, novels to write. For years she traveled constantly, "always arranging with whoever would send me to write what I wanted," she said, accepting brief assignments to cover "what I needed to see and know for myself."

When she slowed down, it was not by choice. At the age of seventy-four, she wrote me from her home in the tranquil countryside of Wales, "I wanted terribly to go to Lebanon this summer, but nobody would send me." Nobody wanted her to get killed or taken hostage in that strife-torn land.

Literary biographers credited Gellhorn with writing novels "of lasting literary merit" for nearly half a century, among them *A Stricken Field*, published in 1940, and *The Weather in Africa*, published in 1978. Dismissing all flattery, she observed that all but two of her books were out of print and said, "I've decided to wait for posthumous fame and glory, much more sensible than worrying about the here and now. . . . The winter here is a shocker, dark at 3:30 in the afternoon; maybe that will be writing time."

10

The Unsinkable
Maggie White

MARGARET BOURKE-WHITE, AMONG THE GREATEST NEWS PHOtographers of all time, was one of the first correspondents authorized to cover the North African campaign in World War II. But the armed forces refused to let her fly to Africa on the grounds that it wasn't safe. Forever protective of women, the military assigned her to a ship early in January 1943. As the newsmen were descending from their plane in Algiers, feet still dry, her ship was torpedoed.

The Army had issued survival kits for just such an emergency. Bourke-White discarded all but one can of food to make space for a camera in her kit; she would rather have starved than fail to get a photograph of the sinking ship. Aware of how little space there was in the lifeboats, she regretfully left four cameras behind. From experience with famine in Russia, she knew how long one could live without food, and as she headed for the lifeboats, she vowed not to open her can of food until the eleventh day.

Although she proudly considered herself a photographer, not a writer, she wrote a heartrending account of what happened next. Of the ship, she recalled, "Her portholes began melting and flowing down great tears of molten glass."

The first five officers of the Women's Auxiliary Army Corps assigned to Africa were aboard her ship, not because commanding officers wanted them in combat but because recruiting officers thought the novelty would help attract women to the typing pool in Washington. (The second-class-status word *auxiliary* was dropped in 1943, and the force has since been known as the Women's Army Corps, the WAC.) Bourke-White told of two young WAACs who approached a lifeboat only to learn it was overloaded. Smartly, the girls stepped aside and waved the others off. "We can't all go," they said.

The ship was traveling in convoy escorted by destroyers. When it was hit, the other ships, following orders to avoid additional torpedoes, sailed away. One destroyer remained in the vicinity just long enough to look for submarines, not to rescue passengers. Miraculously, another destroyer arrived in time to rescue the WAACs.

Not everyone was so lucky. Bourke-White, sitting in her lifeboat in water up to her waist, heard a tragic cry, "I'm all alone. I'm all alone." Their rudder was useless, and they could not turn in the direction of the voice. The desperate call for help was swallowed by the sea.

At last Bourke-White reached Algiers and caught up with Air Force General Jimmy Doolittle. "Well you've been torpedoed. You might as well go through everything," he said. Thus, after months of effort, on January 22, 1943, she became the first woman allowed to go on a bombing mission, even before Sonia Tomara.

Those who think women correspondents, however dissimilar in personality, must have similar interests, should have met Margaret Bourke-White, known to many as Maggie White and to special admirers as Peggy. Her favorite childhood pets were a baby boa constrictor and an elderly puff adder. When she acquired her own photo studio atop the Chrysler Building in New York, she peopled it with two alligators and a bunch of turtles. The alligators ate the turtles.

As a photographer, her first enthusiasm, in the mid 1920s, was taking pictures of factories, most of which were hideous— dusty, smoky, grimy, and dangerous. She relished the challenge to find beauty where nobody else did, in the pouring of metal, the sparks from a furnace, the abstract construction pattern of a trestle. "To me, politics were colorless beside the drama of the machine," she said.

Long before she obtained an assignment in the field of industrial photography, she was climbing to factory roofs and crawling close to furnaces to get pictures portraying the drama and the power of industry. People wondered why she took such an interest in industry, an exclusively male preserve in her day. With sweet reasonableness she explained that she was simply sharing the enthusiasms of the men she loved.

Her father, Joe White, an inventor, was her inspiration. Margaret Bourke White (no hyphen) was born in New York City in 1904 and grew up an only child in New Jersey. Her parents adored her, and they taught her to be fearless. Her father introduced her to snakes. Joe White, fascinated by light, contributed importantly to the development of color film. Then, out of sympathy for those who could not enjoy light, he built the first Braille printing press for the blind. From him his daughter inherited her fascination with the camera, its technical capacities, and the intricacies of film development. Her interest in industry began with a visit to a factory to see his printing press produced.

Her first traumatic experience was finding herself a wallflower at dancing class. When finally she won an essay contest, she was ecstatic just because she was sure that the boys at the party following the presentation would dance with her. They didn't. Rejection fueled her ambition to excel; denied popularity, she insisted on admiration. Her father died when she was seventeen, and her sense of isolation deepened.

A college acquaintance remembered her as pudgy, dowdy, and given to wolfing her food so she could hurry back to her cameras. Among her assets were a perfect profile and soft brown hair. While a sophomore at the University of Michigan, Margaret White, still insecure at nineteen, met and married Everett Chapman, a graduate student in electrical engineering, whose fascination with electric welding techniques she shared. Too young to cope, she encountered a mother-in-law problem, compounded by the financial necessity of sharing a home. The day her mother-in-law said, "I never want to see you again," she ran out of the house. Her husband was at work. Without a nickel for streetcar fare, she walked seventeen miles to find him. That marriage lasted scarcely two years.

For her senior year in college, Maggie White, as fellow students called her, went to Cornell University, where she sold her first photographs, pictures of the campus, to help pay her tuition. After graduation in 1927, she went to live with her mother in Cleveland, Ohio, and the next year her pictures won first prize at the Cleveland Museum of Art. The thought of using a hyphenated name came with her divorce papers, but instead of hyphenating her maiden name with her husband's name, she hyphenated her own name for the more distinctive signature Margaret Bourke-White. Bourke was her mother's maiden name.

Months of prowling around factories and steel mills, where nobody else could detect the beauty, won her an assignment to take photographs of Otis Steel Mills. She soon received a telegram—"Have just seen steel photographs. Come to New York"—signed by Henry R. Luce, publisher of *Time*, the newsmagazine he founded in 1923. She had demonstrated a unique talent, and Luce saw a use for it. In 1929, he was planning *Fortune*, a magazine directed at the top executives in business and industry that would sell for the spectacular price of $1.00 a copy. *Fortune* would tell their story in magnificent pictures as well as text. To start, Luce offered Bourke-White $1000 a month for half her time, a fine fee.

The amount she spent on clothes for the trip to New York is not recorded, but Bourke-White was improving her image with the same insistence on perfection she applied to photography. A slender, stylish young woman stepped off the train in Pennsylvania Station, and her good looks would impress everyone who met her from then on. Her hair was her halo, even as it turned from brown to platinum blond to white. The figure the now-and-forever-after-slender photographer cut in her tailored slacks was as striking as that of Marlene Dietrich in her tuxedo.

While pioneers struggled to establish photography as an art form, Henry Luce elevated the news photographer from the level of reporter's adjunct to master of the art of communication. In 1929, the newspaper reporter told the photographer what pictures to take, and editors wrote the captions from copy submitted by the reporter. *Fortune* photographs were works of art accompanied by text.

The magazine sent Bourke-White to Berlin to photograph factories. It was her idea to haunt the Soviet embassy until, after five weeks, she won a visa, a rare prize at a time the United States still refused to recognize the Communist government. She was one of the few Western photographers allowed into Russia after the Revolution and the first invited to photograph Soviet industry, still in its infancy.

Aware of a food shortage in Russia, she had taken with her a trunk filled with canned food she intended to give to hungry Russians. Her hosts did not even have enough to feed her. On long trips to photograph the factories in Russia, she and her interpreter-guide survived on the canned goods she had brought; for many days they ate nothing but cold beans.

They traveled five thousand miles to photograph the vast new industry being built under the Five-Year Plan. She visited mills, quarries, factories, and farms to record on film the effort to transform Russia from a feudal land into a modern nation, summarizing her impressions in a note: "Little food, no shoes, terrible inefficiency, steady progress, great hope."

Taking pictures that would survive as a chapter in history, she proved herself both a precisionist and a perfectionist. On this trip she also demonstrated that people, if not politics, fascinated her as much as factories; she risked missing a train that ran only once a week to get the perfect shot of an elderly peasant's expressive face.

Under the Communist system, her traveling companion was not only interpreter and guide but responsible for her as well, serving as an intermediary with local authorities suspicious of foreigners and making sure she did not offend camera-shy Russians. Granted the authority to be dictatorial, the Russian woman chose to be diplomatic, winning the photographer's appreciation.

Bourke-White noticed that her guide had converted a cheese can ring into a bracelet and put it on her wrist—the Russians in those days had so little to add sparkle to life. The photographer remembered, and when she left Russian she sent the guide a small gold bracelet.

As anyone would, Bourke-White found steel difficult to photograph. Sometimes she would use a hundred plates in her clumsy camera in hopes that one would be perfect. When she was ready to leave Russia, she had eight hundred film plates to get past the censor, and she insisted upon developing them herself. Her precious film had to be developed by green light, and she worked straight through two days and two nights to complete the job, then left her film with the authorities. If she had tried that twenty years later in the era of the cold war, she might never have seen it again. But the Russians forwarded her film to Paris, and they invited her back.

On her second trip, she made two short documentary movies and on her return to the United States was besieged by film companies wanting to buy them. But she insisted on supervising the editing and took so long that producers lost interest. When the United States finally granted diplomatic recognition to the USSR in 1933, interest revived, and her documentaries were shown all over the world for years thereafter. Success, however, did not sustain her interest in motion pictures, and she returned to her first love, mastering the art of still photography.

Her first book, *Eyes on Russia*, published in 1931, proved that she could write. For her next, she wanted someone to write the text while she concentrated on the photography. At the same time, Erskine Caldwell, whose novel *Tobacco Road* introduced the world to the Southern poor white, was seeking a photographer to collaborate on a book with him. Fellow journalists introduced them, and together they produced three books. The first, perhaps the most famous, *You Have Seen Their Faces*, was another book about the deep South and showed Bourke-White's growing concern about injustice. Caldwell was married when they met, and at first he objected to working with a woman. Whether he questioned the photographer's talent or feared for his marriage, he did not say. The working relationship between writer and photographer gradually developed into something more, and eventually Caldwell obtained a divorce.

Life magazine was launched in November 1936, and Bourke-White not only took the photograph for the first cover, she also wrote the lead essay, about Fort Peck Dam, Montana.

Her next major foreign assignment was to cover the 1938

crisis when Hitler demanded that Czechoslovakia cede the Sudetenland to Germany, and Caldwell went with her. They stayed on in eastern Europe to collaborate on another book, *North of the Danube*. On returning to the United States, they were married on February 27, 1939, in Silver City, Nevada, close enough to Reno to be prophetic.

Traveling by way of war-torn China, the Caldwells went to Russia in the spring of 1941, while the Hitler-Stalin Pact remained in effect. One month after they reached Moscow in May, three million Axis troops invaded Russia.

American ambassador Laurence Steinhardt was eager to evacuate the Caldwells, they being virtually the only ones left to evacuate. He did not understand that they had come for the war and the bombing of Moscow. With each air raid alert, the thorough Russians searched every hotel room to see that all had gone to the bomb shelter. Bourke-White hid under the bed and her husband hid beneath a rug behind a sofa until after the room check, risking their lives to get pictures of the bombings and develop them.

One night in July 1941, the Germans dropped eleven huge parachute flares over the Kremlin, lighting up the whole central section of Moscow. Bourke-White stood at her window watching an enormous cloud rise into the sky, then stones and boards dropping out of it. Her pictures were spectacular.

Her greatest challenge came when she was finally allowed to photograph the Soviet dictator. Joseph Stalin, accused of killing millions in his purges, sat stone-faced until she accidentally dropped some flash bulbs. As they skittered across the floor, he laughed, and she got two perfect photographs.

Bourke-White was the only foreign photographer in the Soviet Union when the Germans attacked, and she managed to get close enough to the front to stand on a hill and watch the Germans incinerate a village. For the rest of the war, the Russians strictly enforced a ban on all foreign correspondents at the front.

It took the Japanese attack on Pearl Harbor to separate the Caldwells. While the War Department was denying transportation to women war correspondents, it asked Bourke-White to go to England to take photographs for the Air Force. Her employers at Time Inc. agreed to an arrangement whereby the War Department would get first choice of the pictures she took, after which *Life* would be able to use them. Thus, in the spring of 1942, she became the nation's first accredited woman war correspondent, an honor that eluded Peggy Hull because World War I ended before she reached Siberia with her accreditation to a war zone. She needed a uniform, and the Army chose her as the model for whom it designed the women correspondent's uniform for World War II, the first firm evidence that others eventually would be allowed to follow her. The uniform was so late getting into production, however, that Bourke-White did not wait to wear it overseas. The Air Force flew her to a bomber base in England, where she photographed the "Flying Fortresses," the B-17 bombers assembling for attacks on the Continent.

Caldwell, a creative genius with a fragile ego, difficult to live with and unwilling to live alone, wanted her to stay with him in the West, in California and Arizona. In retrospect she wrote as if she knew that her departure would end their marriage. But friends in England said she was shattered when she received a "Dear Jane" letter asking for a divorce. Caldwell married for a third time before 1942 was out.

Those who knew them took sides and started an endless argument as to whether she was a cold, calculating careerist or a deeply emotional, passionate woman. Fellow workers found it difficult to get to know her, as she distanced herself from casual companions. Awkwardness in social relationships, forgiven in the child, was not forgiven when she became a celebrity and withdrew from friendly overtures.

Of course she cared. Her photographs possessed the power to make strangers care about every soldier killed in World War II. She fell in love with one of them, an officer in Italy, and was deeply affected when he was killed in action, though she hid her emotions and went on with her work. Her acts of kindness became oft-told anecdotes, but when it came to getting a photograph, her concentration on her objective was so intense that she could be oblivious to the existence, much less the feelings, of anyone in the way.

Bourke-White was assigned to the lead plane in a force of thirty-two B-17s sent from Algiers to destroy the airfield at Tunis, the chief base of the German Luftwaffe in North Africa. Her pilot was Major Paul Tibbetts, who three years later was at the controls of the plane that dropped the atom bomb on Hiroshima, Japan.

Bourke-White did not fear for her own safety, but she was worried by the legend that a woman's very presence in a dangerous situation would so distract the men as to cause fatal accidents. Therefore, it pleased her to see that the men on the mission quickly forgot there was a woman aboard. She gave herself away, however, with some suggestive instructions to her helper, which were heard over the interphones: "Roll me over quick. Hold me just like this. Hold me this way so I can shoot straight down." She caught the bombs bursting on the airfield, the attack response. Two B-17s were shot down, and her plane was hit twice in the wing. This, the key raid in the air war, pushed the Luftwaffe off the North African continent.

For anyone with a death wish, her next assignment, to photograph the war in Italy, would have been made to order. At the front, she quickly learned to appreciate "a nice deep muddy ditch which I could roll into during a shelling." There were no helicopters; to get an air view of the earth, she rode the "Grasshoppers," light and inflammable Piper Cubs. In her airborne "birdcage," she flew over what the soldiers called "Purple Heart Valley" with a pilot assigned to pinpoint enemy mortar fire. She was in the air to see the enemy mortar, called "Screaming Meemie," knocked out of action.

Jealous newsmen joked about the amount of equipment she carried, and wept crocodile tears for the poor soldiers who had to be relieved of their war duties to carry her load. Bourke-White never had a moment's doubt that her pictures were worth all the help she could get from the armed forces. On one occasion, she undertook to photograph a shelling from four different directions with four cameras. This required the assistance of at least three soldiers while she handled the fourth camera and shouted instructions: "Load! Ready! Fire!" She was too busy to greet a brigadier general who happened on the scene. Sizing up the situation, he took the fourth camera from her and fired it as she ordered.

The drama her pictures portrayed in the winning of World War II helped to sustain public support for the war effort. Television cameras later would help turn the nation against war by exposing its horrors. In World War II, the Army could and did censor Bourke-White. Besides glorifying the valiant, she undertook to photograph the horror of war, particularly in a series on American soldiers dying at front-line hospitals. Shells were falling within thirty feet when she and a nurse listened to a wounded soldier's last request, for watermelon. The nurse had to tell him that melon was out of season. They heard him whisper "I'm so cold" before he died. That picture story was lost somewhere in the War Department building, and Bourke-White herself went to Washington in a fruitless effort to trace it.

In recounting the incident, she never hinted at the obvious, that this was not good propaganda. Censors could stop it without confessing they had ever seen her film. It would be a generation before the American public, inured to Nazi atrocity pictures, was fully exposed to the worst horrors of war as seen on the American side.

With General George S. Patton's Third Army, she reached the Buchenwald concentration camp at Weimar in Germany and photographed the piles of naked bodies, skeletons already incinerated, and bodies yet to be burned. Bourke-White had invented the techniques of soft focus and special lighting to dramatize her subjects, but at Buchenwald she cast them aside and used understatement to achieve images a world with a conscience could not forget. "Using the camera was almost a relief," she wrote. "It interposed a slight barrier between myself and the horror in front of me."

Her ever growing prestige was evident at the end of the war when she was able to have Alfred Krupp, the German industrialist who had been taken prisoner, brought to his family mansion for pictures. Bourke-White found him arrogant in denying responsibility for the death of slave laborers under his command, and she had him removed to his servants' quarters, then returned to prison. The twelve-year sentence imposed on Krupp later was revoked, and in less than three years he was back at the helm of his industrial empire. Her enthusiasm for industrial power was waning.

In India after World War II, Bourke-White photographed the most senseless of all slaughter, a religious war between the Moslems and the Hindus. She watched thousands die, as she witnessed "a bleeding Pakistan carved out of the body of a bleeding India." Before she was allowed to photograph the pacifist leader Mahatma Gandhi, she was required to learn to spin, twisting and winding the fibers to produce yarn. As carefully as she prepared for all her photographs, this did not strike her as unreasonable. On the day she photographed the great Indian thinker and leader, he swore he would preach passive resistance, even if threatened with the atom bomb. On January 30, 1948, a few hours after she left him, Gandhi was assassinated.

Family and followers wanted no cameras at Gandhi's bier. But Bourke-White, never one to take no for an answer, stood outside a window and used flash bulbs to get the last photograph of the martyr. Critics cited this as evidence of insensitivity but it was better evidence of her one-track mind, her determination to get her photograph, her conviction that it mattered for all posterity.

Covering a riot can be more dangerous than covering a war, where one can at least identify and locate the enemy. In a riot, you never know who is going to knife you in the back. I finally caught up with Bourke-White in Tokyo on the June 1952 day the Japanese chose to celebrate the end of the American occupation of Japan, by rioting in the streets.

As a correspondent in Europe, I had heard all sorts of stories about Bourke-White the fabulous photographer. Wherever I went, from Moscow to Morocco, she, like the legendary Kilroy, had already been there. My chances of covering an area in the news as soon as she did improved when the United States Information Agency sent me to Japan in February 1952. On independence day in June, my assignment was to escort Norman Thomas, the American socialist, to a platform on the grounds of the imperial palace, where a huge audience had gathered to hear him speak.

Communists started the trouble with a surprise protest demonstration in front of the platform where we stood. Thomas insisted on staying to watch even as the crowd turned into a mob and pushed against the stand, threatening to topple it. As it turned out, this was the safest place to be, for the police moved in to protect the dignitaries on the platform.

In the streets adjacent to the palace grounds, the rioting Japanese overturned automobiles and set them afire, broke windows and used the shattered glass for weapons.

Through it all, Bourke-White sat calmly atop a *Life* magazine station wagon shooting pictures, even as rioters were striking up at her with the staves of their Red banners and the police were fighting back with tear gas. Once again, her practice of carrying half a dozen cameras served well that day, for she had no time to reload. The Japanese, who had been the most docile of people throughout the occupation, erupted on independence day. When night fell, the violence ended as suddenly as it had begun.

A few weeks later, Bourke-White became the first correspondent to reach the forwardmost artillery observation post on the Korean War front. The bunker closest to the enemy, seven miles north of the main line of resistance (MLR), a pockmarked dirt road dividing North and South Korea, stuck out on a war map like a dagger penetrating enemy territory. At that juncture in the two-year-old war, the MLR was fairly stabilized. The fighting had degenerated into an ugly game known as "keeping the enemy off balance." Take a hill, lose the hill, retake the hill. At night the MLR was brightly lighted so that observers could detect infiltrators. By day the noise of shelling was so deafening that it was impossible for a novice to detect an incoming from an outgoing shell. From relative safety, the great guns of the artillery fired over the heads of the infantry. Farthest forward, miles in front of the infantry, artillery observers watched to locate the origins of enemy fire. They called the shots by radio, telling the gunners where to fire.

A mountain protected the approach to the observation post Bourke-White visited. The bunker was located at the peak, and the ascent was so steep that only a trained mountain climber could negotiate it, but she made it. She weighed so little that soldiers could put her in what looked like an oversized grocery basket they had wired to a pulley to deliver supplies to the peak. Swinging in the wind, she ascended seven thousand feet into the sky. At the top, she had to climb out of her basket, get over the peak under enemy fire and slide into the bunker. In Russia, Bessie Beatty had managed to get within one hundred and fifty yards of the enemy. On her mountaintop, Bourke-White was within one hundred yards of enemy snipers hiding in tall grass.

I was at the press camp in Seoul, having quit the government to cover the Korean War for the Overseas News Agency, and there men were telling me what Bourke-White had disproved two decades before, that the presence of a woman at the front would so distract men as to endanger their lives. What she could do, other women could insist upon doing. A week after she did it, I went up the mountainside in the grocery basket, singing all the way, "Rock-a-bye-baby on the tree top, / When the wind blows the cradle will rock." My mistake was to stand up in that bunker. *Pyong* went a rifle. "They are shooting at me!" I gasped in disbelief. Bourke-White had said almost those same words in Italy; by the time she reached Korea, she had acquired the wit to keep her head down.

Bourke-White's clout by then was such that she managed to get a captured Communist guerrilla released from custody so she could photograph his reunion with his mother. Her picture story was a belated reminder that this was more than a case of Communist aggressors invading South Korea from North Korea. It was also a civil war that pitted brother against brother.

With all her sense of mission, Bourke-White found time in Korea to be wonderfully kind. Edward Hymoff, the International News Service bureau chief in Seoul, recalled the day the Eighth Army public information officers challenged the war correspondents to a softball game. Maggie was cheering the correspondents from the sidelines when Hymoff handed her his camera and asked her to shoot some pictures of him as he swung the bat. "She did," he recalled. "I hit one and ran, and there was one of the greatest photojournalists in the world catching me in action."

When he had the film developed, every shot was out of focus. "Maggie, how could you?" he asked.

She offered no excuses, but he made one for her: his thirty-five-millimeter Bolsey was no longer being produced, and she was not acquainted with its mechanism.

"Ed, I'll make it up to you," she promised.

"We happened to be up front together," Hymoff recalled, "and enemy artillery bursts exploded in our area. She caught me diving for cover. As I looked up with mud on my face, she shot yet another picture. I never did wind up with a photo of me banging off a home run; I did receive a set of prints of a rugged war correspondent 'in action.' "

In Tokyo, on that trip to Asia, she first noticed difficulty in walking. It was the onslaught of the Parkinson's disease that ended her career as a war correspondent, but not her work. In addition to the three books she produced with Caldwell, she wrote six on her own. Increasingly, she was aware that photographs could not tell the whole story; the more she saw, the more she realized that writing helped her make sense of her all too vivid impressions.

She lived to see her photographs represented in the Library of Congress, the Brooklyn Museum, the Museum of Modern Art. The world would recall such leaders as Winston Churchill and Franklin D. Roosevelt through her photographs of them. Among the memories she collected were that King George VI of England had admired her hair and Emperor Haile Selassie of Ethiopia had carried her cameras. She won all sorts of awards, among them that of the Art Director's Club in New York and the American Women of Achievement Award, 1951. Her life ended on August 27, 1971.

11

Combat Correspondent

THE MASSIVE MOBILIZATION AMERICA MOUNTED TO WIN WORLD War II created colossal confusion, a situation fraught with obstacles, and sometimes, opportunities for the correspondents. As rapidly as it could, the War Department issued uniforms to correspondents and sent them to war attached to military units, but for the whole year 1942, all combat correspondents were male. Margaret Bourke-White and Sonia Tomara obtained press accreditation to war zones, but they did not travel as members of a military group.

The first two uniformed women correspondents sent to war attached to a military unit, Ruth Cowan of the Associated Press (AP) and Inez Robb of International News Service (INS), boarded ship in January 1943 with the first two companies of the Women's Auxiliary Army Corps sent overseas. Traveling under orders issued by the U.S. War Department, they were subject to court-martial for disobeying an order or violating the rules established by military authorities.

The War Department made it clear that it did not intend to allow women correspondents to cover combat by ruling that they could "go no farther forward than women's services go." Any women correspondents in a war zone were to be accompanied by an officer of no lesser rank than lieutenant colonel. If such officers were not available for escort service, the women would be in violation of the rules the moment they stepped out of the billets the Army assigned them.

Women who disregarded the regulations designed to keep them from covering combat were evicted from press camps and threatened with summary disaccreditation, even court-martial. British and American military authorities in London joined forces to stage one showcase court-martial, but the judges failed to convict the culprit. As often as not, strict enforcement of the rules defeated their purpose. Press officers assigned to combat units fumed because they had no control over women assigned to medical units.

Told that she was being sent to Britain, Ruth Cowan stocked up on woolen underwear. At the staging area in New Jersey, she and Robb were issued mosquito netting as well as gas masks. Not until they were aboard ship did they learn they were headed for Algiers. En route, their ship joined the convoy carrying Margaret Bourke-White, but they didn't know that her ship had been torpedoed until they reached port safely.

In their identical uniforms, the two news agency reporters could have been mistaken for twins. Both, at forty-two, were slender, pretty, blue-eyed blondes, not too tall, with nationally recognized by-lines. Beneath the surface, they were a study in contrasts.

Inez Robb, a Californian assigned to society news in New York, specialized in crashing weddings until she was invited to cover the coronation of King George VI in England and the wedding of Wallis Warfield Simpson to the Duke of Windsor. She was aboard the first plane to carry passengers across the Atlantic, the Pan American Clipper, in June 1939. Her fellow INS columnist, Bob Considine, described her as "a good-looking woman who could type with her long white gloves in place." For North Africa, she had removed them.

Ruth Cowan escaped from the tedium of teaching in Texas by adopting the masculine by-line R. Baldwin Cowan. She was covering the state legislature in Austin for United Press (UP) in 1929 when a top United Press executive dropped in to praise the work, discovered her sex, and fired her. The Associated Press hired her to cover crime in Chicago and promoted her to Washington correspondent in 1940. She was traveling with the endorsement of First Lady Eleanor Roosevelt and Oveta Culp Hobby, the first director of the WAAC.

The women were not expecting flowers, but they anticipated

at least a friendly welcome from fellow correspondents in Algiers; instead they received an icy reception. The woman-hating Wes Gallagher had become chief of the Algiers bureau of the Associated Press, and he accorded Cowan the silent treatment. Even the men called him "Smiling Jack," because he never smiled.

The British ran the crowded Hotel Atlantic where the correspondents were billeted, and they resented having to give up a room to a pair of American women. General Robert McClure, the U.S. Army public relations officer in Algiers, reacted with fury to the arrival of women correspondents.

On one of her first outings, Cowan went to Rabat, Morocco. Frenchmen operating the press corps dining room refused to serve her, using the excuse that it was a stag mess. "It didn't bother me," she said. "My meals were served in my room, and I ate a helluva lot better than the men did."

Americans, not to be outdone in gaucherie, refused to issue a liquor ration to a woman. On that occasion a man showed up his fellows, saying, "Let her have a bottle of booze, for God's sake." She opened it and invited the men to have a drink with her. "I tried to do the best I could with a sense of humor," she said, "and I tried never to ask for special favors."

There was a better way to get respect. Cowan went to the wireless office in Algiers and announced that she wished to send a cable to Mrs. Eleanor Roosevelt at the White House. It said, "Don't encourage more women to come to Africa. The men don't want us here." As she said years later, "I knew the message would never go anywhere." At least it would go no farther than the desk of the top brass for permission to censor. The last thing the Army needed was a bad report card delivered to the outspoken wife of the President. The military response was a personal invitation to Cowan to attend General Dwight D. Eisenhower's press conference. "Ike" was never prejudiced against women, she recalled.

After the aborted cable and the press conference, Cowan and Robb were allowed to visit the front. The British had long been fighting in East Africa, but only on November 8, 1942, did American forces under General Eisenhower's command land in

Northwest Africa. All was going well in February when the women went by plane, with officers on an inspection tour, to the Kasserine Pass in Tunisia. They were in the air when the forces of German General Erwin Rommel attacked. By the time they landed, the American forces were moving out. An army in retreat can be as spectacular as an advancing army. They stood on the side of the road and watched the jeeps, the trucks, the weapons carriers, the tanks, pulling out.

In the confusion, their plane took off without them, and the whole inspection party was stranded without transportation. Trucks overloaded with troops roared by them, and GIs laughed derisively at the spectacle of officers they could leave in their dust. Finally, the men had the sense to put the women forward to thumb a ride, and sure enough a vehicle stopped. They were rescued by a wheat king from Montana who was in charge of food supplies for the area. By March, Allied forces reoccupied Kasserine, and historians would summarize the story by saying that the Allies contained a German flanking attack. As eyewitnesses to the surprise assault, the women scored a beat and established themselves as combat correspondents, War Department orders notwithstanding.

The battle dust still on her uniform, Cowan reached Algiers just in time to attend a reception at the French embassy, where, to her embarrassment, she found others very well dressed. "I was tired. I smelled. I was dirty," she remembered. "But once in uniform, you stayed in uniform, and if you stank, you stank."

At the reception she encountered the formidable General George S. Patton, commander of the Third Army, who enjoyed taunting people. "So you want to be in the war? What is the first law of war?"

"You kill him before he kills you," she replied.

Patton said, "She stays."

Cowan had come to expect praise for her work. For years she had been hearing what editors thought was the highest acclaim they could give—"You write like a man." The table turned, perhaps for all women correspondents, the day AP editors in New York sent a cable chiding their men in North Africa for failing to convey the color she put in her stories. "Why can't you write the way she does?" New York wanted to know.

A censor who read all the copy the correspondents filed was in an excellent position to evaluate it, and he commented, "With the exception of Ernie Pyle, only the women really understand these GIs."

Only Wes Gallagher and General McClure were not reconciled to women war correspondents in North Africa. They made their objections known to Washington, and soon public information officers at the War Department were telling such applicants as Flora Lewis, then with the Associated Press, that they could not have accreditation because the women sent to Africa had behaved like "prima donnas." Cowan was appalled to learn of this, for the first time, four decades later. "I'm sure we gave them plenty of trouble," she commented. "But then, they gave it to us."

The truth, which eventually emerged, was that the women correspondents sent to Africa were tokens meant to allay criticism, not the forerunners of more to come, and the War Department was running out of excuses for its refusal to accredit more women. Robb obliged the War Department by returning to her husband and her job in New York. Cowan went to England in March 1943, and she was there for the arrival of the first contingent of WAACs to be stationed in Britain.

All women overseas were still viewed as a nuisance by the Army, but the War Department was counting on the excitement engendered by the arrival of WAACs in London to give a mighty boost to the recruitment of WAACs for service on the home front. To make sure the press gave it proper credit for this event, the War Department issued accreditation to a dozen women correspondents.

Iris Carpenter, a British correspondent, linked up with the Americans to cover the arrival of the WAACs—a splendid show—for the British Broadcasting Corporation. Carpenter would never forget how the silk stockings of the American women shone in the sunlight as they marched on parade. The British had run out of silk stockings years before.

Alas, the press officers and the censors had neglected to get their act together. Carpenter broadcast the news of the WAACs' arrival to the world, but after all that American press officers had done to arrange publicity, their censors refused to release the news to the American press.

Certainly censoring the arrival of the WAACs was overkill, an error corrected in time. But it was evidence that somehow the British and the Americans had to coordinate their censorship, and the problem was pushed to the top, presented to General Eisenhower, the supreme Allied commander, and even to Prime Minister Winston Churchill.

It was agreed that Iris Carpenter should be accredited to the American forces, subject to American censorship. Carpenter took her chances with the Americans because she had learned that a woman correspondent would get nowhere with the British forces. The British commander, Field Marshal Bernard Law Montgomery, said flatly, "I will not tolerate them."

For American accreditation, Carpenter had to be employed by an American publication, but that was no problem for her. NBC's Blue Network, the *Boston Globe*, and the North American Newspaper Alliance gladly shared her services with the BBC and the London *Daily Herald*. Carpenter and Cowan were two of the most distinguished women correspondents in the business, and eventually they teamed up to cover the war together.

War did make strange bedfellows. Iris Carpenter was truly "to the manor born." The first German bomb dropped on Britain, she reported, landed on her property in Kent. Five German planes shot down over Britain crashed on the estate. Her husband, Charles Scruby, piloted the family yacht in the historic evacuation of British forces from Dunkirk, France, just before it was occupied by the Germans in June 1940, a maneuver so secret that she did not learn of it until he returned with a cargo of soldiers.

The daughter of a cinema magnate, Carpenter was in the tradition of privileged British women whose status could open doors closed to the masses. Still, she had to prove her worth before she could use her connections, and London really was not prepared for her when she started out in 1924, at the age of eighteen, as a film critic for a publication called *The Picture Show*.

An exclusive interview with a reclusive woman movie censor led to a job on the London *Daily Express*. Winning by-lines from the start, she married and had two children before she resigned in 1933 to raise her family.

The day war was declared, a harried spokesman for the Ministry of Information phoned Carpenter with brief instructions to come to the ministry at once, bring clothes, and be prepared to stay. On arrival, she was assigned to broadcast for the BBC.

Surviving the Battle of Britain took courage. Carpenter recalled a woman coming out of shock to see her home destroyed by bombs, while an air raid warden pressed her for information. "Where is your husband?"

"He's at the front, the coward," the woman retorted.

The women who covered the war in Britain all felt they had earned the right to cover the war in France. By the spring of 1944, close to one hundred women correspondents in Britain— British, French, and Polish as well as American—were asserting their right to cover the Normandy invasion. The more women they counted coming forth to demand consideration, the more adamantly the military authorities held to the decision that none would accompany the invasion forces to France.

Women who had reported the war in Italy with distinction viewed the decision as shameful. Iris Carpenter felt she had been double-crossed. Having accepted American censorship with the understanding that she would be allowed to cover the invasion with American women correspondents, she learned that neither the high command in London nor the War Department in Washington had ever considered allowing women to proceed to Normandy.

A blue-eyed blonde with a turned-up nose and a beautiful complexion, Carpenter was distinguished by the tone of authority in her voice, the glint of steel in her eyes, the determination in her stride. In short order she had contrite generals agreeing they owed her one, and she soon found a way to collect.

As it turned out, the restrictions placed on women helped both Carpenter and Lee Carson of International News Service score totally unanticipated news beats. Nurses hit the Normandy beaches on D-Day, June 6, 1944; women correspondents did not. But Carson managed to get a better view of the invasion than most of the newsmen who went in with the troops. Bypassing the press office, she found a group commander at an air base who was happy to help her get a seat aboard a plane and an aerial view of the attack. Her forced early return to base enabled her to cable an exclusive eyewitness report of the invasion.

Some of the newsmen got so far from their lines of communication that they were not heard from for days. When the callbacks came from angry editors, men accused Carson of "batting her eyelashes" to get the story. No one observed that at best this served to even the scales tipped against the sex.

Carson possessed a faculty for causing a storm wherever she went. Tawny-haired and saucy, she was every soldier's pinup girl. She refused to tell her age, but she was probably one of the youngest correspondents to cover the war, which made her somehow suspect. As it happened, her credentials were impeccable. A Smith College graduate, she had studied at the Ecole Anglaise in Paris.

By D-Day plus four, Allied forces had their first air strip in France on a slice of sand between two gullies taken at enormous sacrifice. The first ambulance plane to land brought Iris Carpenter and Cornelius Ryan, whose war books would win him fame. The U.S. Army was atoning for breaking its promise to let her cover the invasion by choosing her to be the first woman correspondent to set foot in France. That was the extent of the gesture. Ryan was allowed to travel in France. Carpenter was restricted to the air strip.

The medical corpsmen had not cleared the beach of the dead when the first plane with wounded survivors took off from Normandy for London, with Carpenter aboard. It was a perilous flight. The runway was so short that the plane barely cleared a hilltop where men were digging graves. Carpenter interviewed the wounded on the way back to England and broadcast their account of the invasion on the nine o'clock news. Again a woman was able to score a scoop because of military restrictions on her movements.

Within a few days, Carpenter obtained orders to visit the

Normandy beachhead by ship. From there she found transportation into the city of Cherbourg. For this, she was court-martialed. Her orders had been issued for the beachhead only. Among her judges she remembered "a vicious, pompous little British chap" and a man she learned to adore, American Colonel Richard Ernest ("Ernie") Dupuy, the public relations officer for Supreme Headquarters Europe and General Eisenhower's liaison with the British Ministry of Information. The British began by demanding to know who had allowed her to go to France. Dupuy replied, "Nobody lets Carpenter do anything. All we can do is try to stop her."

Her fate hinged on an answer to the question "Did the beachhead include Cherbourg?" When it was decided that she had not gone too far, her fellow British tormentor could not resist remarking, "My dear woman, you will never go back."

"But General, I have the orders already," she was able to tell him. The Americans had assigned her and Ruth Cowan to an extended stay with the Ninety-first Evacuation Hospital unit in France.

Not all women were so lucky. As Carpenter recalled, two, one British, one American, were quickly disaccredited, perhaps as a warning to women of both nations. As she saw it, women correspondents faced a choice—they could get the story for their editors or they could abide by military regulations designed to restrict them. They could not do both. Women managed to cover the war because men were divided, she said, citing the six women assigned to a ship carrying General Patton's forces to France. The U.S. Army had ruled that the women could not go aboard, the U.S. Navy that they could. The women went.

Ruth Cowan and Iris Carpenter soon found themselves in France in an area of meadows and orchards where the medics were setting up an eight-hundred-bed hospital. They cooked in trash bins and ate out of mess kits. The Germans bombed them every night, in violation of the rules of war against attacking hospitals. The two newswomen, sharing a tent with two nurses, had only tin helmets to protect themselves from shrapnel, and this provoked debate as to which part to protect. Carpenter put her helmet over her face.

The Army set up comfortable press camps for men only and provided daily briefing on the battles and the location of friendly and enemy troops. For transportation, the men were given their own jeeps. Denied briefings, the women went blindly to the front, risking encounters with the enemy. Denied transportation, they had to thumb rides back to the press camp to file their stories. Then they had to wait until every last man had sent his story, however insignificant, before they could use the communication facilities.

Far from gloating over their privileges, the men were as angry as the women. Their press camps were located as much as forty miles behind the hospitals where the women were billeted. Closer to the front, the women were scooping the men left and right. Priority to use the teletype machine did not help the newsmen missing the action.

Carpenter and Cowan reached the front in ambulances that went out to collect the wounded, but neither would risk being accused of taking a wounded man's place to return that way, even when there was room in a vehicle for them. During the battle for St.-Lo, they were waiting for a ride at a crossroads guarded by a single sentry when he yelled, "For Christ's sake, get in that hole!" As bombs dropped, two stories of the town hall fell in front of them. Cowan escaped unscathed, but one of Carpenter's eardrums was shattered. A lieutenant colonel in a jeep drove up in time to ask, "What in hell are you doing here?" Carpenter told him, "We are war correspondents, but we are just women. We don't rate being taken care of like the men." Still Carpenter had the same assignment as the men, and whether or not the Army provided transport for her, she was going to cover the story. The intrepid Cowan could hardly let her scoop the Associated Press.

Lee Carson also declined to be confined. Traveling to Normandy on a conducted tour in August 1944, she disappeared. The Army issued orders calling for her apprehension and return to London. For two weeks, she escaped capture. By then, the correspondents were racing each other to be first into liberated Paris, their destination the Scribe Hotel, the designated press center. Major Frank Mayborn, the first press officer to reach the

Scribe on Liberation Day, August 25, arrived with orders to find and punish Cowan, and there she stood in the lobby. The major was so happy to see her alive, all he did was smile. "It's good to see you got here safely."

In a jeep with two fellow correspondents, Carson had rolled through the St.-Cloud gate into Paris the evening of August 24, behind the tanks but before the Germans had checked out of the Scribe. Lawrence G. ("Larry") Blochman, a veteran and beloved correspondent, bestowed on her the title of "first" correspondent to reach Paris because she was sitting in the front seat of the jeep. But none of them beat Sonia Tomara of the *New York Herald Tribune*, who had arrived on a weapons carrier.

Iris Carpenter reached Paris by jeep in time to make a historic broadcast for the BBC. Because of her shattered eardrum, she could not hear herself speak. Yet her report of the celebration of liberation, the "wildest party" she had ever seen, was impressive enough to be preserved in the British Archives.

Ruth Cowan arrived on the first train, a dangerous excursion because of the weak state of railroad trestles. The train came under enemy fire as it reached Paris. Nobody caught the gunmen, who could have been German stragglers or French Nazis.

It took Carson and Carpenter, fighting on separate fronts, to break the ban against women in the press camps. In Paris, Carpenter went over the heads of the press officers to General Eisenhower's top aides to complain about the relegation of women to hospital units.

"If you care so much about the safety of women, why don't you look after us?" she shouted. "You send women out with no knowledge of front-line conditions. I want to stop this nonsense." Anticipating the retort that nobody had sent her anywhere, she added, "I am going to get my story. I am going to go whether you accredit me or not."

The women were accredited to the war zones. They did not have accreditation to military units, as required for admission to press camps at the front. Carpenter got her accreditation to the First Army and reported to its press camp in Spa, Belgium. Lee Carson arrived the next day. They met warily, each wondering how the other had managed to get there. This time both had proper orders. They had been so successful at getting major stories without military assistance that the press officers now wanted them in the camps in order to acquire some control over them.

Once Paris had been liberated, the press no longer had to live in tents. As the Allied forces advanced, elegant hotels and villas stretching from Paris to the German border and beyond were requisitioned to serve as press "camps." No longer could military commanders plead a shortage of latrines to exclude women.

Still the Army did not lift its ban against women at the front. It simply made exceptions. Women who had been waiting years to get overseas finally were reaching London and Paris only to be denied permission to go forward. Some who were assigned to press camps found themselves confined to rear areas while other women were given transportation to the front. The offended women protested what they considered worse than sex discrimination, the unequal treatment of women. If some could go, why couldn't all?

Under tremendous pressure, the Army caved in first to the women who shouted loudest and proved most adept at breaking its rules. Also among the privileged were VIPs like Anne O'Hare McCormick of the *New York Times*; others whose publishers could bring pressure to bear, like Sonia Tomara of the *New York Herald Tribune*; and women who could get generals to request their presence at the front, like Helen Kirkpatrick of the *Chicago Daily News*.

Ruth Cowan managed briefly to cover the Battle of the Bulge, the German counteroffensive in December 1944. But the AP recalled her, an action that infuriated her. Wes Gallagher was there and he was gaining influence with the home office. Assigned again to a hospital unit, she found new opportunities to live dangerously. As the Allied forces approached the German border, she joined a group searching for a place to locate another front-line hospital. Eventually, she and her driver found themselves alone in a jeep on an empty stretch of road.

"You know what's funny?" she remarked. "I don't see any cigarette packs." The Americans had not been through there to litter the area. When they reached the village of Stenford, villagers came out and joyously placed a Stenford flag on their jeep. Where was the U.S. Army? the villagers wanted to know. It was not the first time correspondents had found themselves in territory ahead of the armed forces. Like others before her, Cowan asked how long it had been since the Germans had pulled out. In reply, the villagers pointed to a building. The Germans were still there. Cowan and her driver expressed their thought simultaneously: "Let's get the hell out of here." They reached base to tell the tale.

After the war, fellow newswomen elected Ruth Cowan president of the Women's National Press Club. She served as a Washington correspondent for the AP until 1956, when, at the age of fifty-five, she married Bradley D. Nash, deputy undersecretary of commerce. Two years later President Eisenhower appointed her assistant undersecretary of Health, Education and Welfare. At eighty-six, she was still entertaining visitors in a handsome farm house at Harpers Ferry, West Virginia, where her husband served as perennial mayor of the town.

12

The Russians Were Coming!

FOR ONE MOMENT IN HISTORY, THE UNITED STATES AND THE Soviet Union shared a single ambition, to join forces in the heart of Germany and finally put an end to World War II in Europe. Allied armies driving eastward from the Rhine reached the Elbe on April 11, 1945, and halted to await the arrival of the Russians. The Russians kept coming. They surrounded Berlin, and the biggest suspense story of the war began to build. Hundreds of combat correspondents positioned themselves to be first to flash the news of the climax of the war, the meeting of Marshal Ivan S. Konev's First Ukrainian Army with the U.S. First Army.

To the dismay of some and the astonishment of all, the first American to greet the Russians was neither a general nor a foot soldier, but Ann Stringer of United Press. Her successful dash back to Paris with the news of the Russian arrival at the Elbe produced the best scoop of World War II.

Stringer was in the worst of all possible positions to break the news. For disobeying instructions to stay out of danger, she was under military orders to retreat to Paris. As directed, she had left U.S. First Army press headquarters in Germany, but instead of going back toward France, she went forward. Joining forces with Allan Jackson, a photographer for International News Photos and proud possessor of a decrepit Ford automobile, she set out to report on front-line battalions, where field commanders welcomed them. Her problem was that they had no facilities for filing a news story, and she could not go back to the press camp.

Early on April 25, Stringer and Jackson found two pilots to take them up, each in a tiny Piper Cub, for an aerial view of the Elbe River front. Stringer's first inkling that Russians were approaching the Elbe was when the radio in her plane intercepted Russian voices. When the pilots and their passengers saw smoke, they decided to land and investigate. The two small planes landed in a field outside the town of Torgau. The four climbed over army roadblocks and made their way into Torgau. Suddenly Stringer screamed. A man, dripping wet, clad only in bathing trunks and a cap sporting a red star, was coming toward her from the Elbe. "Russians!" she shouted. She recognized the red star. It happened at high noon.

What surprised her most was that she experienced no language barrier. In English and in Russian, they conveyed their jubilation. The Americans climbed into a racing hull and crossed the river to meet the Russian Army. The Russians kept shouting, "Viva Roosevelt!" "Viva Roosevelt!" They did not know that President Franklin D. Roosevelt had died on April 12.

On the way back across the Elbe, Stringer's notes were ruined by water. It did not matter. She had her story; the problem was how to file it. Stringer vowed that somehow she would find a plane to fly her to Paris. Jackson, who had to pick up his Ford and drive it back to the First Army press camp, trusted her to make it and entrusted her with his precious film of the linkup. Back in her Piper Cub, she headed west. Her pilot was first to spot a C-47 on an airfield, and they put down beside it. The big plane was there to fly back some furniture that the GIs were "liberating" from the Germans to furnish the headquarters of an American general in France, a building previously looted by the Germans.

"I just met the Russians," Stringer called to the pilot of the C-47.

"Yeah, and I just met Stalin," the incredulous pilot shouted back.

While men loaded the plane, she sat on the wing typing her story. She aroused the enthusiasm of the crew by including their names in her dispatch. The pilot was convinced, and off they flew to Orly Airport, Paris. Alas, they did not have permission to land, and the tower at Orly turned them away. "Don't you know there's a war on?" "Yes, and we have major news to deliver." It cut no ice. The C–47, lacking priority, landed at a military field outside Paris.

Stringer hitchhiked her way into press headquarters at the Scribe Hotel, Paris. She filed her story and delivered Jackson's film to the censors, then collapsed in the press bar, a nice, dark retreat from the war. Drew Middleton, the respected *New York Times* correspondent, was shocked to see her. "You should have stayed," he told her. "The Russians are coming. That would make a great story."

Stringer merely nodded. Her report of the Russians' arrival was in the censor's basket. Had she given Middleton a clue, the bar would have emptied in a flash, leaving her no assurance that her news flash would be first to reach New York. It was, making extras and headlines across the nation. Germany was cut in two; the war in Europe was all but over.

Iris Carpenter recalled the rage of the whole First Army press camp at getting scooped on Torgau, a story in its own area, yet the First Army correspondents were not far behind. Stringer beat them mainly by flying her copy to Paris while other correspondents spent precious time driving to and from Torgau. "She did it, bless her heart." Carpenter could laugh. She had scored her share of scoops.

Ann Stringer could have played the heroine of a war movie. She was tall and willowy with a lovely figure and long chestnut hair flowing free. Soft-spoken and gentle, she evoked the protective instincts of the men. For a woman determined to make a name for herself, this was a mixed blessing.

Stringer, a Texas native, found the United Press as reluctant to hire her when she graduated from the University of Texas in 1940 as it had been to have a woman on the staff in 1929. United Press did hire her husband, William J. Stringer, and when he was sent to Columbus, Ohio, as chief of the UP bureau, she obtained a job on the *Columbus Citizen*. Her success there won her a job with UP.

The Stringers worked as a team for UP in New York and in

Buenos Aires, Argentina, but they could not persuade UP to send them to cover the war in Europe. Bill Stringer went to France alone as a correspondent for Reuters, the British news agency, and she continued to work for UP until Reuters consented to send her to join her husband. The day she went to work in Reuters' New York office, she received the news that Bill Stringer, driving his jeep through Versailles, had been killed in German crossfire on the eve of the liberation of Paris. His death devastated her, and she passed up her opportunity to go to Europe for the agency.

Then UP had a change of heart. Hugh Bailey, general manager, personally arranged to send Ann to Europe as a UP correspondent. In London, she encountered the Army's reluctance to send a woman, particularly the widow of a war correspondent, to the front. Caught in red tape at U.S. Army press headquarters in London, she haunted the military airfield outside the city, seeking in vain a pilot willing to fly her to France. Too upset to eat, she was chided by the mess officer for letting the food on her plate go to waste when wartime Britain was so short of food. She could only tell him not to serve her so much.

Orders arrived at last assigning her to U. S. Army press camps in Germany, where she met Lee Carson and Iris Carpenter, who had advanced with the First Army from their base in Belgium. Press officers who could find transportation to the front for such women as Carson and Carpenter could not do the same for Stringer. Her assignment to the rear was unintentionally made clear in a reminiscence by Colonel Barney Oldfield, press officer of the U.S. Ninth Army. Stringer, he wrote, "never moved across the rear areas without causing something of a sensation."

Hank Wales of the *Chicago Tribune* was in the jeep with Stringer the first time she heard the chorus of whistles and catcalls she evoked from GIs they passed on the road. Observing her attempt to ignore the ruckus, Wales murmured, "You would think they never saw a jeep before."

Stringer got into trouble when she traveled to the front with James McGlincy, a fellow UP correspondent. They made it into the battered and blasted city of Jülich, sixteen miles northeast of Aachen, and reported the capture of the city. Her story, "With the First Troops in Jülich,'' created a furor. McGlincy and Stringer went in with the flame throwers, on the theory that the firepower would protect them. Brigadier General Frank Allen, in command of public relations for the Supreme Headquarters Allies Expeditionary Force, was appalled. He threatened to jerk Stringer back to Paris if she did not stay in the rear.

Oldfield delivered the reprimand. McGlincy, under a cloud simply for taking Stringer with him, defended her. Nevertheless, she was restricted because she went where newsmen were allowed. She aroused special concern because she was Bill Stringer's widow.

''I really think she wants to get killed, too,'' Boyd Lewis, a leading UP correspondent, confided in Oldfield.

Lewis, in his own memoirs, explained: ''My feelings about having Ann in our theater were mixed. On the one hand, we did need more help at the front from someone with her writing style. She could give us the kind of human interest features about GIs which Ernie Pyle had made famous. On the other hand, Ann was a beautiful, headstrong, bereaved woman.'' He said that some men in the London bureau suggested that Ann might want to join Billy by getting herself killed. She denied it. ''I was only trying to do what Bill and I had planned to do together,'' she said. That failed to reassure the authorities, whose interpretation was that she was as reckless as he had been.

The same men who caused trouble for Stringer by gossiping about her death wish caused grief for Boyd Lewis by telling his family that he was emotionally involved with her. In his recollections, one could detect a slightly nostalgic regret that nothing had come of it. Stringer did not learn of this bit of gossip until Lewis published his memoirs forty years later. She could not help but know she was forever the controversial center of attention.

On March 6, 1945, British Prime Minister Sir Winston Churchill made a visit to the Siegfried Line, Germany's once great defense barrier, which had been breached by Allied troops on November 18, 1944. By March it was no longer a war zone, yet Stringer said she was not allowed to cover Churchill's visit.

Incensed, she did not calm down when she discovered the reason.

When they reached their destination, Churchill, Field Marshal Bernard Law Montgomery, and Field Marshal Sir Alan Brooke opened their flies and proceeded to wet the Siegfried Line. Even mighty leaders would be boys. Some knew in advance what they would do and did not consider it a seemly sight for a lady. Well, they could have let her cover the news event and told her not to watch the men urinating outdoors, something she saw every day as she passed GIs along the road.

· Allied forces reached the Rhine on March 7 and captured the railroad at Remagen, the only bridge across the river the retreating Germans had failed to destroy. Under enemy fire, the U.S. First Army crossed the bridge and established the first Allied bridgehead east of the Rhine. Lee Carson of International News Service reached the Rhine in time to be among the first to report it. Wes Gallagher of Associated Press, already in line to take command of America's major news agency, obtained transportation without question. Stringer could not get a jeep to approach the scene.

Refusing to be left behind, Stringer stalked out of the press camp looking for a ride. She hailed a general in a tank, and he took her in. By tank was the safest way to go if you had to get to the Rhine. They were stopped repeatedly. Three Allied armies were converging on the Rhine for a massive assault against enemy lines across the river, and the traffic jam was unique in history.

From the tank, Stringer transferred to a jeep and reached the bridge while German armies were threatening the American beachhead across the river, and again trying to destroy the bridge with artillery fire and dive bombers. Shortly before her arrival, a German shell hit a jeep attempting to cross the bridge and incinerated its two occupants. Since her jeep would be too large a target, Stringer got out and calmly walked across the railroad trestles of the bridge to explore a tunnel on the other side. Major Charles Gillette, press officer of the Ninth Armored Division, saw her for the first time when she entered a small building that served as a headquarters on the east bank of the Rhine. "He told me he almost fainted when he saw me," Stringer recalled.

More than forty years later, Gillette, president of the New York City Convention and Visitors' Bureau, remembered that Stringer was severely criticized for crossing the bridge and defended her right to do it. Howard Cowan of the Associated Press (no relation to Ruth Cowan) crossed the bridge before she did, Gillette said. "You could get killed out there," he said. "Some parts of the bridge were half out. Their planes were in dogfights with our planes. But it was like a big celebration," the firing of a salute to the crossing of the Rhine.

Americans had saved the bridge by cutting wires attached to explosives left by the retreating Germans. Having sustained three corps of the U.S. First Army's crossing it with their heavy equipment, the bridge collapsed peacefully into the water on March 17.

With the news that Allied armies were about to cross the Rhine en masse, Stringer reached the press camp and filed her story ahead of Gallagher. There remained the devil to pay. For ignoring commands and risking her life, she was ordered back to Paris. Again she defied the authorities to break the news of the Russians' arrival at the Elbe.

As she and Allan Jackson crossed the Elbe in their racing hull, it seemed for a moment as if she was in more trouble than she had been at Remagen. For the Russians let loose with a burst of machine gun fire. "I had been under enemy fire, and it can be terrifying," Stringer recalled. "Why I didn't get scared to death on the Elbe, I don't know. But there was a sense of friendship, exhilaration, and joy."

The Russians across the Elbe greeted them with new cries of "Americanski! Americanski!" and invited them to lunch.

While Stringer was having lunch with the Russians, Jack Thompson of the *Chicago Tribune* arrived with expectations of scoring the biggest exclusive of the war, and he might have pulled it off had she not flown her copy to Paris while he was driving back to the press camp. At a reunion luncheon forty years later, he recalled the incident and his anger. "I could have slit her throat."

Hitler committed suicide in his ruined chancellery in Berlin five days later, and the German armies began surrendering on May 4. Stringer was in Munich on May 7, preparing to return to Paris, when victory in Europe was announced. That day she witnessed the contrast between the beaten, hopeless Germans in their bomb-battered city and the joy erupting in Paris. Back at the Scribe Hotel, she raced from one balcony to another to get the best view of the parades, the swelling excitement of the victory celebration.

Edward Kennedy of the Associated Press was first to flash the news of the unconditional surrender of the Germans. He did it by breaking a release date, for which the AP fired him. Kennedy aroused little sympathy among fellow correspondents, who had known as much as he but abided by instructions on the timing of the announcement.

Newsweek bestowed its honors on Lee Carson, Iris Carpenter, and Ann Stringer in an article entitled "The Rhine Maidens." "In the strictly male army view, the three women were out of bounds," the magazine reported, but it gave them credit. "They dug their own foxholes. They asked no favors and gave none."

As it turned out, hole digging was about the only skill they did not need. Foxholes, used for cover on Pacific islands, would have been of little use against the might of the German Wehrmacht. Instead of digging their own latrines, the women were allowed to use the general's facility, provided a soldier stood guard. Years later, Carl Freund, a Texas newsman who had served with the 104th Infantry (Timberwolf) Division during the push to link up with the Russians, saw an article recalling Stringer's coverage of the historic event and wrote her.

You were responsible for the high spot of my Army service. It came at Weisweiller, just before we crossed the Roer and took Düren, when I told General Terry Allen, our division commander, that he could not enter his own latrine. He looked at me as though he thought I had gone off the deep end and asked, "Have you lost what little sense I gave you credit for having?" Then I pointed out that, if he did enter, he would find himself confronting one very angry female war correspondent. He left muttering something about having women in a combat zone, but I know from his comments at other times that he really had a lot of respect for your journalistic abilities. So did the other correspondents who spent time with us.

Stringer cited the letter as an example of how women were treated at the front—"nice but awkward."

Carson, whose articles were featured in the Hearst newspapers, was a formidable rival, but she was not Stringer's chief competitor. For Stringer, AP's Gallagher was the man to beat. The major newspapers in America subscribed to both AP and UP. Many of them featured AP and used UP only as a backup service for stories the AP missed. If only out of deference to her status as a war widow, Gallagher would speak to Stringer, "but you could see it hurt," she said. When finally scooped by a woman, he managed to keep his poker face. He would take his revenge against the sex when he took over AP and could see to it that few women got a chance to compete.

The shout "Bring the boys home" erupted with V-E Day, and Lee Carson went home with them. She married twice and pursued a successful magazine career for two decades before, again too young, she died of cancer.

Iris Carpenter's husband died of cancer before World War II ended. With the German surrender, she became the only woman assigned to accompany the U.S. First Army to the Pacific for a final assault on Japan. Carrying her own duffel bag and typewriter, she reached the United States by ship, and she never left. The atom bomb had been dropped on Hiroshima; Japan surrendered. The *London Daily Express* assigned her to open a Washington bureau. Her second marriage, to an American colonel she had met in Germany, was not a success, but it completed the Americanization of Iris Carpenter and changed her by-line to Iris Carpenter Akers. The Voice of America accepted her ideas for a radio show, "World Opinion Roundup," and hired her away from the *Daily Express* to produce it. Her son and daughter joined her in the United States, and she settled in a pink brick house with blue shutters close to a lake in Virginia.

Of the three Rhine maidens, only Stringer reported the aftermath of World War II in Europe. She was with the Allied forces when they liberated the Nazi death camp at Nordhausen and found people, still alive, buried beneath the decomposing bodies of the dead. It was the first time she was truly shaken. A GI tried to send her away. "How can your husband allow you to see such a thing?" When the soldier learned what had happened to Bill Stringer, he contritely escorted her through the concentration camp. Ironically, among the few buildings to survive the Allied bombing of Nordhausen was the seventeenth-century Rathaus with its oaken Roland monument, an ancient symbol of civil liberty.

Stringer reached Vienna in July with the first convoy of Western correspondents the Russian occupiers allowed into the Austrian capital. In the dining room of the hotel that served as a press camp, she overheard two waiters talking about Vaslav Nijinsky, the great Russian dancer. "Is he alive?" she asked. The threat of insanity had ended his career in 1917, and his Western friends assumed the Germans, who exterminated the mentally ill as well as the Jews, had done away with him. Stringer discovered Nijinsky and his wife in the hotel behind her own and got the story of how they had hidden from the Nazis and escaped the Allied bombs that destroyed much of the city. The Russian couple had been hiding out in the woods, sleeping beside a bonfire, when they heard Russian voices, the first they knew that the Russian Army was approaching Vienna. In celebration, the famous ballet master danced with the soldiers around the bonfire.

Before anyone could stop her, Stringer took off by jeep for Budapest, Hungary, crossing the Danube six times on a circuitous route and stopping short only where the bridges across the Danube between Buda and Pest had been destroyed. The once blue Danube was filled with corpses floating on the water. She could not find out whether they were two weeks or two months old, but the river reeked of death. A nunnery provided haven for the night before she sped back to Vienna to file her eyewitness report of the devastation. Stringer would never forget the reaction of Colonel Stanley Grogan, the American press officer in Vienna, when he learned of her unauthorized journey by reading her copy. As she put it, "Grogan had a fit."

The next time she went to Budapest without permission, she described a city nursing its wounds and added to her lead the phrase "travelers reported." The last line of her story explained that "among the travelers was this correspondent." Grogan apparently did not read the story through, for when she asked permission to go to Sofia, he said yes. "He probably thought it was in the Vienna woods," she said.

With Seymour Freidin of the *New York Herald Tribune* and an American driver, Stringer headed south through Yugoslavia toward the capital of Bulgaria. Needing a permit to get by Russian roadblocks, she found a red and black wrapper for Octagon soap and pasted it on cardboard. Russian soldiers unfamiliar with the Western alphabet turned the card upside down trying to decipher it, conferred over the impressive lettering, and finally motioned them through. When the roads became so treacherous that the driver balked at going any farther, Stringer took over and drove the jeep into Bulgaria and on to Sofia.

No less dangerous was her flight with an Air Force pilot to get an aerial view of Romania. On the way back to Vienna, they ran out of gas and had to make an emergency landing in a field in Transylvania out of sight of civilization. While the pilot went in search of help, she guarded the plane. Having waited alone for hours, she began to wonder if anyone would ever find her, when at last the pilot appeared over the horizon, rolling a barrel of gas.

Jeeps were more dependable, and Stringer finally reached Bucharest, the Romanian capital, by driving across Hungary. In the city where caviar had been plentiful when Sonia Tomara of the *Herald Tribune* left the still neutral country in 1940, Stringer felt fortunate to share K rations, cheese, and crackers with the small American contingent stationed there.

The iron curtain was descending, and while she was in Bucharest, Prime Minister Winston Churchill made a speech which so angered the Russians that Romanians decided it was too dangerous for her to drive back through Russian-occupied territory to Vienna. Her greater fear was that Grogan would kill her if she did not return the press camp jeep. The Romanians solved her dilemma by flying her to Naples, Italy, where she was able to borrow a surplus jeep from an army unit and drive it back to Vienna. Grogan never noticed the difference.

In Nuremberg, Germany, for the war crimes trials, she was walking through the rubble with Dan DeLuce, a senior AP correspondent; both were depressed by the total desolation around them when they heard music. "No buildings were left standing. Yet the birds were singing for the first time since the war," Stringer remembered.

It seemed time to start life anew. Impulsively, she agreed to marry DeLuce.

That marriage lasted six weeks. DeLuce had been married before, and men who knew and liked his first wife gossiped maliciously about Stringer. She was paying the price of her celebrity status, invasion of privacy. "I wanted marriage, but I wasn't ready for it," she admitted. "I saw him as a father figure."

There was no time to dwell on her personal troubles. In addition to reporting for UP, she was broadcasting for CBS and writing for the *Saturday Evening Post*. CBS, which had deemed the sound of a woman's voice unsuitable for reporting war news in 1941, was happy to hear from Ann Stringer whenever she cabled that she had another exclusive story for them. From the Nuremberg war crimes trials, she broadcast live the day the Nazi defendants entered their pleas of innocent to the slaughter of the innocents. New to the medium, she had carefully rehearsed what she intended to say as she watched the proceedings from the gallery of the courtroom. Rudolf Hess, Adolf Hitler's deputy, threw her off balance by marching before the judges and shouting just one word, *"Nein!"* Other defendants had made lengthy speeches in self-defense and self-righteous indignation. No one in the court was prepared for this enigmatic brevity. It took some fast ad-libbing to explain to her audience overseas that he was saying no to the charges against him and no to the jurisdiction of the court.

From Dresden, she broadcast her commentary on what she saw as another war crime, this one committed by the Allied powers, the phosphorus bombing of that beautiful and historic city on February 13, 1945. Dresden, known as the Florence of the Elbe, had been crowded with refugees who thought it was one place the Allies would take care to preserve. Thousands who survived a direct hit were eaten alive by the phosphorus burning into their skin.

The heart of Berlin was also destroyed, and rubble blocked the route to town when Stringer arrived to establish her headquarters there. The first correspondents to reach the former German capital slept in crowded quarters and ate in a canteen called Uncle Tom's Cabin at the bombed-out suburban Zehlendorf subway station. Always a light eater, Stringer let the Americans pile food on her plate, then scooped it up and gave it to starving Germans.

Accommodations for Americans improved rapidly as the U.S. Army moved into West Berlin and confiscated the best housing left standing for its officers and the correspondents. The luckiest Germans were those allowed to remain in their homes as servants to the occupiers. Stringer rated a charming house of her own, with a German maid, a driver, and a secretary she later took to the United States along with the secretary's mother. Hers was a modest staff compared to the retinues others employed at a time the U.S. Army paid them in worthless currency and the Germans worked willingly for one square meal a day.

Her driver was essential because a U.S. Army ruling forbade American women to drive any vehicle in occupied Germany. Other women correspondents protested that newsmen were being allowed to scoop them on news that broke after their drivers left for the day, but for once Stringer did not add her voice to the chorus. She had done her share of driving across Europe, and besides, she was constantly flying to other European cities on assignment.

Twice in Rome she obtained audiences with Pope Pius XII. The first time she was appropriately attired in uniform. For her second audience, she was wearing civilian clothes and only at the last minute realized she had nothing with which to cover her head—no hat, no veil. Some covering was de rigueur to show respect for the pontiff; on this occasion it was particularly imperative because the Pope had granted her the honor of an exclusive audience, so her costume could not possibly go unnoticed. Resourceful in an emergency, she fashioned a cap out of a pair of black lace panties.

The Pope received her in his private study, where women were not known to intrude, and talked of his concern about the many thousands of refugees left homeless by the war. In time, he stood and extended his hand, a gesture of dismissal. Although he may have expected her to kiss his ring, she shook his hand, then sat down again because she hadn't finished asking her questions. Graciously, he allowed the interview to continue until she got her story.

The story she filed produced a ''rocket,'' a word reserved for a furious query from the home office, to her competitors at the Rome bureau of the Associated Press, and they immediately issued a denial of her story. Her account of a private audience in the private study of Pope Pius struck them as so unbelievable that they assumed she had fabricated the whole episode. Stringer, however, was able to show her appointment on the Pope's calendar.

Henry (''Hank'') Ries, a handsome photographer for the *New York Times*, had invited Stringer to lunch after her audience with the Pope, and she saw more of him in Berlin. Until the wives arrived in the fall of 1946, and the Army opened food commissaries for them, all the correspondents ate breakfast, lunch, and dinner at the Berlin press center, except for an occasional invitation to some officers' mess. No Germans were allowed across the threshold of the press center, and that made for an insular society.

In Berlin in winter, the sun did not rise until 9:00 A.M., and it set at 3:00 P.M. Germans stole the coal as fast as the U.S. Army delivered it to American billets. For correspondents, it was a time of macabre joviality, and attention focused on the minority of women at the press center bar, which also happened to be the best place to keep warm. Stringer was the loveliest to look at and the most talked about, as I found out when I arrived in Berlin in October 1946 as a correspondent for the U.S. Army newspaper, the *Stars and Stripes*, providing a new captive audience for oft-told tales. In a backhanded tribute to Ann Stringer's magic, the newsmen blamed her both for Dan DeLuce's divorce from his first wife and for his divorce from her.

Most of the correspondents were covering the same story, the new war, the cold war between the Soviet Union and the Western powers. All Gaul had been divided into three parts, but Berlin was divided into four sectors—Russian, American, British, and French. Germany was divided into four corresponding zones, with Berlin an enclave surrounded by the Soviet zone. Stringer covered the growing animosity of the four powers in the Allied Control Council, culminating in the Berlin blockade, the Soviet refusal to allow access to Berlin through the Soviet zone, and the American response, the Berlin airlift.

Ann Stringer and Hank Ries were married in 1949. A man with an athletic build and the temperament of an artist, Ries was born in Germany of Jewish parents. His family had escaped the Nazis in the 1930s, and he returned to occupied Berlin as an American citizen. When the marriage was announced, newsmen taking wagers at the Berlin press center bar gave it six weeks. To their surprise, it lasted thirty years.

Together the Rieses produced *German Faces*, a book with his photographs, her text. When the occupation of Germany ended, she gave up her career to devote her talents to building his reputation as a commercial photographer in New York. More than a career, she wanted children, but they had none. After three decades, the marriage ended in anger. The divorce case dragged on for years, with many ugly accusations traded in court. Her regret was that she had not pursued her career. Her message for a new generation of women was "Develop your own talents. Make your own way. No one can take that from you."

At a time when others were retiring, she began writing again. She served with distinction on the Overseas Press Club awards committee. Ralph D. Gardner, an advertising man who had met her when he served as a corporal in World War II, renewed acquaintances with her at the club and, in a column for the *OPC Bulletin*, suggested that her memoirs would make a best seller. She was way ahead of him. Having recalled her war days for me, she was writing a book of her own about those momentous years.

13

No Peace in the Pacific

WOMEN ALSO SAW THEIR SHARE OF ACTION IN THE PACIFIC THE-
ater during World War II. Like the War Department, the Navy
Department sent no women correspondents overseas until 1943,
and then it sought to confine them to hospital ships. The Japanese introduced the women to war by attacking hospital ships
as readily as they attacked warships. Once the women were out
there getting torpedoed, field commanders realized that they
would be as safe ashore as aboard ship and allowed several to
accompany the assault troops.

Patricia Lockridge of the *Woman's Home Companion* was
among the women who reached Paris in World War II without
obtaining orders to cover combat. When the war began, prospects in the Pacific were no better. Women assigned to hospitals
in France could hope to escape to the front. It was worse to be
confined to a hospital ship, a tiny island usually out of sight of
land, removed from the fighting and from the admirals conducting the war. But having seen as much of the European war
as she could, Lockridge headed for the Pacific, and there she
scored, by convincing officers that she might as well be a running target on land as a sitting duck aboard ship.

"Marines piling ashore at Iwo Jima found Patricia Lockridge
there to greet them, besmudged but clearly female," fellow correspondents reminisced in *Off the Record*, a book published by
the Overseas Press Club. The anecdote, however amusing, was
slightly distorted. She beat the newsmen, not the Marines, to
shore.

What the correspondents had to report from Iwo Jima was

stark tragedy. Two divisions of Marines storming the beaches between February 19 and February 21, 1945, suffered heavy casualties in one of the fiercest and most costly battles of the war. Arriving aboard the hospital ship *Solace* on D-Day plus four, Lockridge did not see the Marines coming in. She saw the wounded being carried out. A third division would arrive to end the battle and secure the strategic island some seven hundred miles southeast of Tokyo, but not until after the *Solace* had left with all the wounded it could carry.

To take on casualties, the *Solace* maneuvered around warships offshore to within one hundred yards of land. As small boats brought hundreds of the wounded to the ship, Lockridge worked as hard as the nurses, comforting those in pain, bringing them water and fruit juice. Someone pinned a bandage to her arm with her rating, ''Water tender, first class,'' painted on it in mercurochrome. By the second day, ''the ship began to smell of blood, disinfectants, gangrene and death,'' she wrote.

It seemed impossible that the beach would be worse than the ship, but it was. Japanese mortar shells still were hitting the blackened and littered shoreline as Lockridge went in on a landing boat, and the confusion was incredible. Wounded Marines waiting for transport to the *Solace* were wounded again, and some were killed. The Japanese, so entrenched in caves that weeks of bombardment had failed to dislodge them, would hold out for almost a month.

Back on the *Solace*, it was still only once, when a red-haired corporal choked out the words ''They got me when they killed John.'' John was Gunnery Sergeant John Basilone, a Congressional Medal of Honor winner for his bravery in the battle for Guadalcanal. His fellows had thought John was invincible.

For Lockridge, the worst moment came when a corpsman told her of a man who ''says he knows you.'' She said she discovered that ''it was Bill, a lieutenant I had danced with just a few short days before at division's farewell party on Guam. . . . A shell fragment had severed his spinal cord.''

When every inch of space on deck and below was occupied by the wounded, there came the heartbreaking decision to up anchor and head for Saipan, leaving behind wounded men waiting to come aboard. "Don't go. Don't go! If I had my rifle I'd shoot you. Come back!" cried a youth they left behind.

One could hope he would be picked up by the *Samaritan*, the ship just behind the *Solace*, with photographer Dickey Chapelle aboard. The *Solace* would return as quickly as it could deliver its cargo to Saipan. Of the twenty-one thousand American casualties on Iwo Jima, more than forty-five hundred died.

Lockridge's next journey was aboard a C-54 plane carrying wounded from Saipan to Honolulu. Braced for the ever present danger that Japanese fighter planes would attack, they faced more peril when a smoking engine forced them to return to Saipan. Aloft again, Lockridge found herself changing the sheets of an inconsolable blind soldier. During the American invasion of Guam, he and four friends had found and drunk some whiskey the Japanese had poisoned. His friends died and he lost his sight. "How am I going to tell my parents?" he asked. "They don't drink. They think I was wounded in action." Another soldier, his legs shattered, was clinging desperately to a pair of boots; they were all he had to sustain his hope that one day he would walk again.

Lockridge shared with Martha Gellhorn a capacity to write with such compassion of the wounded that her readers would weep forty years later. While Gellhorn had to endure the assumption, made even by Lockridge, that she owed her success to her husband, Ernest Hemingway, Lockridge and other correspondents for the women's magazines had to deal with the equally wrong assumption that correspondents sent to war by magazines known mainly for covering food and fashion would not portray the war realistically.

In the Pacific and in Asia, there was a brief pause for a glorious celebration to make the end of World War II, but the fighting never ceased. In China, the defeat of the Japanese freed the Nationalists and the Communists to war against each other. With the help of U.S. Air Force and Navy planes, the Nationalists were taking over key cities. The Communists were occupying much of the hinterland. Among women correspondents, there was a changing of the guard.

Milwaukee-born Charlotte Ebener, having served in India for the American Red Cross during World War II, arrived in Chungking in October 1945 to report for International News Service at a salary of $75 a week, serving as a stringer for *Newsweek* as well.

The Russians had entered the war in the Pacific only days before the Japanese surrendered. In February 1946, nine American correspondents, Ebener the lone woman among them, boarded the Mukden Express and traveled in fourteen-degree-below-zero weather to see what the Russians were doing in Manchuria. She and her fellow correspondents found the Russians stripping Chinese factories of their machinery and preparing the Chinese Communists to rule the land they had taken over from the Japanese. The information was not easily acquired.

The Americans arrived in Mukden at 3:00 A.M. Lacking permission to enter Soviet-occupied territory, they argued that their visas for China should suffice. Russian officers, obviously uncertain as to how Moscow would react, put them up in a hotel, served them a banquet, then confined them to the hotel. Eventually word came that they could see what the Russians chose to show them.

To celebrate Red Army Day, the Russians gave a party. While the men were consuming vast quantities of vodka, Ebener sought to escape to her room. A Russian colonel, Ivan Kravchenko, followed and embraced her with a frightening bear hug. She kicked him, then escaped down the back stairs to the kitchen. Scullery maids, quick to grasp the situation, hid her in a potato bin. When the coast was clear, she met with fellow correspondents recovering from vodka paralysis, and they agreed to get out of town.

The correspondents took the first train out, to Ch'ang-ch'un, two hundred miles north and deeper into Manchuria. The Russians there were decidedly unfriendly. Ebener, suffering from chest pains, was seen by a Japanese physician who told her she had pleurisy. She later learned what the trouble really was: the Russian colonel, with his bear hug, had cracked three of her ribs.

A plane attempting to return the group to Peking made an

emergency landing in a Manchurian field. That night they spent in a hospital memorable for rats and bubonic plague patients. The only available train took them back to Mukden where they saw the Russians moving out. Nobody seemed to know why, but everybody was scrambling to get out at the same time. The correspondents knew that in the vacuum left by the Russians, war would erupt there between the Communists and the Nationalists. The Americans climbed onto another train. Chinese who could not find seats climbed to the roof. After twenty hours of numbing cold, they arrived in a town called Chinchow, outside the Russian-occupied area. Ebener climbed off in time to see a conductor carrying the body of a Chinese woman who had frozen to death on the roof of the train, a whimpering baby still in her arms.

Ebener reached the American military hospital in Peking by Marine plane. Her ribs taped, she returned within a month to Ch'ang-ch'un to witness the Russian withdrawal from that city. Among her traveling companions on these journeys were Reynolds Packard of United Press and Philip Potter of the *Baltimore Sun*. Ebener had eyes only for George Weller of the *Chicago Daily News*. On a plane flying them to Peking, she watched Weller typing his story, then typed a message to herself: "Charlotte, you are in love, and he doesn't give a damn." All they needed was time.

In Ch'ang-ch'un, as the last Russian car rolled out, a battle began between the Chinese Communists and the Nationalist troops of Chiang Kai-shek. Artillery and mortar shells exploded. The lights went out. The water went off. Communist tanks rumbled through the streets. The Russians had not allowed the Nationalists to have them.

"Is this the way a battle is when it's real?" Ebener whispered to Packard.

"Little girl," he said, "no battle was ever realer than this one."

"We correspondents never know what the hell is happening," Weller told her. "We just try to save our own necks and record the tiny personal victories and defeats in front of our own eyes. Later the generals add them up and announce who won and what the strategy was." Ebener would have to prove her mettle in Korea and in Vietnam before her future husband whispered anything more intimate.

As a result of World War II, Korea stood divided between Soviet and American occupiers at the thirty-eighth parallel. In South Korea, Syngman Rhee served as chief of state, having been placed in power by the Americans after thirty-five years' exile in the United States. When Ebener arrived in Korea in 1946, she encountered rioting in the streets of South Korean cities, where many were killed and wounded and thousands arrested. She saw hungry children with distended bellies and rickety legs.

Ebener assessed Rhee as totally corrupt and inept. The Americans had confiscated large estates owned by the Japanese rulers of Korea before World War II and turned them over to Rhee to distribute to peasants as a land reform measure. Instead, he used the property as his private pork barrel to deliver to his supporters, Ebener reported. Rhee also decimated the South Korean Army the Americans were attempting to train by rejecting officers strong enough to challenge him, she said.

As she also wrote, the U.S. military government issued an order that sharecroppers need pay only one third of their crop to their landlords, but it neglected to implement the law. The sharecroppers were forced to deliver half their crop to their landlords, leaving them without enough to feed their families. Far from penalizing the landlords, the military government hired them because they spoke English.

In American-sponsored elections, only the island of Changji-do, controlled by women pearl divers, dared elect two opponents of Syngman Rhee to the provisional government. When Ebener requested permission to visit the women leaders there, she was informed that there were "no facilities for women." No facilities for women on an Amazon island? Beyond that, her accreditation was withdrawn, and she was forced to leave.

From Korea, she flew to Cambodia in December 1946. On December 19, Viet Minh guerrillas crawled out of the sewers of Hanoi, Vietnam, and massacred every French citizen in sight. Ebener arrived before the stinking corpses were buried.

This was the beginning of the end for French rule in Indochina. Again, American editors could not have cared less. On a trip to the United States, she found the editors were only reflecting the indifference of the American public.

With George Weller, Ebener covered the civil war in Greece. When he went home, she flew on to report the turmoil in the Middle East. She and Phil Potter were in Amman, Jordan, when an Arab mob attacked, protesting American support for creation of the state of Israel. From Boston, Weller wired, "Come on home and marry me before you get yourself killed."

As Ebener wrote, the Soviet Union and the United States withdrew from Korea, and the United Nations sponsored free elections for South Korea in June 1950. Syngman Rhee lost his majority in the legislature. A week after the elections, before a government supported by the voters could be organized, North Korea invaded South Korea, and the South Korean army Rhee kept too weak to defy him fled rather than fight. Ebener was appalled when U.S. General Douglas MacArthur arrived and embraced Rhee soon after the invasion, in spite of his defeat at the polls.

Scores of American women correspondents covered the war in Korea, a fact later obscured by the celebrity status accorded Marguerite Higgins of the *New York Herald Tribune*. Foremost among them was Esther Van Wagoner Tufty, founder of the Tufty News Service in Washington, D.C., whose by-lined articles appeared in three hundred newspapers at the peak of her career. A woman so regal that everyone called her "the duchess," she wore her gold hair wrapped in braids around her head to form a coronet. She was fifty-five by the time she covered the war in Korea and seventy when she did the same in Vietnam.

Like Ebener, Tufty covered Korea before the war began there. At the home of her first cousin, Ethel Van Wagoner Underwood, and husband, Horace Underwood, missionaries and educators in Korea, she met with opponents of the Rhee regime. When the North Koreans invaded South Korea, they entered the Underwood home and shot and killed Mrs. Underwood, who may have been the first American casualty of that war.

Doors opened automatically for Tufty when she returned to cover the Korean War. She had more connections and background than her competitors. In Korea, she covered the war for two hundred fifty newspapers serviced by Central Press, a King Features affiliate. In addition, she broadcast spot news for NBC television. Nobody in sight boasted such an audience.

Tufty epitomized the globetrotters. In command of her own bureau, she was not dependent on editors for assignments. She could go where she chose, and she never failed to show up for a disaster. She covered the war in Britain and rode the Berlin airlift sitting on a load of coal. In Vietnam, the enemy fired and hit the wing of a helicopter taking her to visit a Vietnamese hospital. ''We were a sitting duck. It was an awful feeling,'' she recalled. ''Then I reminded myself, 'You didn't have to come.' ''

So long as newsmen with the stature and the status of Bob Considine of the Hearst newspapers and Phil Potter covered the Korean War, men and women correspondents worked together. But after the first year of warfare, the first team was withdrawn. The replacements, by and large, were youngsters in their twenties with little news and no war experience. Female competition was the last thing they wanted.

As late as 1952, newsmen in Tokyo were warning women against going to Korea, saying they would be raped. In Seoul, securely behind the lines, they told women they had no business going to the front and tantalizing those sex-starved soldiers. When this failed, they sought to arouse guilt. At division headquarters, a woman's tent had to be guarded, and that meant taking a soldier away from the war. The solution was to fly over division headquarters to regimental headquarters, so close to the front that the whole camp had to be guarded against North Korean infiltrators. Even closer to the front, at battalion headquarters, within mortar range of the enemy, colonels welcomed women for bringing a reminder of home to the warfront, and Army commanders paraded them to restore morale.

Before I left Tokyo to cover the war as a correspondent for the Overseas News Agency, I was told not to wear a dress in Korea lest I unduly excite the men. Thus I arrived at a reception given by President Syngman Rhee in Seoul wearing Army issue khaki trousers, only to find the newsmen who had told me not to dress escorting Korean beauties in fluffy white national costume.

Newsmen pulled dirty tricks on each other all the time, and extending them to women was a backhanded way of treating them as equals. Their advice on what to wear to war was at best a new twist on an old trick, telling a man a party was informal, then arriving in black tie to watch the butt of the joke squirm in his beach wear.

The young correspondents in Korea knew when to stop. Indeed, they treated senior correspondents like Tufty with proper respect. Times had changed since the days when newsmen seriously believed that women correspondents could disrupt a war.

14

The Outrageous
Marguerite Higgins

MARGUERITE HIGGINS, A TALL BLONDE WITH THE FACE OF A Barbie doll and the mannerisms one might expect of the little girl who owned it, arrived in Japan in disgrace. For antagonizing fellow *Herald Tribune* correspondents as well as the opposition, she was demoted from chief of her paper's Berlin bureau to correspondent in Tokyo, where only the cherry blossoms attracted attention in the spring of 1950. Weeks passed before she filed a news story, and that was about elections in Korea.

The world would not soon forget what happened next. A force of sixty thousand North Koreans attacked South Korea on June 25. Of a defending force of one hundred thousand South Koreans, eighty thousand fled rather than fight.

With three other correspondents, Higgins reached the South Korean capital of Seoul two days later aboard a plane sent to evacuate civilians. By the time they arrived, the invaders were within seven miles of the city. She was billeted with Colonel Sterling Wright, acting chief of the U.S. Military Advisory Group. Aware that they might have to flee during the night, she lay down fully clothed.

Almost immediately, she was awakened with the news "They've broken through." Soon mortar shells were bursting around the billet. As the Americans raced by jeep toward the Han River Bridge, their escape route to the south, an orange flame tore through the rainy darkness. South Koreans in a panic were blowing up the bridge while truckloads of their own troops were trying to cross it, and many were killed. Higgins managed to get across the river by ferry, then confronted the ordeal of walking fourteen miles across a mountain trail to the town of Suwan. Along the way, she saw Korean soldiers throw down their weapons and run simply at the sight of Americans walking toward them.

The American Army moved in under the umbrella of the United Nations, and eventually many nations sent military units to support the U.N. command. From the start, Higgins witnessed the horror of the war, and she did not spare her readers. On the outskirts of Seoul she came upon a wounded Marine Corps medic whose jeep had been blown up. She saw the will to live staring out of his eyes. He made no cry. ''There was only the burbling of blood on the shredded lips as he gasped hard, his breath forming red bubbles.''

At the beginning, she had to fly to Tokyo to file her stories and fly back the next day. When communications finally were established in Korea, there were endless delays. In those days of rout, there were no beds, no toilet facilities for the correspondents. They slept in jeeps or on the ground and used bushes. At best, when they found shelter, Higgins slept on a table. Far from causing trouble in Korea, she astonished field commanders by her coolness under fire. In one dangerous spot, a medic administering plasma to the wounded ran out of supplies. While he raced back for more plasma, she administered the lifesaving fluid.

In Korea, women correspondents were still resented by their male counterparts, Bob Considine, the prize-winning correspondent of the International News Service, observed. It was unnerving, he said, ''to be huddling in a hole, frightened, and look up long enough to see a good-looking babe moving up closer to the fighting.'' About Higgins, Considine told this story. On a dangerous patrol action, the troops were pinned down by a heavy mortar attack. She and a soldier hit a ditch simultaneously. As enemy shells came closer, Higgins was quoted as saying, ''I've had a full life. I don't mind dying.'' At this, above the sound of exploding shells, the soldier yelled, ''Maybe so lady. But goddamnit, don't go including me.''

Marguerite Higgins risked her life repeatedly to cover the war in Korea, for which she won national acclaim. The Overseas Press Club presented her with the George Polk Memorial Award for overseas reporting requiring exceptional courage. With five fellow correspondents, she shared the 1951 Pulitzer Prize for international reporting.

Yet Higgins never could resist exaggerating her considerable achievements. Publishers, publicists, biographers, and lovers joined in the game of embellishing the truth. Her enemies, and she made many, conspired to tear her down. She became the most controversial personality in the press corps. Some have attempted to describe her as a golden girl, successful at everything she attempted. In creating a myth, they destroyed the drama of her struggle for success.

Like Marilyn Monroe, she was pretty, talented, sexy, and painfully insecure. Each made a tremendous splash in her profession. Both died tragically when they were much too young. Nobody paid them the respect of attempting to place them in the history of their professions. Marilyn was no Sarah Bernhardt. Marguerite was no Margaret Fuller, neither an innovative thinker nor a pioneer in her profession. After World War II, a world weary of tragedy chose heroines with feminine wiles. As superstars, their audiences invented them.

In her autobiography, Higgins revealed more of herself than others attempted. Her father, a World War I pilot, married a French woman in Paris and took his bride to Hong Kong, where Marguerite was born. As a baby, she was sent to a health resort in Vietnam to recuperate from an illness. After these exotic beginnings, the small family came down to earth. Marguerite grew up in what she remembered as a dreary middle-class suburb of Oakland, California, with an alcoholic father and a mother addicted to fainting spells when crossed. The child saw herself as under enormous pressure to realize the shattered dreams of her parents. "I don't recall there was any time at all to have fun," she said. Her mother taught French at a fashionable girls' school, and Marguerite attended the school on scholarship, forever struggling with a sense of inferiority to her wealthy classmates.

Those who knew her as a student at the University of California at Berkeley said her self-esteem was so low that she did not bother to wash or change her clothes. At the Columbia University Graduate School of Journalism, where I met her in the fall of 1941, she was neat enough but cold toward women students.

A male classmate at Columbia helped Higgins obtain a job as campus correspondent of the *New York Herald Tribune*, and she concentrated on it to the extent that she did not do as well in her studies as she later pretended. Elie Abel, who would achieve prestige as a correspondent and dean of the School of Journalism, won a Pulitzer Traveling Fellowship, and Higgins told the world she was his alternate. In truth, Higgins ranked fifth among thirteen women in the class of 1942, behind Jane Dealy, who won a Pulitzer Fellowship, and three women who won other travel awards.

Not that she had time to travel. A June graduate and a June bride, Higgins married Stanley Moore, a Harvard University philosophy professor, a week before he was drafted into the Army. After a brief honeymoon, they were separated while her husband went through basic training and reunited for an even shorter holiday on Nantucket before he was shipped overseas. Moore was sent to Russia, and Higgins, envisioning him having affairs with beautiful ballerinas, talked openly about her own infidelities, an indiscretion the marriage could not survive.

The love of her life was the news business, and when she was put on the city staff of the *Herald Tribune* at the age of twenty-one, her marriage ceased to matter. Attributing her good fortune to the fact that men were being drafted, she described herself as a war profiteer.

Still eager for parental approval, Higgins wrote her mother that she was "the second woman ever to be hired as a straight news reporter on the *Tribune*," a bit of childish braggadocio memorable mainly because her biographer quoted it with a straight face. In contrast to the *New York Times*, the *Tribune* had employed women news reporters ever since it hired Emma Bugbee in 1911 and Ishbel Ross in 1919. Fay Wells, Tanya Long, and Sonia Tomara were *Tribune* foreign correspondents a few years before Higgins. Long had recently served on the city staff; Tomara and Ann Cottrell were there when Higgins arrived.

Real competition and basic insecurity combined to keep Higgins running scared. As a cub reporter on the *Herald Tribune*, she was sent to Hyde Park, New York, where women reporters had been invited to meet the First Lady, Eleanor Roosevelt. Higgins was caught, her competitors said, reading their copy in the telegraph office before she filed her own.

Big blue eyes, a high-pitched little girl's voice, and sex appeal were part of her arsenal. As a last resort, she used her head. When her editors at the *Herald Tribune* refused to send her overseas, Higgins went over their heads to Helen Rogers Reid, the feminist wife of the publisher, and in August 1944, she finally won permission to travel to London. An attempt at reconciliation with her husband in London failed, and she spent the last months of the war in Europe working in the Paris bureau, where her knowledge of French helped her do well.

The flamboyant Marguerite her fans would adore emerged on a jeep trip into southern Germany as the Nazis were collapsing. A rumor that American troops were about to liberate the concentration camp at Dachau inspired Higgins and Sergeant Peter Furst of the *Stars and Stripes* to cut across six miles of territory still held by the enemy to reach the prison compound. Along the way, they passed group after group of fully armed Wehrmacht soldiers prepared to surrender even to them. Infantrymen surrendered as many weapons as their jeep could hold, and German villagers actually cheered them.

At the town of Dachau, some miles from the concentration camp, they learned that Americans were still fighting SS troops in the vicinity and had yet to reach the prison camp. But Germans had seen white flags on the southern edges of the huge camp area. So they pushed ahead until they encountered an SS general staggering under a heavy white flag on a pole, and they accepted his surrender. Alas, the German commandant did not know whether SS guards still manning watchtowers were as ready as he to surrender. There was only one way to find out, and the two correspondents jeeped off to the watchtower area, where they decided to reconnoiter on foot.

As Higgins was turning a corner into a courtyard, Furst spotted SS guards on a tower with a machine gun trained on her, and he shouted frantically for her to return to the jeep. As she told the story,

> I looked up. There was a watchtower crammed with . . . SS men. They were staring intently at me. Rifles were at the ready, and the machine gun was trained on me. God knows what prompted me other than the instinctive feeling that there was absolutely no point in running. Instead of heeding the frantic sergeant, I addressed myself to the SS guards. "Kommen Sie her, bitte. Wir sind Amerikaner." Come here, please. We are Americans.

Whereupon twenty-two SS guards came down from the tower and surrendered to her.

Furst and Higgins chose one SS guard to lead them to the prison barracks. At sight of Americans, prisoners exploded out of their quarters in hysterical frenzy, embraced all three newcomers, and hoisted them on their shoulders. The Americans lost sight of the German at first mistaken as a liberator, but he was soon found out. Later in the day, Higgins stepped over a body outside the prison gates. It was the SS guard whom the prisoners had beaten to death.

What should have been a day of jubilation turned into stark horror when the American forces arrived at Dachau and prisoners wild with excitement were told they would have to be inoculated and quarantined before they could be released. At this they rioted. In suicidal protest, a half dozen threw themselves against the electrically charged fences, electrocuting themselves. Higgins and Furst managed to get on the loudspeaker system and, in German, appeal to the prisoners for calm. An American general tried to eject Higgins from the camp, but she would not leave. After calm was restored, that same general saw to it that she won the Army campaign ribbon for outstanding service under difficult conditions. For the story, the New York Newspaper Women's Club gave her its award for best foreign correspondence of 1945.

During the liberation of Buchenwald concentration camp, Higgins came upon twenty American soldiers methodically taking turns beating six captured Germans. The bloodied and battered prisoners were teenagers, fourteen to seventeen years of age, recently drafted into forced labor battalions, not the SS guards responsible for conditions at that camp. A fellow correspondent, Percy Knauth, found an officer to put a stop to the brutality.

"You know what will happen if we say anything," Higgins remarked to Knauth. Generals who would not have countenanced such behavior nevertheless managed to punish correspondents for reporting anything detrimental to the armed forces. Higgins not only reported the incident, she delved for its meaning. Convinced by what she had witnessed that Americans could be as brutal as Germans, she found the difference between a fascist society and the American way in the democratic system of checks and balances, the free press, the legal safeguards, the reins on absolute power.

Demonstrating no proper regard for personal safety, she took off alone by automobile for Warsaw, ignoring the warnings of fellow correspondents that she would be robbed, raped, and shot along the way. Against Army regulations, she chose to drive through the Soviet zone of Germany, where spare parts for her automobile remained nonexistent, and into Poland, still in a state of civil war. While World War II had ended, Polish patriots persisted in fighting a Communist government. She found the roads deserted and made it to Warsaw in record time.

In 1947, at the age of twenty-six, in the tradition of Sigrid Schultz and Dorothy Thompson, Higgins was named chief of the Berlin bureau of the *Herald Tribune*. Far from gaining self-confidence, she confessed to moments of inner panic.

I felt if I made the slightest mistake my new job might be taken away from me. I can't explain this continuing lack of self-confidence. But I'm not exaggerating it. . . . For a long time when any one of my competitors produced a major scoop, I took it as a personal disaster. That sort of reaction makes for a chaotic emotional life, but it does generate lots of nervous energy. And this motivation— partly fear—kept me doggedly and singlemindedly occupied with my job.

The 1948 Russian blockade of Berlin, calculated to starve the Germans into submission, came as a relief to her. "I thoroughly enjoyed the excitement and even the hard work," she said, "partly because it left no time for the introspective brooding toward which I have a pronounced tendency." She remained a classic case of success anxiety.

As Higgins saw it, aloneness was the price she paid for success. Most correspondents would recall Berlin after World War II as a wonderfully social setting for them. Even as she turned to a procession of personable fellow correspondents to relieve moments of depression, Higgins insisted her job was "too demanding to permit other involvements."

Her incredible competitiveness provoked the feud that eventually caused the newspaper's editors to send Higgins to Coventry in Tokyo. Among her chosen enemies was Drew Middleton, the distinguished Berlin bureau chief of the *New York Times*. Never a team player, she made enemies even of fellow *Herald Tribune* correspondents. There were endless anecdotes of petty behavior, such as the one about how she tagged along on an interview with a fellow correspondent, then filed his story as her own. Men accused her of hyping her stories beyond their importance to make page one, then having the gall to criticize them for not exaggerating. "She was a dangerous, venomous bitch and a bad reporter" is the way *Tribune* correspondent Stephen White summed up the charges against her.

Her enemies accused her of sleeping with men to get her stories, but her lovers were mainly fellow correspondents. One could as well accuse them of sleeping with her to get their stories. Never truly promiscuous, she fit the pattern of the young woman so insecure she doubted men would care for her unless she gave them sex. The gossip increased to outrageous proportions when she settled on one man, Major General Wilson Hall, who had a wife and four children in the States. The double standard was never more evident than in the fact that newsmen who cheated on their wives and children back home aroused no criticism.

Her editors nevertheless concluded that Higgins was overintense, overeager, and incapable of getting along with fellow reporters. Over her protests, they delivered the injunction: go to Tokyo or quit.

When she refused to stay put in Tokyo and went on to Korea, both the U.S. Army and the senior *Herald Tribune* correspondent, Homer Bigart, undertook to banish her. She was doing a commendable job when U.S. Lieutenant General Walton H. Walker issued an order banning all women from Korea on grounds that "there are no facilities for ladies at the front." From the day the war began, women correspondents clamored to cover it, and the Army was not accrediting them. For the sake of consistency, Walker sent Higgins back to Tokyo.

Helen Rogers Reid, by then president of the *Herald Tribune*, appealed the decision to the commanding general, Douglas MacArthur, an action recalling the way she went to bat to get accreditation for Sonia Tomara in World War II. MacArthur immediately overruled Walker, and the good news was awaiting Higgins when she arrived in Tokyo. Part of the consequence was female competition for Higgins. This was easier to handle than Homer Bigart.

When the war erupted, the *Tribune* rushed Bigart, a famous war correspondent, to Korea, and he ordered Higgins back to Tokyo. But she had been there first, and she refused to go. In anger, he told her she would be fired if she did not obey his orders, and he added his opinion that she did not have a single friend in Tokyo. Forever aware of her own deficiencies, she later admitted, "He was probably right."

Higgins blamed the animosity toward her on a misunderstanding. She was accused of breaking an agreement to delay filing a story about American bombings of North Korea. Her version was that she made no such agreement. Besides, she could not recall filing the story.

Higgins won permission to remain in Korea from the home office. The story was big enough for two, but instead of sharing the assignment, these two competed fiercely to produce the bigger news story. Fellow correspondents, relishing the dispute, hired Korean urchins to gather outside Bigart's billet at a time he needed his sleep and chant "Homer loves Maggie! Homer loves Maggie!" As those who taunted him knew, Bigart was no more a team player than Higgins.

Ansel Talbert, noted for his reporting on aviation, was also there and wrote more benignly than most about the famous Bigart-Higgins feud. "Both Homer and Maggie were exceptionally talented, courageous and resourceful, and both were motivated by a burning compulsion to go where the biggest news was, regardless of danger, to get a story," he said.

Higgins usually managed to get closer to the front than Bigart, and one way she did it was to join forces with Keyes Beech of the *Chicago Daily News*, the proud possessor of a jeep. "The front is no place for a woman, but it's all right for Maggie Higgins," he said.

She was alone, however, on September 15, when she covered the Inchon landing, a naval assault calculated to cut North Korean forces in two and a turning point in the war. Press officers, intending to relegate her to a hospital ship, made the mistake of issuing orders intended for men, allowing them to board "any Navy ship." In the staging area she made her way aboard a troop transport, one of 260 ships involved in the action, and four days later she hit the beach with the fifth wave of assault troops.

With the troops, Higgins descended from the ship to a landing boat in a cargo net. In a surprise attack, earlier waves of Marines had made it to shore safely. But now the enemy was mustering all its firepower. As she wrote,

> The channel reverberated with the ear-splitting boom of warship guns and rockets. Blue and orange flames spurted from the Red Beach area and a huge oil tank on fire sent great black rings of smoke over the shore. Then the fire from the big guns lifted and the planes that had been circling overhead swooped low to rake their fire deep into the seawall.

As their craft wove its way toward the seawall, a news photographer with her said, "I've had enough! I'm heading back to the ship, are you?'' He intended to return to the ship with the landing craft after it dropped off the Marines. Instinctively, Higgins said, ''No, I'm going ahead.'' As she later admitted, the decision was not rational. ''Instinctive pride,'' she called it.

Enemy tracer bullets cut across their bow. ''The quake and roar of the rocket ships was almost unendurable,'' she wrote. Somehow she managed to hold on to her typewriter as she jumped from the boat into three feet of water. Thirty Marines and three correspondents climbed ashore and snaked their way on their stomachs over boulders to a hiding place, where they could watch wave after wave of Marines hitting the beach behind them. In the confusion, Americans fired on their own forces. And worse, she reported:

> Suddenly a rush of water came up into the dip in the wall and we saw a huge LST rushing at us with the great plank door half down. Six more yards and the ship would have crushed twenty men. Warning shouts sent everyone speeding from the seawall searching for escape from the LST and cover from the gunfire. The LST's huge bulk sent a rush of water pouring over the seawall as it crunched in, soaking most of us. . . . Two Marines in the back were caught and their feet badly crushed before they could be yanked to safety.

By 7:00 P.M. the shore was fairly secure, and Higgins boarded the flagship *McKinley* to file her story. The correspondents who had covered the landing gathered in the wardroom, and she discovered that the *McKinley* even had a ladies' room. To her horror, she also encountered the officer who had consigned her to a hospital ship from shore. While she was allowed to spend that night on the *McKinley*, the Navy decreed the next day that women would not be allowed aboard ship between 9:00 P.M. and 9:00 A.M. So while male correspondents went ashore and returned to the ship to sleep in comfort, take a morning shower, and breakfast on scrambled eggs, she had to sleep on the dock with the troops and breakfast on cold rations. What mattered more to her was that for those twelve hours she could not use the cable facilities. In addition to the possibility of missing a major news story that might break at night, she frequently spent half the night writing her story and needed to file it as quickly as possible to meet her deadlines.

Despite the obstacles, she felt she did her best reporting at Inchon. For that alone, she earned her Pulitzer. Shouts of "first woman to win," by now a cliché of the profession, helped her sell a book and book a lecture tour. It was a reminder that the *New York Times* had to issue a correction in 1937 when it described Anne O'Hare McCormick as the first woman to win a Pulitzer. A Pulitzer Prize for meritorious public service had been awarded to Minna Lewisson in 1918 for a history of services rendered to the public by the American press during 1917, the year the United States entered World War I. Where McCormick single-handedly won the first Pulitzer awarded a woman journalist, coverage of the Korean War was so spectacular that the judges honored six correspondents—Keyes Beech and Fred Sparks of the *Chicago Daily News*, Homer Bigart and Marguerite Higgins of the *Herald Tribune*, and Relman Morin and Don Whitehead of the Associated Press. Publicists could always find a way, and they came up with the information that Higgins was the first woman to win for combat correspondence.

When Chinese forces entered the Korean War on November 26, 1950, Higgins advocated using the atom bomb. The prospect of covering a war for the Chinese mainland struck her as more inviting than reporting stalemate in Korea.

After eight months in Korea, she returned to the United States and married General Hall. Their first child died at birth, but they soon had two more. Without letting her family interfere with her career, Higgins circled the globe and interviewed chiefs of state for the *Herald Tribune*. By 1954 she was in Vietnam to cover the French defeat in the battle of Dien Bien Phu, the end of French colonialism in Indochina, the beginning of American involvement in the area.

Between assignments, Higgins wrote books, six in all. When *Herald Tribune* editors failed to give her assignments she wanted, she covered events for magazines and filed sidebars to the paper. While assigned to the Washington bureau, she was more her own boss than she really enjoyed. This was one way of easing her out, and soon after President John F. Kennedy's inauguration in 1961, she quit the *Tribune* to write a syndicated column for *Newsday*, the Long Island newspaper.

In mid-1963 Higgins went to Vietnam for *Newsday* and wrote, "Like almost every American in Southeast Asia, I believe Vietnam to be as much a front line of freedom as Hawaii or San Francisco." This was before Congress passed the Gulf of Tonkin resolution enabling President Lyndon Johnson to escalate the war in Vietnam, and already other American correspondents in Vietnam were warning against it.

Her advocacy of American involvement in Vietnam sparked a feud with David Halberstam of the *New York Times* that put her fight with Homer Bigart in the shade. As Halberstam told the story,

> A well known journalist from Washington named Marguerite Higgins, who was very much a voice of the Pentagon, came out to Saigon for a brief tour. She soon went around telling other reporters what she had been told by a Marine general in Washington. Halberstam, she said, quoting the general, had been shown a photo of a bunch of Vietcong bodies, and he had burst into tears. Tears were for women, of course, and not only had I wept, but I had wept for the other side.

Halberstam confronted her. "I know what you've been saying to reporters in Washington about me crying over seeing a bunch of bodies, and it's crap. Do you hear me? Crap! I've been on more than fifty missions in this country, and I've seen a lot of bodies, and I don't cry." Two decades later, Halberstam would say he was sorry only for having failed to weep for the dead on both sides of that war.

Outrageous was the word for the escalation of their personal war. Halberstam described Higgins and Joseph Alsop, syndicated columnists, as "not among resident correspondents but visiting journalists . . . who were there not so much to report on the war as to strengthen policy." Higgins said that correspondents who refused to fight were cowards, ignoring the fact that correspondents were in constant danger and frequently getting killed.

Her Vietnam credentials predated his. While never permanently assigned to Vietnam, she was on her ninth trip to the area when they locked horns. Alas, her French background, her early associations with Vietnam, her military marriage, conspired to leave her dreaming of what might have been under mandarins and cultivated Frenchmen rather than what was possible after 1963. Those who had known Asia longest loved it most and insisted it should not change. Their twofold error consisted of the notion that the United States somehow could keep Asia the way they remembered it and their emotional conclusion that it was vital to American interests.

On her tenth trip to Vietnam in 1965, Higgins contracted a tropical disease. In one book she had said that her grandfather died of battle wounds received in Vietnam, in another, of a tropical fever. Whatever the truth, it should have served as a warning. She was flown to Walter Reed Hospital in Washington for medical treatment. Then, without the permission of physicians or family, she had herself wheeled out of the hospital to appear in New York on the television show "Today." It was her last hurrah. Soon after her return from New York, she died at the age of forty-five.

Those who knew her speculated that if she had only conserved her strength, she might have lived another forty years. Those who knew her best knew there was no way of stopping her. They recalled that she had been in a jeep accident with Keyes Beech in Korea, suffering a severe blow to the head and a possible concussion. Refusing a stretcher when the ambulance arrived, she insisted on riding in the front seat. Walking into the hospital, she collapsed on the stairs. The next day she forced Beech to smuggle in some clothes so she could sneak out of the hospital against doctor's orders.

She would be remembered not for brilliance but because she was fearless. As a correspondent, she made it because she was as intelligent as her competitors and would rather die than face defeat. As a woman, she was reckless because what mattered more to her than life was winning.

15

Last Stop, Vietnam

THEY TOLD HER NOT TO DO IT.

"No daughter of mine is going to set foot in an airplane."

The year was 1935, and Dickey Chapelle was sixteen years old when her mother issued the edict. The attitude was old-fashioned, but the mother knew her daughter. Give the child a scenic flight over Milwaukee and she would escalate it into a flight over the South Pole.

At eighteen Dickey could pilot a plane. During the fighting for Okinawa in World War II, she moved into no man's land with the Marines under enemy fire to rescue the wounded, an infraction that got her evicted from the Pacific war. The one thing no woman, not even Dickey Chapelle, managed to do in World War II was parachute with the troops, but that was only the first of three wars and four revolutions she covered. During the war in Vietnam, she parachuted into jungle territory held by the Communist Vietcong.

While her mother taught her caution, Dickey's father, a salesman of construction equipment, taught her how to walk across high boards and roof beams at building sites. "Don't look down. Look ahead," he told her.

Dickey learned not to look down and more. She learned a way to get ahead: never pause to calculate the consequences. Although she called herself a tomboy, she was better described as a tomgirl, for she didn't want to be a boy. She just wanted to do the things boys get to do. Nobody said she was pretty, but she had an open face, a wide grin, and sparkling eyes. As an adult, she wore her long hair wrapped in a bun and, even in Marine combat issue, never went without two tiny pearl earrings.

A whiz at math, she entered the Massachusetts Institute of Technology at sixteen on a full tuition scholarship. But when she should have been studying, she could be found at an airport watching the planes take off. Eventually a pilot let her board a plane taking off to deliver relief supplies to a flooded city. Remembering Mama, she paused halfway up the ladder, but only for a moment. Next she was flying with a stunt pilot, then learning to fly the plane. When she flunked out of MIT, she landed a job in airline public relations.

At nineteen, Dickey, born Georgette Meyer in Milwaukee, Wisconsin, married her photography teacher, Anthony ("Tony") Chapelle. A perfectionist twice her age, he taught her how to sell her picture stories to major magazines. During World War II, he joined the Navy, and Dickey followed him to Panama as an accredited correspondent for *Look* magazine after the Navy had evacuated wives. This arrangement blew up literally, the day she photographed Secretary of the Navy Frank Knox, who was making an inspection tour in the Canal Zone, and the flashbulb on her camera exploded like a pistol shot. Knox, the former publisher of the *Chicago Daily News*, did not complain. Besides, the Navy Department could not withdraw the accreditation the War Department had given her. But having separated the rest of the Navy officers in Panama from their wives, Tony Chapelle's superiors shipped him to New York, and again Dickey followed.

When the Navy decided to send Tony to Chungking, China, Dickey applied for navy accreditation to cover the Pacific war for Fawcett Publications, whose magazines included *Woman's Day* and *Popular Mechanics*. Since she could not work in the same war theater with her husband, she chose the war front closest to him. Her orders arrived in ten days, well before his, and this time the husband saw his wife off to war.

In California the Navy informed her that she could serve as a reporter or as a photographer, but not as the reporter-photographer Fawcett wanted. The Navy would let her use its facilities to transmit articles or photographs, not both. She chose to be a photographer because there were no women competitors in sight.

On the flight to Honolulu in February 1945, the radio was sputtering news of serious American casualties in the assault on Iwo Jima. Although the Navy had not promised to send her west of Hawaii, it took only hours to put her on a plane to Guam with a group of American nurses. There she learned she could ship out at dawn aboard the hospital ship USS *Samaritan*, en route to Iwo Jima.

At sunrise, she found the big ship painted gleaming white with red crosses four decks high on either side. The first exercise was a battle drill.

"Isn't this ship protected by the Geneva Convention?" Dickey asked.

"You know any Japanese ever heard of it?" a Navy corpsmen replied.

At dawn the next day she was awakened by the alarm klaxon— the Japanese were attacking the unarmed vessel. While others ran for cover, Dickey raced for the ladder and up to the flying bridge. From her perch she shot the attacking plane with her camera just as it swerved off course under fire from a neighborly destroyer. The *Samaritan* survived the attack, and six days after the Marines had stormed Iwo Jima, the hospital ship arrived to take aboard the wounded.

"A part of the deck was for the stretchers of the men who had died in the boats on their way to us," Dickey wrote. But they soon ran out of space.

Time and again, I would hear the doctor, his face stiff, hoarsely tell a boat crew that one of their casualties had reached us too late. "Take him back, cox'n. We only have space for the living." Often the boat crew refused to believe the doctor. "He isn't dead, Doc," they insisted. "You can save him." At last, the doctor would simply wave them away.

The dead were carried back to the beach.

Dickey did not anticipate that a picture she snapped routinely as the wounded were lifted aboard the *Samaritan* would become one of the most famous pictures of World War II; she labeled it "The Dying Marine." Deeply cut by a shell fragment, the Marine had been bleeding for five hours before her camera recorded his condition.

The next day she encountered a bright and vital youngster, Private First Class Johnny Hood from Waycross, Georgia. "Hey, you made my picture yesterday," he remembered. At first, Dickey did not recognize "The Dying Marine," restored by fourteen pints of blood. She took a second picture, and for the next decade, her pair of contrasting photographs spurred blood donor drives across the United States.

The nationwide response to the pictures inspired both Dickey and the Navy to concentrate on a common goal, to increase the contribution of blood to save the wounded. Assigned by the Navy to photograph its casualties, she could not resist pursuing a goal the Navy declined to share with a woman, portraying the courage of the United States Marines in action.

On her second trip to Iwo Jima, she experienced in one gruesome day the three progressive stages of covering a war under enemy fire: first, the long-range but deadly artillery fire; next, the medium-range and constant mortar barrages, and finally, firing her camera back within rifle range of Japanese snipers.

The Air Force sent planes to Iwo Jima to pick up the wounded Marines for whom there had been no room on the hospital ships, and by D-Day plus twelve Dickey was aboard a DC-3, circling the one airport on the island the Marines had captured, looking down at blossoms of dust caused by Japanese artillery shells exploding on the field. When they had not seen any blossoms for ten minutes, they landed. The Japanese lobbed mortar shells over a ridge and into her path on the way to two tents that served as a field hospital.

A soldier with a broken, twisted leg watched from a stretcher as she photographed a surgeon operating with a few medical instruments, no hospital equipment. Noticing that she had no gun, the soldier fumbled at his belt and gave her his trench knife. "Where I'm going, I won't need one. If you ever do, you'll need it bad."

Marines in a weapons carrier drove her forty minutes away from the hospital, to a point where she could hear rifle shots. For a picture of Marines firing from foxholes, she climbed a ridge. Because she was scared, she kept telling herself that the Marine lieutenant who had brought her would call her back if she went too far. Instead, he waited until she returned to explode. "Do you realize that all the snipers on both sides of this fucking war had ten full minutes to make up their minds about you?"

With the Allied invasion convoys off Okinawa in April 1945, Dickey wheedled permission to go ashore at Brown Beach for only an afternoon to photograph one man getting a blood transfusion. The driver of an amphibious tractor took her to Orange Beach instead and left her stranded for the night. Two Marines took her up a coastal road to General Lemuel C. Shepherd, commander of the Sixth Marine Division. Although he knew she had no permission to be there, he was neither surprised nor sorry to see her. Women correspondents bolstered morale just by being there and demonstrating that the world cared what happened to men risking their lives in war.

On the way to the forwardmost medical aid station the next day, her jeep passed in front of a tank firing at the Japanese. The tank crew elevated the barrel to let them by, then lowered it to fire again without missing a shot. That night in the aid station she discovered a need for the trench knife the wounded Marine on Iwo Jima had given her. A Marine pharmacist showed her to a cot and said, "Just sleep in your helmet and keep your knife out of the sheath and in your hand."

The people of Okinawa were Japanese nationals living just 350 miles from the home islands of Japan, and children begging candy from the Marines would tell Japanese soldiers where to find Santa Claus, enabling the enemy mortars to fire with deadly accuracy. Dickey roamed the front with the medics, rescuing the wounded.

Never fearless in the way Marguerite Higgins was fearless, Dickey confessed that she was scared half to death half the time. She equated courage with overcoming fear. Identifying with the courageous Marines, she was not about to let them down.

Not until she had been on Okinawa for five days did she learn that the Marines had been hiding her from Navy officers broadcasting repeated orders to arrest her on sight. One Marine swore the first order was to ''shoot on sight.'' When she was sure she had pictures enough to inspire the American public to give rivers of blood for the wounded, she surrendered. Confined to an LST, a small Navy vessel, she lived through the worst Japanese kamikaze attack of the war on the American fleet, then was delivered to the airport on shore at the point of a gun, her departure from the war as abrupt as her introduction to it. Okinawa was not secured until June.

For nearly a decade after World War II, Dickey and Tony Chapelle roamed the world. *Look, Life*, the *National Geographic, Cosmopolitan* magazine, *Seventeen*—virtually every outlet for first-rate photography used their pictures of a suffering world. They also worked with the Quakers, for expenses only, to publicize the needs of the refugees. ''The wreckage resulting from man's inhumanity to man . . . was the litany I wrote and the subject I photographed,'' Dickey said.

But by 1955, when I met her at the Overseas Press Club in New York, her marriage was breaking up. She never said why. Others saw it coming. ''Tony was earthbound,'' a photo editor commented on the man and his work. Dickey was the one with imagination, dash, and glamour. The daughter Tony had married had grown up. The pupil became the celebrity of the team. Financial troubles brought emotional strain. Perhaps Tony felt he no longer was needed, but if so, he was wrong.

She was living in an apartment the size of a cell in an East Side New York tenement. There was no room for an easy chair, scarcely space for her typewriter. Her pictures, beautifully mounted, competed for space with albums of impressive picture stories. Having established herself as one of the best photographers in the news business, she had to face reality in the decade of the fifties. Nobody was hiring women photographers; the war was over, and hiring women was out of style.

For security there was no better job than the one I was leaving to return to Europe. So Dickey followed me as public information director of the Research Institute of America, a large business advisory organization. The fascination of the job for her was working with Leo Cherne, who was both executive director of the Research Institute and chairman of the International Rescue Committee (IRC), aiding refugees around the world.

In November 1956, Russian forces crushed a revolt against the Soviet-dominated regime in Hungary, and refugees began pouring out of the country. Leo Cherne went to Vienna to negotiate delivery of IRC medical supplies to the wounded in Hungary through the International Red Cross, and Dickey went with him, traveling on assignment for *Life* magazine to photograph refugees arriving in Austria.

While Cherne's efforts in Vienna to get medical supplies into Hungary progressed slowly, Dickey met refugees at the Austrian border and listened, as long as she could take it, to their stories of the suffering of Hungarians they had left behind. The Russians were laying minefields and establishing lines to prevent others from escaping. Alone and on her own, Dickey located men whose mission was to guide the refugees through the minefields to freedom, and with them she slipped into Hungary at night. Wearing a Hungarian peasant costume, she carried a small camera, infrared bulbs for night photography, and as much penicillin as she could handle, to be used for the wounded.

The Russians captured her quickly and confined her to a Budapest prison, where she languished while Americans virtually disowned her in their rush to deny any knowledge of or involvement in her mad scheme. Before she crossed the Hungarian border, *Life* magazine had managed to get a staff correspondent accredited to Budapest. To protect his status, the magazine declined to defend her unauthorized journey. As for her mercy mission, the medical supplies she carried could not have made a dent in the problem. Her excursion had jeopardized the efforts of the International Rescue Committee to obtain permission to deliver truckloads of supplies to the wounded. Leo Cherne could do nothing for her because to go to her defense would have been to invite the Russians to believe that the IRC had connived in her escapade.

The American embassy in Vienna wanted no part of her problem. Since Americans prized their right to hang any foreigner penetrating their defenses in wartime, the State Department was not about to defend an American caught red-handed sneaking across borders to photograph a revolution. The photographers Dickey had tried to scoop were less than sympathetic.

This was not her finest hour. As a photographer, she had violated the first commandment of her profession: calculate the risk. Her mission was to return with pictures, not to risk her life with the freedom fighters. Some said she had acted out of desperation, and they made a case that this was her bid to return to the profession of photography as a star for a death-defying performance.

For three months she languished in jail, denied enough to eat and harassed by her guards. The worst of it was seeing the plight of her fellow women prisoners and beginning to believe they would all rot in jail for all anyone cared.

The person who finally did most to obtain her release was Carl Hartman of the Associated Press in Vienna. I was in Italy as a correspondent for North American Newspaper Alliance when I heard belatedly of Dickey's incarceration and did what I could by cabling Hartman, a fellow graduate of the Columbia University School of Journalism. Hartman visited Dickey in jail in Budapest, and after weeks of neglect, the American press headlined Hartman's news of Dickey Chapelle's ordeal in a Communist prison. One definition of news is "what the Associated Press finally decides to report." At last the world was aroused, and the Communists let Dickey go.

However foolish her behavior, her bravery brought her national acclaim. The *Reader's Digest* printed her story, and she started work on her autobiography. Risking her life had become a way of life, but after Hungary, she showed extreme caution on one score, going out of her way to assure that nothing she did caused trouble for anyone else.

What no one else would do, Dickey did. In 1957, Algerian revolutionaries fighting for independence from France smuggled her from Morocco across French lines to their secret headquarters deep in Algeria. To reach the front, she rode mules and climbed mountains with the men. Along the way she collected evidence that the French were dropping bombs supplied by the North Atlantic Treaty Organization for the defense of Europe, not for a colonialist war in Africa.

Perhaps her most traumatic experience was stumbling on a teenaged Arab prisoner and being asked if she wished to witness his execution. "Not unless I cover the trial," she said, hoping to prolong his life. To her horror, the Arabs immediately organized a tribunal, and she feared that their speed for her benefit would hasten the boy's death. She heard the boy confess to the brutal slaughter of women and children taken prisoner by the French, for which their captors had paid him. Besides, he said, they had held a gun to his head. Now that he had been taken prisoner by the Algerian rebels, he wanted only to die, and his wish was granted in short order. Dickey's picture of the executed boy was her statement against capital punishment, colonialism, and war.

Her success as the first American to cover the Algerian fighters' side of that war inspired several newsmen to follow in her footsteps, even though the French appeared to control all access to Algeria. The Algerians finally won their independence in 1962.

After Algeria, wherever a gun was fired, Dickey was there. In 1958 she landed with the Marines in Lebanon. Then she flew to Cuba, where the rebel forces of Fidel Castro were in revolt against the dictatorship of Fulgencio Batista, again slipping through government lines to photograph the war from the rebels' side. By 1959 she was in Korea, parachuting from an Air Force plane, a practice jump for the next Asian war.

When President John F. Kennedy took office in January 1961, he faced a crisis in Indochina. For five years, the United States had been training the army of South Vietnam with little success toward the goal of defeating Communist insurgents. When Kennedy sent in squadrons of American helicopters and airplanes, Dickey Chapelle went with them.

Her credentials were superior to those of most photographers for major news agencies, and the Defense Department was prepared to accredit her, the remaining obstacle being the reluctance of employers to assign women as combat correspondents. "You'll get yourself killed," editors told Dickey, as if she had not been risking her life at every opportunity since she had gone off to cover World War II. Of course, they had not known she would reach the front in that war. As for Algeria and Cuba, desk-bound editors somehow failed to notice that small wars are as dangerous as big ones. They did know that Vietnam was a jungle, and she could not get a photographic agency to send her there.

She went as a free-lancer, having obtained the endorsement the armed forces required from two news outlets, WOR-RKO Radio and the *National Observer*, the weekly newspaper published in Washington, D.C., by the *Wall Street Journal*.

Once in Vietnam, she used her parachute training to do what fellow photographers were not yet trained to do. In September 1961, she made her first jump with full equipment, accompanying troops of the Fifth Battalion, Vietnamese Airborne Brigade. From her practice jumps in Korea, she knew what to expect, a sensation she described in her autobiography, *What's a Woman Doing Here?* An airman slides open the door from which they are to exit,

> and the hurricane wind out there almost out-thunders the engines. . . . I remember how I once marveled that jumpers over target seemed anxious to leave the haven of the plane. Suddenly, with the sin of pride, I realize that this has happened to me. My mind is reaching out of the racketing plane into the dark stillness I know lies just beyond the hurricane of the slipstream. It will be so quiet out there.

It was also quiet, too quiet, on the ground. At sight of the planes, the Vietcong melted into the jungle. They never gave the Americans the sort of battle they were prepared to fight. The very nature of the war seldom afforded the kind of action shots photographers gladly risked their lives to get. As in World War II, Dickey photographed the casualties, the men shot in the back by a sniper, the men who stepped on land mines. She made some thirty jumps on five separate trips to Vietnam.

President Kennedy also inherited a messy war in Laos, which kept getting worse. About two hundred Americans serving as civilian instructors were training the army of Laos to resist Communist attack. When Dickey sought to join them, a crusty colonel asked her, "Will you eat bats?" "Yes, sir," she said. Thus she found herself attached to a team that had actually been eating bats whenever its supply helicopter was downed by the rainy season.

For five weeks she shared their field rations, jungle posts, patrols, and fire missions deep in Laos. The small American force could only counsel, never lead, the Lao battalions. "Yet the effort was a proud thing to see," Dickey recalled. It was so effective that the Communists were offering a price of $25,000 a head for each American instructor captured. None was delivered by the Laotians.

For her coverage of the fighting in Vietnam and Laos, Dickey won the 1962 George Polk Award given by the Overseas Press Club "for the best reporting, any medium, requiring exceptional courage and enterprise abroad." In 1963, the U.S. Marine Combat Correspondents Association gave her its highest award, also for her courage and sympathetic reporting on the Marines in combat. From the beginning, the majority of American correspondents took a dim view of American involvement in the war in Vietnam. The troops sensed that their sacrifices were not appreciated, and morale suffered. Whatever the grand strategy, Dickey chose to focus on the heroism of the men.

President Lyndon Johnson sent the U.S. Marines into the Dominican Republic in the spring of 1965. Although his action later was denounced as unprovoked intrusion, Dickey was there to convince the world that the Marines were behaving splendidly.

President Johnson also presided over the escalation of American involvement in Vietnam in 1965, and Dickey returned to the front. In early November, she was covering a large-scale Marine operation near Chulai Air Base. Reporters could get the news at military briefings in Saigon. Dickey, her cameras strung over her shoulder, was marching with the Marines when she stepped on a booby-trapped land mine. Four Marines were wounded. Dickey, still wearing her little pearl earrings and with a small white flower in her helmet, was the first American woman combat correspondent killed in action.

At the age of forty-seven she had risked her life so many times, it was a wonder she had survived that long. Yet who was to say that she took unnecessary risks? Forty-five correspondents were killed covering the war in Vietnam, and many more risked their lives to get the story.

Her obituary made the front page of the *New York Times*. She would have written it just the way it appeared. She had made that much clear after seeing the chief of the Cuban Air Force killed in a plane crash during an air show. Dashing to file the story, she had paused to wonder,

> Could any cold sentence like the one I had just composed be a proper requiem for the warm human being who had elected to take that final fatal chance because his pride was more important than his survival? The answer came to me like a cold wind blowing from a city room in Boston. Yes, it was.

More than pride was involved. Dickey equated courage with the capacity to overcome fear. A pacifist at heart, she was drawn to war by her admiration for the courage of the young fighting men she covered.

Richard Tregaskis, prominent foreign correspondent and author, wrote the final salute to Dickey for the Overseas Press Club.

> Dickey Chapelle knew the combination of the big war, had learned some of the new ones and had retained the basic lessons. But Dickey also knew that the most dramatic and exciting stories in war are found where the action and danger are. That day chance was against her, and she was killed by an anti-personnel mine. It was the same with Ernie Pyle back in 1945 on the island of Ie Shima when he lifted at the wrong moment and got a machine gun bullet in the forehead—the most honorable death for a correspondent. All of them, those who were lucky and those who weren't, took many calculated risks. The risk was and still is to cover the hottest story in the world, where the action is hottest and chances the shortest; but the great game, we know, is worth the candle.

Tregaskis, too, took many risks. Ironically, he drowned while swimming off the shores of Hawaii. He would have preferred to die in action, as Dickey did.

16

A New Cast of Characters

THE CHANGING STATUS OF WOMEN FOREIGN CORRESPONDENTS from pathfinders to accepted professionals became evident after World War II. The surge of women reaching Europe as that war ended produced a new peak in the number of women correspondents that would not be equaled again until the 1980s.

Women reporters had kept the city rooms of the nation functioning during the World War II manpower shortage, and as many as could collected their reward in the form of overseas assignments. Others trained during the war gave up secure jobs to take their chances on making connections overseas. Countless interviews with men returning from combat zones left them feeling that they had covered the world from behind a post and must finally see it for themselves.

The press still needed military accreditation to get into occupied Germany, and the War Department did not relax its rules. Nevertheless, a few of the first correspondents arriving in Frankfurt, Berlin, and Munich were wives of officers and newsmen who managed to get accreditation and join their husbands two years before the Army provided facilities for families. Several were as successful as veteran reporters, and at least one divorced her husband, the better to pursue her career. Transportation bottlenecks and a shortage of accommodations delayed for months the arrival of other women assigned to cover postwar Europe. In Paris, one of the few major cities that had not been severely bombed, many hotels continued to be requisitioned by the U.S. Army.

After spending some time getting organized, the Army

opened four first-class press centers in Germany: a suburban mansion in Berlin, a once elegant hotel in Frankfurt, a palace featuring a ballroom in Nuremberg, and a schloss confiscated from a Nazi propagandist in Munich. All issued weekly lists of correspondents in residence, but nobody kept count. While the names changed constantly, the numbers remained fairly steady, often with more than one hundred in Berlin, usually fewer than fifty in Frankfurt and Nuremberg, seldom more than fifteen in Munich. It is a fair estimate that by mid-1946, 15 to 20 percent of the correspondents were women.

Among the first to arrive in Germany was Kathleen McLaughlin of the *New York Times*. McLaughlin, who had established her reputation as a crime reporter on the *Chicago Tribune* in the 1920s, personified the accepted professional. Despite her lack of sympathy for the Germans during the war, she was appalled by the behavior of the occupiers after it. Russian soldiers, out of control, raped German women. American soldiers, amply supplied with cigarettes and nylon stockings, bought them and were repaid with a soaring venereal disease rate. Using cigarettes to barter, the victors stripped the vanquished of their valuables. The damage was done when anyone with something to sell, from cameras to diamonds, used cigarettes to buy food and coal on the black market. Ration cards became as worthless as the currency. Those who had gained the least under Nazism suffered most under the occupiers.

Kathleen McLaughlin exposed the black market in print and shunned it in her personal dealings. Yet when a fellow correspondent praised her for it, she blushed, and her sense of humor surfaced. "How do you suppose I got this?" She laughed, pulling out a Russian samovar. It had been a gift, but she knew it had come from the black market. There was no avoiding it.

Newsmen facing serious competition from women accused everyone in sight, except McLaughlin, of using sex appeal to get the news. Still blond and slender in her late forties, she had earned acceptance. When the *New York Times* hired her in 1935, she was the only woman in the city room and, as she recalled, "You could have cut the ice with a hatchet." The men relaxed only when she was promoted to women's editor in 1941. The

Times sent her to Washington in 1943 to cover Eleanor Roosevelt. Her persistence in pursuing an overseas assignment took her to London in February 1945.

From her German secretary in Berlin, McLaughlin heard a story that would become a classic. Frau Freida Stinsky came to work one morning with the news that Russian soldiers billeted in German homes were removing faucets from bathrooms to take home with them. The soldiers were under the impression that the bathroom fixtures would make water spout from the wall. Nobody had told them that the faucets would not work without plumbing.

The Soviet blockade, which prevented trains from bringing supplies to the Western sectors of the city, began on April Fools' Day 1948. The Russians thought they could force the Western powers out of the city and run it their way. The American response, the Berlin airlift, came as a relief to many correspondents, because for the first time in three years they could write with pride of American behavior in Germany. It also brought a new influx of women correspondents, more than one could count, to cover those turbulent times.

The crisis lasted for more than a year, until the Russians lifted their blockade of Berlin in the summer of 1949, and the Western powers began turning authority over to a civilian government in West Germany. Kathleen McLaughlin, like others who came to cover the occupation, continued to report from Germany until the summer of 1951, when the United States established diplomatic relations with the Federal Republic of Germany and she was reassigned to the United Nations in New York. It was the end of an era.

With the end of the occupation of Germany and Japan and the wind-down of the Korean War, the profession was faced with a surplus of foreign correspondents, but you would never have guessed it from the size and complexion of the press corps in Paris.

The American-funded Marshall Plan for the reconstruction of Western Europe was in full swing, and Europeans from Bergen to Belgrade were working for the Yankee dollar. The fifties were the glory days for women free-lancers overseas. The American dollar was so strong that one could live delightfully in Paris for half what it cost to live modestly in New York. With military accreditation no longer required, such news feature agencies as the Women's News Service, the Worldwide Press Service, and the North American Newspaper Alliance gladly provided accreditation to experienced women in partial payment for their articles, and the magazine market was thriving.

Anyone who could get a visa to the Soviet Union had it made; for covering confrontations with the Russians, only Moscow provided a better vantage point than Berlin. But editors were slow to assign any woman to Moscow on a permanent basis because the Russians strictly limited the size of news bureaus. Senior correspondents vied for the post, and Communist tactics made this the most difficult of all foreign assignments, as Aline Mosby discovered when United Press International (UPI) sent her to Moscow in 1959.

MOSCOW CORRESPONDENT DRUGGED BY KGB! A story which could have made that lurid headline was never printed in the United States for substantial reasons, the most personal of which was that Mosby, the victim, did not propose to allow the incident to drive her out of the Soviet Union. It took place after a period of detente between the United States and the Soviet Union turned into one of extreme tension when, on May 1, 1960, an American high-altitude reconnaissance plane, a U-2 piloted by Francis Gary Powers, crashed in the USSR, and the Russians discovered that American photographic missions had been spying on them for at least three years. A scheduled Paris summit meeting collapsed before it began. Correspondents had to contend with the possibility that Russians who were offering information or asking for help were really trying to entrap them, to establish grounds for their expulsion or blackmail them into becoming spies.

At a British exposition, some youths who identified themselves as students clustered around Mosby, an attractive blonde reared in Missoula, Montana, and invited her to dinner. "It was so difficult to speak to Russians, especially students, that I was excited by the prospect," she said. On second thought, she realized that the boys could be setting her up, and she did not show for the appointment. But when one of them called to express his disappointment and mentioned that they had even brought her flowers, she gave in and agreed to meet them at a restaurant. As a precaution, she told a colleague that if she was not back in good time, he should call the American embassy. Unfortunately, her friend neglected to make the call.

Her hosts, two young men, ushered her to a table reserved for them in a crowded restaurant and ordered a liter of Armenian cognac. When she took only a sip, the men ordered champagne and, while she was in the ladies' room, mixed it with cognac. One sniff sufficed to identify it.

"That is called a French Seventy-five," she told them, "and it can be lethal." When she refused to drink it, her escorts tried to sell her black market icons, which angered her. As she looked in her Russian dictionary for the word *despicable*, all she could see were solid black lines. To be civil, she tasted the food and, at their insistence, joined in one last toast. That did it.

"My mouth was like cotton, my field of vision was blocked, and I had only cameo vision," she recalled. Realizing that she had been drugged, she fled to the street, where a waiting photographer snapped her picture. The two "students" came out to watch, then vanished with the photographer. A traffic policeman took her in hand.

The next day she awakened in her own bed to find a physician from the American embassy, an embassy attaché, and UPI bureau chief Henry Shapiro at her side. "Those guys slipped me a mickey," she murmured. Her hosts had added a sleeping potion to her drink. The doctor diagnosed drug poisoning and said she was lucky it had not caused permanent damage. Overnight, the hair on half her scalp turned white, apparently from the shock.

Her friends, both Russian and Western, immediately suspected the KGB. The table reserved in a crowded restaurant was an oddity in Moscow and the quantity of liquor served illegal. The photographer waiting outside was there to trap her. The U.S. ambassador, Llewellyn Thompson, told Mosby that he thought the KGB was attempting to blackmail her into spying.

After she told the ambassador, keeping no secret she could be blackmailed for, the Soviet government newspaper, *Izvestia*, printed the photograph of her leaving the restaurant with a front page story accusing her of having been drunk. Its editor, Alexei Adjhubei, "had never liked me," Mosby said.

The incident was reported to President John F. Kennedy, and Ambassador Thompson made an oral protest to the Soviet government. While diplomatic protocol does not require a reply to an oral protest, Foreign Ministry officials unofficially told Shapiro that they regretted the incident.

Mosby's case was not an isolated one. Harrison Salisbury, veteran correspondent of the *New York Times*, reported "a rash of knock-out drop attacks on Americans, correspondents and Embassy personnel." Some men awoke to find themselves in bed with a sex partner, photographs having been taken.

At the request of UPI, American correspondents in Moscow did not file the story of Mosby's drugging. But then a Communist newspaper in East Berlin printed the *Izvestia* account of the incident, and the *Chicago Daily News*'s George Weller felt free to write Mosby's counterstory. Again at the request of UPI, the *Daily News* did not print it. Weller related that the story appeared in a London newspaper six months later. He concluded that the UPI was not so much interested in protecting a woman as making sure its veteran correspondent, Shapiro, did not also get expelled in a fracas.

Even twenty-five years later, Mosby had to get UPI's permission to confirm the story. "A journalist must judge whether the story she wants to write is worth the risk of being expelled," Mosby said, adding, "I don't hold anything against them. Every country has its security agency. Lots use dirty tricks."

Mosby had spent more than a decade working for the United Press in Seattle, San Francisco, Phoenix, and Los Angeles before the agency sent her to London in 1958, then on to Moscow, and in 1960, at the age of thirty-eight, she was not ready to give up a chance-in-a-lifetime assignment.

The Russians put Powers on trial for operating his spy plane over the Soviet Union, and Mosby covered the case. Sentenced to ten years in jail, Powers was later exchanged for Rudolf Abel, a Soviet spy held in the United States.

Although Mosby refused to be forced out of Moscow, she tired of the tension of covering the Soviet Union in an atmosphere of mutual distrust. On a local bus in Sukhumi, Soviet Georgia, Sonia Tomara's hometown, she was robbed of her passport case. The police found it but refused to return it until she signed a statement that she had "lost" it, thus precluding her from writing that she was robbed in the Soviet Union. The police followed her so constantly that a Soviet Foreign Ministry official she met at a reception could tell her in detail all her movements in the Soviet Union. Having successfully fought expulsion, she requested a transfer when the decision became hers to make.

After Moscow, Mosby covered Paris, Vienna, and then Eastern Europe, dividing her time between Prague and Bucharest. A Ford Foundation fellowship enabled her to study Chinese history and language, and in 1979 she was among the first four Americans admitted to the People's Republic of China as permanent correspondents since the revolution of 1948. For fourteen months she worked seven days, eighty hours, a week. In Peking, as in Moscow, opportunities to get to know the people were limited. She took special pride in discovering and writing about Chinese Jews, who maintained their religious and cultural identity long after intermarriage had erased any physical identity with Jewish forefathers who had settled in China. She earned what she requested next, permanent assignment to Paris.

Mosby was promoted to the prestigious position of Paris bureau chief and ran the UPI operation for a year before she retired in 1985. Instead of returning to her home in Montana, she became attached to the Paris bureau of the *New York Times* as a special feature writer, a part-time assignment freeing her to write as she pleased without the pressure of constant deadlines.

Once accepted as professionals, women aspired to rise to the top of their profession, and Flora Lewis epitomized the women who did, first as chief of the Paris bureau of the *New York Times* and then as its syndicated columnist on foreign affairs with Paris as her base. She was the first woman to achieve such stature since Anne O'Hare McCormick and only after the lapse of a generation.

Mort Rosenblum, when he was editor of the Paris *International Herald Tribune*, described Lewis as "the virtuoso of nuance. . . . She unravels the tangled snarls of summitry, macroeconomics, North-South confrontations and multilateral disarmament."

Marguerite Higgins and Flora Lewis met as fellow members of the class of 1942, Columbia University School of Journalism, and considered sharing an apartment. Had I overheard the conversation (I was also in the class), I would not have believed my ears. Poised, sophisticated, and well dressed, Lewis, a graduate of the University of California at Los Angeles, possessed all the social amenities Higgins lacked. Typically, Higgins isolated herself in Greenwich Village while Lewis joined the campus community.

As graduation approached, the Associated Press called to ask Columbia for an applicant to fill an opening for a copy editor, but when Lewis arrived for an interview she was told that women were a distracting element in the area of the cable desk or the general news desk. A man chosen for the job she sought did not work out. Besides, he was homosexual, and the editors decided that a real woman could not be more distracting. Thus she landed the job.

Lewis spent her three years at the Associated Press in New York trying to get sent overseas. She finally won a prized assignment to London, where she inaugurated a distinguished career as a foreign correspondent. She remembered that when she arrived there, on the day of victory in Japan that ended the war, "the trees on King's Row were festooned with toilet paper, the only thing people had left to throw." During her tenure in London she married Sydney Gruson of the *New York Times*, a beau since her days at Columbia.

Her career almost foundered when the AP ordered Lewis home for declining an assignment in Paris. Instead, she went with Gruson to Poland, where for a decade, she said, "I worked for everybody," including the London *Observer*, the London *Economist*, the *Financial Times*, *France Soir*. Although the *New York Times* refused to hire the wife of a correspondent, the paper's Sunday magazine provided a steady outlet.

Her first close call came when *Life* magazine assigned her to work with a photographer it sent to Warsaw in the winter of 1946-1947. "He might have been a good photographer," she conceded, "but he couldn't brush his own teeth." Those were tense times, the people opposing a Communist-imposed government, and when a crowd gathered around the *Life* representatives, militiamen arrested both Lewis and the photographer. A Polish driver for the American embassy witnessed the scene and reported it to the embassy, but when an American came to the jail the police denied that they were there. The Americans might have been held incognito for days except that Lewis, in a back room, overhead the conversation and spoke out loudly in English to the police. The American heard her and obtained their release.

Lewis was immensely pregnant when she went to Iran for the London *Daily Express* to cover the marriage of Shah Mohammad Reza Pahlavi to the Princess Soraya. The shah's twin sister chose for her costume a magnificent dark gown trimmed in fur and, two weeks before the wedding, decreed that other women would have to wear pastel afternoon dresses. Lewis, who could have concealed her pregnancy in an evening gown, pinned a satin sash to a borrowed afternoon dress to make her condition less obvious. When she left Iran to have her baby, the *Daily Express* sent an extremely fat man to replace her.

Within weeks Lewis, having had her baby, was back to cover the first Iranian oil crisis in 1951, when Parliament under Premier Mohammad Mossadegh nationalized the oil industry. Between news breaks she went to a jewelry store to buy opal cuff links for her husband and waited while a courier for Mrs. W. Averell Harriman, wife of the distinguished American diplomat, purchased rubies and sapphires galore. When her turn came, Lewis warned the salesman that as a journalist she could not pay the prices he charged diplomats. The jeweler, who found journalists strange, was inspired to remark, "Do you know what the London *Daily Express* did? It sent a pregnant woman to cover the shah's wedding. Then it sent a pregnant man to replace her."

In 1956 Lewis won the Overseas Press Club award for best interpretation of foreign affairs, and in 1958 she became the first woman foreign correspondent for the *Washington Post*. The *Post* was just beginning to develop a foreign service, and she was the third correspondent hired. For the *Post*, she served as chief of bureau first in Bonn, then London. In 1960, the Overseas Press Club gave her its award for best reporting of foreign affairs, and her alma mater, the Columbia University School of Journalism, during the celebration of its fiftieth anniversary, bestowed its Honor Award on her.

By then the Grusons had three children, and the more recognition she won, the more people asked how she managed both family and career. For years, she answered with a flip "By neglecting both." For those who remained dissatisfied, she might add, "The real secret is the right nanny." After two glasses of wine, she would say, "You run twice as fast and work three times as hard."

Her debut as a syndicated columnist came in 1966, when she left the *Post* to join *Newsday*, the Long Island newspaper that had syndicated Marguerite Higgins. At the start of the six-day Arab-Israeli war on June 5, 1967, Lewis was the last person through the Mandelbaum Gate in Jerusalem, separating Jordan from Israel, before that gate was closed. Because a woman attracted so little attention unless she was the "first" to do something, it amused her to be last for a change.

Arriving without accreditation to the Israeli armed forces, she rented a car to reach the front where Egyptian forces were attacking in a futile effort to retrieve territory they had previously lost. For three days she traveled alone, while newsmen avoiding her went out together. One day the men found a back way to reach the town of Bethlehem ahead of her, and that night she finally asked one of them why they did not take her with them. "It's too dangerous," he said. "We are scared. You would probably panic." The newsmen didn't know she had been covering the same territory without the safety of numbers.

Covering the Vietnam War in 1968, she found herself caught in the midst of a battle for the Vietnam delta. With a dozen others, she was in a tiny press camp when the lights went out. To watch incoming rockets, they climbed to the roof. A youth next to her, accredited to a group of university newspapers, confided, "I want the other side to win." Lewis shuddered. As she saw it, his heart was with the enemy, and he belonged on the other side of the guns. The American military lied extravagantly and distorted the truth, she said, but the boy's reaction inflicted her with "an extraordinary sense of the abnormal."

The articles she wrote from Vietnam focused on military strategy rather than battlefield drama. "By the time I got to Vietnam, I found the battlefield stories no longer very interesting," she explained. "I was tired of reading about bullets that whoosh and Marines screaming in anguish, and I didn't want to write it yet again." What she tried to do was to give some context to the spot news coverage, to tell in depth what was happening in Vietnam rather than to focus on the small amount of land that changed hands constantly over the years.

What was happening disturbed her, and her disapproval of American policy reached a peak in 1969 when she discovered that the United States, in spite of repeated denials, was conducting "secret" bombings of neighboring Cambodia. The enemy knew it was being bombed. The only people deceived were American voters who might object to this extension of the war and would, when they learned of it, feel betrayed by their leaders.

Writing from Paris on March 13, 1982, Lewis drew on her Vietnam experience to defend correspondents covering revolution in El Salvador when they were attacked for lending credence to guerrilla propaganda.

This wasn't a problem in Vietnam because the U.S. press had virtually no access to the Vietcong. But it is a result of Vietnam, because there the press learned the hard way to detect the symptoms of official lies and distortions, and to notice that opposition propaganda can contain some facts just as our own does. It was a vital lesson.

Lewis also commended David Halberstam of the *Times*, the bitter foe of Marguerite Higgins, for reminding the world "how much is at stake when the people at the top begin to lie and manipulate to suit their views."

Their children grown, the Grusons marked their twenty-fifth wedding anniversary by getting a divorce, which exempted her from the *Times* ban on hiring the wives of correspondents. The newspaper put her on its staff as Paris bureau chief in 1972 and promoted her to European diplomatic correspondent in 1976.

As a columnist, Lewis was especially concerned with the need to create a climate in which the United States and the Soviet Union could negotiate a reduction in nuclear weapons. At a time when Ronald Reagan, first as candidate and then as President of the United States, seemed bent on confrontation, she called for moderation. "It is a fallacy to say the Soviets were the great beneficiaries of detente," she wrote. What was required, as she saw it, was

> an urgent, determined effort to reduce arsenals by agreement. It means accepting Soviet security concerns, being selective about new weapons and not trying to unsettle the Soviet regime, however hateful. The task of reforming it belongs to its own people. Ours is to maintain peace and win time for them to find a way.

In a column dated August 2, 1983, she castigated President Reagan's administration for "gross mismanagement" of United States relations with Central America. She accused the government of "brinksmanship" against Nicaragua and deplored "the evidence that this brinksmanship isn't even based on a policy except trying to patch things together for a while longer."

Because her columns tended to be temperate, even cautious, she was taken all the more seriously when she chose to criticize. Readers were appalled during the 1987 Iran-Contra scandal when she quoted Iranian exiles as saying that in 1980 Republicans asked them to delay the release of American hostages until after the November elections, in order to help Ronald Reagan defeat President Jimmy Carter.

In October 1987, returning to the United States to promote her new book, *Europe: A Tapestry of Nations*, she summed up her experience by saying "Truth is the hardest substance in the world to pin down. But the one certainty is the awesome penalty exacted sooner or later from a society whose reporters stop trying."

17

Bearers of Bad Tidings

TREATED AS EQUALS AT LAST, MEN AND WOMEN COVERING THE war in Vietnam and Cambodia shared the agony of reporting defeat and the ordeal of finding themselves caught in controversy over whom to blame. While the correspondents fought among themselves over what was right and what went wrong with that war, none escaped the accusation that their negative reporting contributed to the defeats they recorded. Their best defense was that they were there, and they reported what they saw.

This was another Thirty Years' War, and women covered the turmoil from the end of World War II to the fall of Saigon in 1975, including the French war to regain control of all Indochina (Vietnam, Cambodia, and Laos) and the American war in Vietnam. Elizabeth Becker of the *Washington Post* returned to Vietnam twice after the Communists won.

Nobody knows how many correspondents covered the war, but interviews with information officers and correspondents stationed there at various times indicate that at least two hundred fifty women were among them in the ten years 1965 to 1975. Although a relatively small minority, women were ever present everywhere. The Associated Press, United Press International, the *New York Times*, the National Broadcasting Company—all major outlets sent women to Vietnam.

Beverly Deepe of the *New York Herald Tribune* arrived in Vietnam in 1962 and spent more than four years reporting the war, time enough to witness a transformation in the attitude of the military toward women correspondents. One can pinpoint the historic day when women achieved full equality to cover combat: November 2, 1963, the day South Vietnamese President Ngo Dinh Diem was assassinated. Until then, women had been advised to remain in Saigon, the South Vietnamese capital, for their own safety. That day Deepe's apartment, a half block from the presidential palace, was riddled with machine gun bullets and looted by government troops fleeing a military coup. Gratuitous advice on safety zones ceased. All could empathize when she wrote,

> Maybe it's my feminine outlook, but to me the war is not simply a war but a hellish dancing madness. I live in a brown half-house made of teak, in a world made of tears, shattered dreams and everywhere the dead and the almost dead, where the American men are lonely and the Vietnamese are sad. My major personal difficulty is to laugh—if only occasionally—for all of Vietnam cries.

Television brought war into every American living room for the first time, in an award-winning performance provoking as much blame as praise. Liz Trotta, a member of the NBC staff in New York, wanted to cover the Vietnam War long before she dared ask. Friends advised, "Don't ask. Tell everyone what you want to do." The word would reach management. An NBC vice president eventually came to her with the question "Do you think you can handle this?" She could and she would. But the Saigon bureau chief cabled, "If you put a woman on that plane, I shall quit, whoever she is."

"I was brokenhearted," Trotta reported. "But I was mad, too. And I went on a campaign."

Her luck changed when the Saigon bureau chief was replaced by an old friend, Frank Donghi. In addition, Chet Huntley, the celebrated NBC news commentator, supported her. Editors who trusted her to report the news worried about sending her out with an all-male camera crew to televise a war. Television news had to be visual, so TV correspondents not only had to get the news, they had to work with and frequently direct the cameramen.

To the surprise of her editors, Trotta won the Overseas Press

Club Award for best television news reporting from abroad in 1968, more than she expected of herself. The week she arrived in Saigon she witnessed a rocket attack on the city by Vietcong and North Vietnamese forces. "I was paralyzed," she said. "They set the opera house on fire. They killed a Japanese correspondent next door to me. Others were running and screaming. I was afraid every minute, every second. People thought I was brave when I was in a trance."

Trotta got along well with the camera crews by not ordering them about. "We talked it out," she said, and they worked together. She wanted to get along with everybody, and if this had been World War II, where the press corps cheered at every strike against the enemy, she would have succeeded. One way to keep friends was to stay out of controversy, and she tried, but as hard as she tried she could not stay out of the dispute within the press corps over what America was doing in Vietnam.

Since few of the correspondents were paid to express their opinions, they fought it out at the bar. In an argument over the bombing of North Vietnam, Trotta found herself pegged as a clinging vine of the establishment. As she told the story, some correspondents accused the United States of "terror bombing," needlessly killing the innocent. She investigated and decided that American bombing was "most strategic, most humane." Recalling the argument after the war, she described reports to the contrary as "utter hogwash, the sort of propaganda that helped us lose the war."

Trotta was criticizing a few individuals, not indicting the press corps. Indeed, she was generous in her praise for her competitors, especially Peter Arnett of Cable News Network and Walter Cronkite of CBS. Nevertheless, she opened a can of worms with the revelation that at least one respected correspondent accepted the view that antiwar propagandists, some of them in Vietnam, shared responsibility for America's defeat.

What the correspondents saw depended on when they were in Vietnam. Civilian populations were not spared by the bombers when I was there in 1967 as a correspondent for the *Reporter* magazine. By December 1967, the United States had 475,000 troops in Vietnam, and all of North Vietnam was subject to massive and continuous bombing. In a bid for peace, President Lyndon Johnson curbed the bombing on March 31, 1968, about the time Trotta arrived in Vietnam. The bombings she observed were indeed "surgical," as she described them, and by the end of October 1968, all bombing ceased for the duration of her duty in Vietnam. President Richard Nixon resumed the bombing, and the criticism began again.

Television, more than any other medium, was blamed for turning the American public against the war. It was not the message Trotta, for one, intended to deliver. Her experiences instilled in her tremendous respect for America's armed forces, and she conveyed it. With an NBC camera crew, she flew to a special forces camp at the front, where she found the famed Green Berets "brave and terrific." Soon they were under heavy enemy fire; North Vietnamese surrounded the camp, and the order came to abandon the position. At an escape briefing, they were told how to cut through barbed wire and tell directions in the jungle. To their relief, they escaped being tested in the jungle when their plane took off safely. But she and the NBC crew were listed as missing for something like seventy-two hours, and fellow correspondents thought they were dead.

While her audiences heard her cheers for the pilots and the Green Berets, the camera was showing them that no act of war can be humane. For NBC, CBS, and later Cable News Network, Trotta covered a world haunted by war and hunger, but nothing was more traumatic for her and others than the war in Vietnam.

More than Liz Trotta, Gloria Emerson of the *New York Times* wanted to identify with the establishment. She first went to Saigon in 1956 as a free-lancer and remembered it as a city of trees, boulevards, and flowers. When she returned for the *Times* in 1970, she took with her an impression of the U.S. Army as "lovable and self correcting . . . a warm hearted, gallant, resourceful army led by officers who preferred to die rather than be dishonored." What she saw in Vietnam turned her admiration to contempt. Only a woman who had once believed in the American dream could feel so betrayed. Her reaction to what went wrong was so violent that she eventually quit the newspaper business.

"After Vietnam it wasn't possible to function as a foreign correspondent," she said, "because I could not possibly conceal my own views and beliefs." While she was there, she functioned so well that she won the George Polk Award for excellence in foreign reporting. Her *Winners and Losers* won the National Book Award in 1978.

Emerson was among those who blew the whistle on false body counts. It would have been difficult to overestimate the numbers of Vietnamese killed and wounded. The problem, as she saw it, was that women, children, and friendly villagers in the line of fire were counted as enemy soldiers killed, giving the impression that the U.S. Army was destroying the enemy at a time the Communists were gaining strength.

Enlisted men in the Awards and Decorations Office at Bienhoa revealed the practice of bestowing medals on high-ranking officers without bothering to determine if they had done anything to earn them, and Emerson wrote the story. As casualties and real heroes went unsung, the GIs were ordered to prepare a citation justifying the award of a silver star to a brigadier general. "There was nothing to go on, not a date or a scrap of information or eyewitness report on what the general might have done," Emerson discovered. So the GIs made up a magnificent story and said it all happened on June 9, because that was the twenty-first birthday of a youth who assisted and also the birthday of his wife.

Her criticism attracted so much attention that she later was asked to lecture at the U.S. Naval War College. "I spoke," she said, "of a lack of truthfulness and honor among the career military in Vietnam, of a tendency in them to cheat, citing how the nation's most esteemed medals were handed out like salted peanuts to field grade officers."

A tragic aspect of the Vietnam War was that the soldiers who survived it felt the war's critics failed to appreciate their sacrifices. Emerson, one who cared, told of a wounded soldier brought aboard a helicopter.

I wanted to hold his hand, but once I had done this. The G.I. had died, his fingers curled with mine, and I had not wanted to let go, thinking the life would pass from me to him, until someone yanked my arm and parted us at last.

His suffering was all the more heartbreaking to her because she failed to see what such sacrifices were accomplishing. Contrasting wartime Saigon with the gaiety of the city she remembered from 1956, she wrote,

Saigon was never a gay city during the war. It was malignant, cruel, crowded, costly and furtive, but never gay. . . . The Americans were there because they had learned nothing from the French. All that mattered was that the French had failed, not the reasons why.

Eventually Emerson faced the accusation that the correspondents had been so opposed to the war that they helped to lose it. As she remembered, "The daily briefings—the meaningless recitals of the military—had been a sham, but no one refused to write them."

Most correspondents struggled to be objective and factual, if only because their editors insisted on it. They found themselves hampered because they had access to spokesmen for only one side of the story, and any facts they reported contrary to the official version of events produced accusations that they took it upon themselves to undermine the government position. The strain of covering what some saw as a futile involvement produced a new and anguished look at the meaning of objectivity. "Quote a lie with as straight a face as you quote the truth" was one definition of it.

The United States lost Vietnam to the Communists by its support of French colonialism after World War II, and the more Vietnamese we killed the more enemies we made, Frances FitzGerald wrote. For her articles published by the *Atlantic* and other magazines, she won the 1967 Overseas Press Club Award for best interpretation of foreign affairs. Her book about Vietnam, *Fire in the Lake*, won the Pulitzer Prize, the National Book Award, and the Bancroft Prize when it appeared in 1972.

In Vietnam in 1953, I had been the only correspondent to witness the defeat of the French Foreign Legion in the battle for the Nassan Valley of Haut Tonkin. The next year, the press arrived en masse to attend the hanging and record the death of French colonialism in Asia with the inevitable and final defeat of the French in the battle of Dien Bien Phu.

In Saigon in 1967, I watched more than two hundred correspondents arrive for the "five o'clock follies," as they called the daily briefings by the military, and was reminded that the media never sent so many correspondents overseas to cover anything less than a disaster. The Overseas Press Club said that they gave the world the most extensive news coverage of any war in history. If the power of positive thinking could have changed the outcome, it would not have been that big a story. Correspondents sent to report disasters seldom arrived in time to prevent them. The purpose of foreign policy was to prevent disaster, and governments failed when they ignored opportunities and reacted only to crises. Bad news was big news, and it was the media's business to report it.

The war in Vietnam spread to neighboring Cambodia on March 18, 1970, when General Lon Nol, commander of the Cambodian armed forces, overthrew Cambodia's chief of state, Norodom Sihanouk. Sihanouk had tried to keep his nation neutral; Lon Nol accepted United States assistance. On April 30, President Richard Nixon announced that U.S. troops would march into Cambodia to destroy North Vietnamese Communists sanctuaries along the border with South Vietnam.

Elizabeth Pond of the *Christian Science Monitor*, Richard Dudman of the *St. Louis Post-Dispatch*, and Michael Morrow of Dispatch News Service International were covering the invasion when two men with rifles, one Cambodian, one Vietnamese, stopped their automobile near the Cambodian provincial capital of Soal Rieng and took them prisoner on May 7.

Captured by the enemy, threatened with rape, and intimidated by terrorists, women correspondents covering the war in

Cambodia remembered Vietnam as a piece of cake in comparison.

Traveling with their captors by foot, bicycle, and truck, Pond and her fellow correspondents found themselves in a village surrounded by an ugly mob. "We were blindfolded—tightly—and led off the truck, stooping to descend the plank. I was kicked once on the way. . . . My sense was that we might be close to being killed," she reported.

Pond was separated from her companions, then denied water to drink. An angry man snatched off her sandals and threw them against the wall. Her "guard" took her rings and next tried to attack her. "I said aloud—in French—that this was not necessary, that he was my brother and I was his sister. Nothing happened for a few minutes, and then he replaced the rings on my fingers," she said.

The worst was over. Under interrogation, the correspondents expressed regret for the invasion of Cambodia by American and South Vietnamese forces and hope that as journalists they would be able in some way to alter American policy. They said no more than they believed.

For several weeks they were kept on the move, marching at night from one Cambodian house to another. After five and a half weeks of captivity, they were released on June 14. A crowd of a thousand Cambodians gathered for a farewell celebration carried banners thanking the American people who opposed aggression by the Nixon administration.

Pond learned that she owed her release to Prince Norodom Sihanouk, who had found refuge in Peking, the People's Republic of China, and from there was directing the Cambodian National United Front in opposition to Lon Nol.

Elizabeth Becker was still in high school in 1965, taking a course in Asian studies, when the teacher scribbled on the blackboard, "President Johnson just sent the Marines into Vietnam. This is going to change your life." At the University of Washington in Seattle, Becker specialized in South Asian regional studies. After a year in India, she arrived in Phnom Penh, Cambodia, in time to celebrate New Year's 1973.

The last U.S. combat troops had left Vietnam in 1972, and on January 27, 1973, a cease-fire agreement designed to end the war in Vietnam was signed in Paris. But the fighting continued in Vietnam and Cambodia. In February, the United States resumed its bombings of Cambodia. Massive American military support for the South Vietnamese fighting Communist North Vietnamese continued.

Becker began by writing for the prestigious *Far East Economic Review*, published in Hong Kong, and soon was serving as a stringer for *Newsweek*, the National Broadcasting Company, and the *Washington Post*.

The U.S. Congress, under immense public pressure to get American forces out of Asia, forbade the use of American advisers in the war for Cambodia, but this did not stop the Defense Department. Becker was first to report that American advisers were still being used in Cambodia, in violation of the law.

Hearing that the town of Kampot, Cambodia, was surrounded by enemy forces, she arranged for a helicopter pilot to take her to the scene. A helicopter right behind hers brought an American lieutenant colonel. Becker went off on her own, encountered enemy fire, and hit the ditch. Things were worse than she had been told. She made it back to the Cambodian military base and was trying to sleep when the Khmer Rouge, the Cambodian Communists, attacked at 2:00 A.M.

Becker struggled to her feet and ran to the command post, where she found the Cambodian commander writing in his diary while the American colonel directed the fire. The next afternoon, she escaped by helicopter. She had qualms about writing the story. The American colonel may have saved her life, but as she saw it, American participation in that war was disastrous, and the public had a right to know that U.S. Army advisers continued to operate in Cambodia in violation of the law.

She wrote the story, which created a nationwide sensation. Defenders of the Army said that she did not know enough French to understand what the colonel was saying. That did not wash because she could speak French and Hindi. The *Washington Post* was so impressed by her scoop that it put her on its staff.

Becker left Cambodia in 1974 when she saw that Lon Nol

was losing the war and there was nothing left to do but record the inevitable victory of the Khmer Rouge in 1975. Persistent reports that the victorious Khmer Rouge brutally destroyed at least a million inhabitants of that small country impelled her to return in 1978.

The Khmer Rouge government still was denying all visa applications from Westerners, but it finally admitted three—Malcolm Caldwell, a British scholar of Marxist persuasion, Richard Dudman, and Becker—for a two-week visit. They were treated properly by a government out to show them what it had done right.

What they were not shown convinced Becker that the reports of a holocaust were true. Thousands were said to have died when they were forced to leave Phnom Penh and march into the countryside. Becker made repeated efforts to find people she had known in 1974 before she was allowed to talk to just two former inhabitants of the city. She could not escape the conclusion that most of the dispossessed died of hunger and disease.

The night before the correspondents were scheduled to leave for Peking by plane, a terrorist entered the guest house where they were staying on Monivong Avenue in the government compound near the old presidential palace. Becker, sleeping in a room on the ground floor, was awakened by a loud crash in back of the house, followed by a pistol shot. She threw on some clothes and ran into the dining room, square into the cocked pistol of an intruder.

"I remember he looked more frightened than I felt," she said. "Then he pointed the pistol at my face, and I screamed, 'No, don't!' " She ran into her bedroom, then into her bathroom and locked the door. While she crouched in the bathtub, loud shots rang out overhead. "I was totally and completely terrorized," she recalled. "My legs collapsed from under me." She crouched there for hours before she was rescued by a Foreign Ministry official, Thiounn Parsith. He told her that the intruders had shot three times at Dudman but missed him. They killed Malcolm Caldwell, whom they shot at pointblank range.

Cambodia's only connection with the outside world, a weekly plane to Peking, was held up for a day so the journalists could first identify Caldwell's body, then fly out with their stories. Theirs was the last plane out. Within a week, Vietnamese forces attacking the Khmer Rouge captured the Cambodian capital.

The Vietnamese blamed the defeated enemy for Caldwell's death and showed visitors a blood splattered room in the Royale Hotel where they said Caldwell had died. But as Becker reported, Caldwell died not in the hotel but in a poorly secured guest house. She won an Overseas Press Club citation for her coverage of the story.

At a 1986 reunion of Vietnam correspondents sponsored by the Overseas Press Club in New York, Tad Bartimus of the Associated Press recalled that at one point the AP's Cambodian war coverage was handled entirely by three women, Edith Lederer, bureau chief, Christine Spengler, photographer, and she herself.

Outside the hall, men wearing jungle camouflage uniforms picketed the press for losing the war. Inside, the correspondents, in a rare display of modesty, recalled the more important role played by 47,381 Americans killed in combat between 1960 and 1974 and 254,259 South Vietnamese dead.

Bartimus quoted her friend Edie Lederer.

There might be other wars, but there would never be the schizophrenia of Vietnam. . . . We couldn't ignore the death and destruction. But living became paramount, and there was an intensity about everything. . . . We all left a little bit of our souls in that tortured land. One day, hopefully, we shall return to reclaim them.

The Incas once killed the messengers who brought bad news. The pickets departed quietly before the reunion ended.

18

Full Circle

SINCE THE DAYS OF NELLIE BLY, LATIN AMERICA HAD SERVED editors as a place to send women who insisted on being foreign correspondents. Compared to Europe, South America was considered close to home, and for a century it was seldom dangerous. Ambitious newsmen were not all that interested in banana republics and coffee dictatorships. Women covered the building of the Panama Canal, the occupation of Haiti by the United States Marines, the rise to power of Juan Perón in Argentina. By the 1980s, women were the accepted authorities on Latin America, and they appeared in force to cover repression in Chile, strife in El Salvador, and the war of the contras against the Sandinista government in Nicaragua.

Shirley Christian, with the Associated Press, staked out Latin America when it was considered less than a choice assignment. When revolution and terrorism promoted the story to page one, her reputation soared. Returning to the region for the *Miami Herald*, she won the Pulitzer Prize for international reporting in 1981, the first time it was awarded for coverage of Latin America.

Before Georgie Anne Geyer branched out to cover the world, her articles for the *Chicago Daily News* helped put Latin America on page one. Geyer and Henry Gill, a *Chicago Daily News* photographer, slipped into Guatemala in 1967 and traveled with guerrilla forces while the Guatemalan Army, led by American officers, pursued them. Her stories dramatized and drew attention to the developing crisis. Her initial success in Latin America led eventually to a three-times-weekly column distributed by

Universal Press Syndicate to more than one hundred newspapers. She also achieved celebrity status as a panelist on the television show "Washington Week in Review," produced by the Public Broadcasting System.

Again by no coincidence, Christian and Geyer were in the forefront of the women's liberation movement. Of her career, Geyer wrote,

> In my curious lifetime I went from the beginning . . .
> from the point where women like me were so considered
> misfits and freaks (and everyone kept wondering when we
> were "ever going to settle down" or who would have us)
> to a point where we became extremely fashionable and
> were ironically and incongruously called "role models,"
> to the third point which is where we are now, where women
> are trying desperately to have everything.

If it did not all happen in her lifetime, it may well have seemed that it had. Born in 1935, Geyer grew up in a decade of reaction, the 1950s. Rosie the Riveter of World War II fame was "out," raising families "in." The children rebelled in the 1960s as if they had invented rebellion. Aspiring journalists did not know enough of the achievements of women in their profession to build on them or even to approach the job market with any confidence.

Geyer accepted a job as a society reporter on the *Chicago Daily News* in 1959, and her autobiography conveyed her impression that she was the third woman ever promoted to the city staff. Vulnerable to such remarks as "I hope she doesn't cry," she might have felt less insecure if anyone had told her that there were seven women reporters in the city room in 1944.

Most newspapers and news agencies stopped hiring women at the end of World War II, and some even fired them in anticipation of a surplus of veterans returning to reclaim their jobs. No excess materialized, but the pattern was reestablished. A genuine glut of foreign correspondents at the end of the Korean War in 1953 cut most women out of overseas assignments. By the time demand revived with the Vietnam War, there were not that many women trained and eligible for overseas assignments in the pipeline. The majority of women who covered that war went on their own, the only way they could get there.

Helen Kirkpatrick, as a foreign correspondent in World War II, had brought great prestige to the *Chicago Daily News*, but as late as 1964, the *Daily News* had no intention of sending another woman overseas. Geyer went to Peru on a Seymour Berkson foreign assignment grant and began filing stories the *Daily News* could not resist. For example, Pensacola, Florida, was planning to donate a stadium to its sister city, Chimbote, Peru, and Geyer discovered that Chimbote's vice lord had donated the land for the stadium. The architectural plans revealed numerous cubicles within the stadium, little rooms where he proposed to locate his whores. That ended one effort at international good will.

Having learned Spanish in six months, Geyer extracted from her reluctant editors an assignment to cover revolution in the Dominican Republic, and she went on from there to assignments in the Soviet Union, Angola, Lebanon, Vietnam. By 1975 she was writing a weekly column as well as new stories for the *Daily News*. When the newspaper refused to syndicate her column, she transferred to the *Los Angeles Times* for a three-times-weekly column. She left in 1980 for a better offer from Universal Press Syndicate.

Shirley Christian joined the Associated Press in 1966 and by 1970 was covering the United Nations in New York. Yet as she saw it, the AP paid women poorly and failed to promote them on merit. In 1972, seven women employees of the AP, led by Christian, joined with the American Newspaper Guild wire service unit to file a complaint with the U.S. Equal Employment Opportunity Commission on behalf of women and blacks. The Newspaper Guild filed suit against the Associated Press in 1973.

Winning recognition one way if not another, Christian received a Nieman Fellowship in 1973 and spent a year studying at Harvard University. She came home to the AP in 1974 only to realize that "the executives would have been happier if I had not returned." While she was assigned to the cable desk, the AP sent Tad Bartimus to Anchorage, Alaska, and Edie Lederer to Lima, Peru, as its first two women bureau chiefs, bypassing Christian. Wes Gallagher, promoted in 1962 to general manager of the AP, "was determined I should not go," she said. "I was one day away from quitting when they sent me to Santiago, Chile" in 1977. In 1979, after twelve years with the AP, she resigned to join the *Miami Herald*.

She was awarded the Pulitzer Prize for reporting the human dimensions of political strife and revolution in Central America. Among shocking events, she wrote of the murder of three American nuns and a woman lay worker by National Guardsmen in El Salvador. "That really shook me up," she said. "As both foreigners and women we had thought we were exempt." After winning the Pulitzer, Christian joined the Washington staff of the *New York Times*.

It took a decade for the Associated Press to settle the sex and race discrimination case against it. Rather than face trial, in 1983 the AP submitted two consent decrees to the U.S. District Court in New York, agreeing to launch an extensive affirmative action program.

Another sex discrimination case, this one against the *Washington Post*, helped other women get foreign assignments. The *Post* even made Karen DeYoung a foreign editor after she scored as a correspondent in Nicaragua. Although DeYoung later chose to return to the field, her appointment was considered an important milestone by women aware that they would never achieve complete equality until more women did the hiring.

By 1987 women held an estimated 20 percent of the foreign correspondent staff positions worldwide and made up a larger percentage of the correspondents working as free-lancers and independents. AP's Nathan Polowetzky said that the increase in two-career marriages made it more difficult to recruit foreign correspondents of either sex. Couples in differing professions could not so easily pull up stakes as men once did when families depended on a single income and the dollar purchased more abroad than at home.

Actually, the economy was forcing changes in recruiting policies bound to benefit women. Employers traditionally reserved foreign assignments to reward reporters for twenty years' faithful duty on the local staff. Even as fewer members of their news staff clamored for overseas assignments, editors raised their requirements. They were demanding two degrees—one in a specialty such as international relations and one in journalism—a foreign language, and some overseas experience before training candidates on the cable desk or in the city room. The highly qualified woman no longer was losing out to the merely adventurous male.

A trend certain to change the way the American public obtained its knowledge of world affairs was the enormous increase in correspondents traveling by jet on brief assignments. Only seventeen hundred Americans were accredited by the War Department to cover all of Western Europe for the duration of World War II. By comparison, the count of 792 correspondents simultaneously covering a revolution in tiny El Salvador in 1982 was overwhelming.

There was a limit to what could be learned in the glitter and exhaustion of a presidential junket to the Great Wall of China or a jet trip to an economic summit in Venice. But for women, the opportunities to travel briefly were a godsend. They could keep their families firmly rooted in Washington or New York or Detroit and still compete for assignments to cover historic events from Panama to Paris to Peking. Thousands of women reporters based in the United States could aspire to cover world capitals, however briefly.

As opportunities for women in the profession improved, it became fashionable to suggest that the whole female sex was cracking up because, in the words of Georgie Anne Geyer, "women are trying desperately to have everything." Again society was underestimating the capacity of women. Granted choices, were women incapable of choosing? As important as anything the women correspondents ever wrote was their success in overcoming barriers and demonstrating that women could choose their way of life for better or for worse.

Granted but one life to lead, the women who made it as foreign correspondents took all sorts of risks rather than confine themselves to limited horizons. The majority married men they never would have met in their hometowns. The birth rate dropped, and the divorce rate soared, but that happened everywhere. As the job market opened up, conventional wisdom changed from ''You couldn't handle the job'' to ''You wouldn't be happy.'' Conventional wisdom rang as false as ever. However distinctively individual, the women correspondents were highly motivated to experience all of life and to convey what they learned to their fellow men and women.

The celebrity status accorded the few who rose to the top did not do justice to their sex. The tendency to feature them as singular achievers in a man's world not only left the impression they had no female competition but discouraged young people, who were presented with icons when they needed role models. Carving a path others could follow took time, and it took persistence by all sorts of women whose only common denominator was their curiosity.

To get overseas, the women correspondents had to be nonconformists, so naturally they did not conform to preconceived visions of the sex's either elevating the tone of international discourse or lowering the standards of objective reporting. No two were alike in style and technique. What the women contributed, they contributed as individuals, not as representatives of their sex.

The foreign correspondents of both sexes were not typical or average; they were exceptional. The women could no more stop wars than newsmen could win them. They did contribute enormously to the nation's knowledge of world affairs. For survival, the human race needed to use the best brains it produced. When Horace Greeley published Margaret Fuller, he made a start.

SOURCES

2. A MAN'S AMBITION, A WOMAN'S HEART

Joseph J. Deiss, *The Roman Years of Margaret Fuller* (New York: Thomas Y. Crowell Co., 1969).

Mason Wade, *Margaret Fuller: Whetstone of Genius* (New York: Viking Press, 1940).
> These biographies were major sources for my report on the career of Margaret Fuller.

Leo Hamalian, ed., *Ladies on the Loose: Women Travellers of the Eighteenth and Nineteenth Centuries* (New York: Dodd, Mead, 1981).
> Contains a choice selection of Margaret Fuller's letters. I quote from two describing events of the revolution in Rome during March and November 1848.

Paula Blanchard, *Margaret Fuller: From Transcendentalism to Revolution* (New York: Delacorte, 1978).

R. W. Emerson, W. H. Channing, and J. F. Clarke, *Memoirs of Margaret Fuller Ossoli* (Boston: Robert Brothers, 1874).

John Hohenberg, *Foreign Correspondence: The Great Reporters and Their Times* (New York: Columbia University Press, 1964). The classic history of foreign correspondence.

Ishbel Ross, *Ladies of the Press* (New York: Harper and Brothers, 1936). The classic history of women journalists.

Margaret Fuller, *Woman in the Nineteenth Century* (Columbia: University of South Carolina Press, 1980).

Barney Oldfield, *Never a Shot in Anger* (New York: Duell, Sloan and Pearce, 1956).

Sara Jane Lippincott, *Haps and Mishaps of a Tour in Europe* (Boston: Boston Stereotype Foundry, 1853).

Edward T. James, ed., *Notable American Women* (Cambridge, Mass.: Belknap Press of Harvard University, 1971).

Mignon Rittenhouse, *The Amazing Nellie Bly* (New York: E. P. Dutton, 1956).

Iris Noble, *Nellie Bly* (New York: Julian Messner, 1956).

3. WORLD WAR I:
THE SILENT TREATMENT

Mary Roberts Rinehart, *My Story* (New York: Rinehart & Co., 1948). The autobiography is my major source on her journalistic career.

Jan Cohn, *Improbable Fiction: The Life of Mary Roberts Rinehart* (Pittsburgh: University of Pittsburgh Press, 1980).

Barbara Gelb, *So Short a Time* (New York: Berkley Books, 1981). A wonderfully readable biography of Louise Bryant.

Louise Bryant, *Six Red Months in Russia* (New York: George H. Doran, 1918).

Louise Bryant, *Mirrors of Moscow* (New York: Thomas Seltzer, 1923).

Bessie Beatty, *The Red Heart of Russia* (New York: Century Co., 1918).

Rheta Childe Dorr, *A Woman of Fifty* (New York: Funk & Wagnall's, 1924).

John Reed, *Ten Days That Shook the World* (New York: Penguin Books, 1977).

Phillip Knightley, *The First Casualty* (New York: Harcourt Brace Jovanovich, 1973).

4. THEY WERE SURVIVORS

Eleanor Bogart and Dr. Wilda Smith, "Peggy Hull: On the Border with Pershing," in *The Prairie Scout*, vol. 5, ed. Leo E. Olive et al. (Abilene: The Kansas Corral of the Westerners, 1985), 19–33.

David Len Jones, "And Peggy Hull Was There" (Master's thesis, University of Texas at Austin, 1980). Available on interlibrary loan.

Emmet Crozier, *On the Western Front, 1914–1918* (New York: Oxford University Press, 1959).

Harry J. Lambeth, "Peggy Hull," *Editor and Publisher*, May 6, 1944.

Lenore Hershey, "Les Girls" in *Dateline* (New York: Overseas Press Club, 1968).

Marion Marzolf, *Up from the Footnotes: A History of Women Journalists* (New York: Hastings House, 1977).

Robert Spiers Benjamin, ed., *Eye Witness*, by members of the Overseas Press Club of America (New York: Alliance Book Corp., 1940).

Irene Corbally Kuhn, *Assigned to Adventure* (New York: J. B. Lippincott, 1938).

Interview with Irene Kuhn.

5. THE DRAGON LADY FROM CHICAGO

Sigrid Schultz, *Germany Will Try It Again* (New York: Cornwall Press, 1944).

Dickson Hartwell and Andrew A. Rooney, eds., *Off the Record* (Garden City, N.Y.: Doubleday, 1953).

Sigrid Schultz, "The Final Hours of Adolf Hitler," in *I Can Tell It Now*, ed. David Brown and W. Richard Bruner (New York: E. P. Dutton, 1964), 104–115.

William L. Shirer, *The Nightmare Years, 1930–1940* (Boston: Little, Brown, 1984).

Letters from Sigrid Schultz to me and reminiscences of Madeline Meyer and members of the Overseas Press Club.

6. ANNE O'HARE MCCORMICK AND THE CHANGING TIMES

Harrison E. Salisbury, *Without Fear or Favor* (New York: Times Books, 1980).

Meyer Berger, *The Story of The New York Times* (New York: Simon and Schuster, 1951).

Susan W. Dryfoos, *Iphigene, Memoirs of Iphigene Ochs Sulzberger* (New York: Dodd, Mead, 1981).

Marion Turner Sheehan, ed., *The World at Home by Anne O'Hare McCormick* (New York: Alfred A. Knopf, 1936). This collection of McCormick's columns is the source of two quotations.

John Hohenberg, *Foreign Correspondence: The Great Reporters and Their Times* (New York: Columbia University Press, 1964).

Richard Kluger, *The Paper: The Life and Death of the New York Herald Tribune* (New York: Alfred A. Knopf, 1986).

Barbara Belford, *Brilliant Bylines* (New York: Columbia University Press, 1986).

For this chapter, I was allowed privileged access to the files of *The New York Times*.

7. THE BLUE-EYED TORNADO

Marion K. Sanders, *Dorothy Thompson: A Legend in Her Times* (Boston: Houghton Mifflin, 1973). This definitive biography was a valuable source of information on her career.

Vincent Sheean, *Dorothy and Red* (Boston: Houghton Mifflin, 1963).

Dorothy Thompson, *The New Russia* (New York: Henry Holt, 1928).

Dorothy Thompson, *Let the Record Speak* (Boston: Houghton Mifflin, 1939).

Dorothy Thompson, *The Courage to Be Happy* (Boston: Houghton Mifflin, 1957).

Dorothy Thompson, "On Women Correspondents and Others," *The Nation*, January 6, 1926.

A. M. Sperber, *Murrow: His Life and Times* (New York: Freundlich Books, 1986).

Personal reminiscences.

8. THE WORLD AT WAR

Ann Denton Behlen, "Mary Marvin Breckinridge Patterson" (Unpublished thesis, Harvard University, 1982).

Olivia Phelps Stokes and Mary Marvin Breckinridge, *Olivia's African Diary* (Arlington, Va.: American Council on Education, 1979).

Helen Kirkpatrick, *This Terrible Peace* (London: Rich & Cowan, 1939).

Helen Kirkpatrick, *Under the British Umbrella* (New York: Charles Scribner's Sons, 1939).

A. M. Sperber, *Murrow: His Life and Times* (New York: Freundlich Books, 1986).

Interviews with Marvin Breckinridge Patterson and Helen Kirkpatrick.

9. ASKING FOR TROUBLE

Martha Gellhorn, *The Face of War* (New York: Simon and Schuster, 1959).

Martha Gellhorn, *Travels with Myself and Another* (New York: Dodd, Mead, 1979).

Mary Welsh Hemingway, *How It Was* (New York: Alfred A. Knopf, 1976).

Sonia Tomara granted me the last personal interview she gave before she died. My report on her is based on that interview and her unpublished memoirs. Correspondence with Martha Gellhorn is quoted.

10. THE UNSINKABLE MAGGIE WHITE

Margaret Bourke-White, *Portrait of Myself* (New York: Simon and Schuster, 1963).

Margaret Bourke-White, *Eyes on Russia* (New York: Simon and Schuster, 1931).

Winfred and Frances Kirkland, *Girls Who Became Artists* (Freeport, N.Y.: Books for Libraries Press, 1934).

Madelon Golden Schilpp and Sharon M. Murphy, *Great Women of the Press* (Carbondale: Southern Illinois University Press, 1983).

Vicki Goldberg, *Margaret Bourke-White: A Biography* (New York: Harper and Row, 1986).

Personal reminiscences.

11. COMBAT CORRESPONDENT

Iris Carpenter, *No Woman's World* (Boston: Houghton Mifflin, 1946).

Joseph J. Matthews, *Reporting the Wars* (Minneapolis: University of Minnesota Press, 1957).

Dickson Hartwell and Andrew A. Rooney, eds., *Off the Record* (Garden City, N.Y.: Doubleday, 1953).

Inez Robb, *Don't Just Stand There* (New York: David McKay, 1962).

Bob Considine, *It's All News to Me* (New York: Meredith Press, 1967).

Personal interviews with Ruth Cowan Nash and Iris Carpenter and my reminiscences of Lee Carson.

12. THE RUSSIANS WERE COMING!

Boyd DeWolf Lewis, *Not Always a Spectator* (Vienna, Va.: Wolf's Head Press, 1981).

Barney Oldfield, *Never a Shot in Anger* (New York: Duell, Sloan and Pearce, 1956).

Ann Stringer and Henry Ries, *German Faces* (New York: William Sloane Associates, 1950).

"The Rhine Maidens," *Newsweek*, March 10, 1945.
Interviews with Ann Stringer.

13. NO PEACE IN THE PACIFIC

Patricia Lockridge, "Solace at Iwo," *Woman's Home Companion*, May 1945, 4ff.

Patricia Lockridge, "Flight for Life," *Woman's Home Companion*, January 1945, 24–25.

Charlotte Ebener, *No Facilities for Women* (New York: Alfred A. Knopf, 1955). One of the best books written by a woman foreign correspondent.

Members of the Overseas Press Club of America, *Deadline Delayed* (New York: E. P. Dutton, 1947).

Dickson Hartwell and Andrew A. Rooney, ed., *Off the Record* (Garden City, N.Y.: Doubleday, 1953).

Interview with Esther Van Wagoner Tufty. George Weller contributed information on his wife, Charlotte Ebener. Phil Potter also contributed.

14. THE OUTRAGEOUS MARGUERITE HIGGINS

Marguerite Higgins, *News Is a Singular Thing* (New York: Doubleday, 1955).

Marguerite Higgins, *War in Korea* (New York: Doubleday, 1951).

Marguerite Higgins, *Red Plush and Black Bread* (New York: Doubleday, 1955).

Antoinette May, *Witness to War: A Biography of Marguerite Higgins* (New York: Beaufort Books, 1983).

Marguerite Higgins, *Our Vietnam Nightmare* (New York: Harper and Row, 1965).

David Halberstam, *The Powers That Be* (New York: Alfred A. Knopf, 1979).

Richard Kluger, *The Paper: The Life and Death of the New York Herald Tribune* (New York: Alfred A. Knopf, 1986).

Several correspondents who worked with Marguerite Higgins contributed; my reminiscences.

15. LAST STOP, VIETNAM

Dickey Chapelle, *What's a Woman Doing Here?* (New York: William Morrow, 1962). Chapelle's autobiography is the principal source for her World War II experiences.

Dickey Chapelle, "The Trouble I've Asked For," in *How I Got That Story*, ed. David Brown and W. Richard Bruner (New York: E. P. Dutton, 1967), 293–306.

Dickey Chapelle, "The Unconventional Americans," in *I Can Tell It Now*, ed. David Brown and W. Richard Bruner (New York: E. P. Dutton, 1964), 295–302.

Richard Tregaskis in *Dateline* (New York: Overseas Press Club, 1966).

Information provided by the U.S. Marine Corps and friends of Dickey Chapelle; my reminiscences.

16. A NEW CAST OF CHARACTERS

Aline Mosby, *The View from #13 People's Street* (New York: Random House, 1962). A lively account of her experiences in the Soviet Union.

Mort Rosenblum, *Coups and Earthquakes* (New York: Harper and Row, 1979).

Harrison E. Salisbury, *A Journey for Our Times* (New York: Harper and Row, 1983).

Dateline (New York: Overseas Press Club, 1984).

Jean E. Collins, *She Was There* (New York: Julian Messner, 1980).

Flora Lewis, *New York Times*, June 20, 1980.

Flora Lewis, *New York Times*, April 4, 1982.

Personal interviews with Kathleen McLaughlin, Aline Mosby, and Flora Lewis.

17. BEARERS OF BAD TIDINGS

Beverly Deepe, "The Woman Correspondent," in *Dateline* (New York: Overseas Press Club, 1966).

Gloria Emerson, *Winners and Losers: Battles, Retreats, Gains, Losses and Ruins from a Long War* (New York: Random House, 1976).

Frances FitzGerald, *Fire in the Lake* (Boston: Atlantic-Little, Brown, 1972; New York: Vintage Books, Random House, 1973).

Elizabeth Pond, articles on Cambodia, *Christian Science Monitor*, June 22, 1970, 1–2.

Elizabeth Becker, *When the War Was Over: The Voices of Cambodia's Revolution and Its People* (New York: Simon and Schuster, 1986).

Interviews with Liz Trotta and Elizabeth Becker; information obtained from United Press International, the Overseas Press Club, and Gloria Emerson.

18. FULL CIRCLE

Georgie Anne Geyer, *Buying the Night Flight* (New York: Delacorte, 1983).

Jane Carolyn Erlick, "Women as the New War Correspondents," *Washington Journalism Review*, June 1982.

Interviews with Georgie Anne Geyer, Nathan Polowetzky, and Karen DeYoung; information from Shirley Christian.

INDEX

About the Author

Julia Edwards, a foreign correspondent for twenty-five years, has covered wars, riots, revolutions, and what passes for peace in more than 125 countries. She knows most of the women correspondents of her generation and has worked with many of them. A resident of Longboat Key, Florida, she regularly serves as a judge on the Overseas Press Club awards committee.